I0812380

IMAGES
of America
ELK GROVE

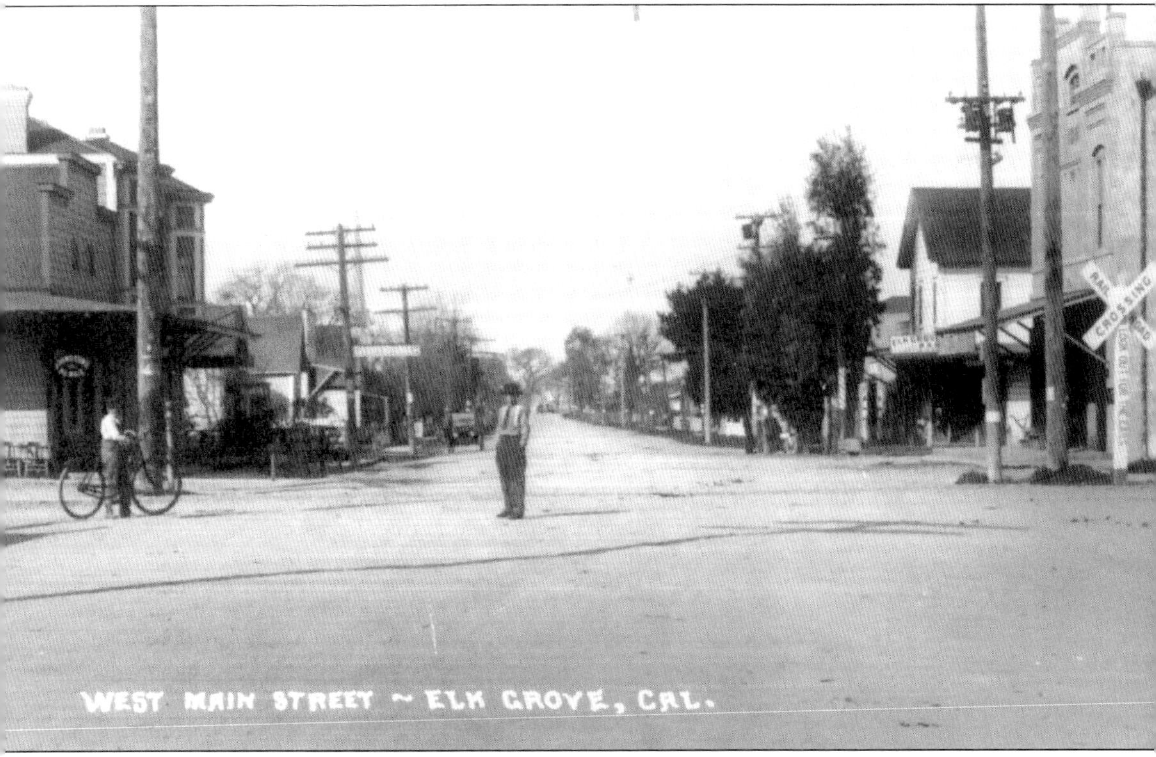

This is Elk Grove's Main Street in the 1920s. Main Street is known as Elk Grove Boulevard in 2006, and this part of the city of Elk Grove is known as "Old Town."

On the Cover: Elk Grove's Main Street is pictured here in 1925. (See page 65.) (Courtesy of Bob Batey.)

IMAGES
of America

ELK GROVE

Elizabeth Pinkerton

ARCADIA
PUBLISHING

ISBN 978-0-7385-3128-1

Published by Arcadia Publishing
Charleston, South Carolina

Printed in the United States of America

Library of Congress Control Number: 2006920549

For all general information, please contact Arcadia Publishing:
Telephone 843-853-2070
Fax 843-853-0044
E-mail sales@arcadiapublishing.com
For customer service and orders:
Toll-Free 1-888-313-2665

Visit us on the Internet at www.arcadiapublishing.com

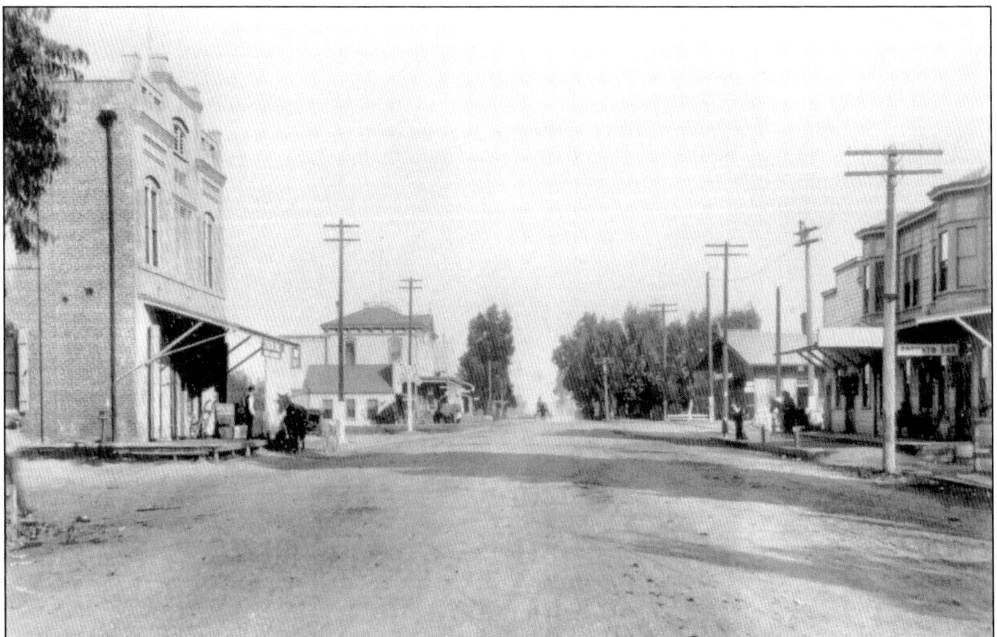

Pictured here is Elk Grove's Main Street in the 1920s. Today this road is Elk Grove Boulevard in Old Town.

Contents

ACKNOWLEDGMENTS

The new city of Elk Grove, even though it is only six years old, is well represented through the collection of photographs in this volume of Images of America. I am grateful for the loans of photographs and other materials from the Elk Grove Historical Society; Anita Peters, the current president; and the board of directors. I am greatly appreciative of the loans of photographs for this book from Tom Russell, Ellen Rosa, Virginia Signorotti, Dave and Jane Morse, Jim and Virginia Ring, Lucile Christesen, Gerald Derr, Bob and Olga Batey, Hal and Wayne Bartholomew, and Dennis Buscher. And to the many other local folks who contributed to my collection of local history and my knowledge of local events over the years, I am forever indebted.

A large part of the work in preparing the photographs for publication was done by Tom Russell, past president of the Elk Grove Historical Society. I thank him greatly for his fine work, his assistance, and his general support for the project. The owners of photographs in the book are credited. The photographs that have no credit noted are mine, either given to me by local residents or taken by me.

The *Elk Grove Citizen* newspaper has been a strong supporter of local history with weekly articles in a column that I have written, entitled "History Happened Here," for the past 23 years. The *Citizen*, under the leadership of Roy and David Herburger, has helped to create a community-wide interest in the past that is valued by old-timers as well as the many newcomers to the area. My three books, *We the People, a Story of Internment in America* (with Mary Tsukamoto) and the two *History Happened Here* books (*River, Oaks, Gold* and *Fields, Farms, Schools*) continue to have wide community support. The proceeds from the *History Happened Here* books have provided scholarships for 19 students through the Elk Grove Community Foundation. I also commend the city of Elk Grove for its support of local history and its recent preservation efforts.

Finally, I would like to thank my family—my husband, Tom, and Mike, Connie, Willie, Kevin, Pat, Barbara, Abbott, David, Patrick, and Sarah—for their continual support of my local history projects.

—Elizabeth

Introduction

The new city of Elk Grove lies in the shadow of the state capitol in Sacramento. There is much to gain from being so close to Sacramento and its fascinating history, but in many ways, Elk Grove has been overlooked in the story of California. The tales of the missions, Sutter's Fort, the forty-niners, the railroads, and the growth of this great state are well known to most Californians because they are the story of California. The historical background of Elk Grove, though not as dramatic as the story of Sacramento, is not well known, but it is comprised of a fascinating set of stories. Much history did happen in our very own backyards, and much of it parallels what happened in the rest of Northern California.

Elk Grove's past is a tribute to the leadership of the people who lived here before. The efforts of local citizens, who are residents now, brought the community into the 21st century. That strong leadership continues.

On July 1, 2000, Elk Grove became the first new city of the 21st century in California because of its historic foundation, made up of vision, determination, and hard work of the pioneers, settlers, and entrepreneurs who were here first. From their work came the historical and successful vote for independence from county governance. In order to move ahead at this historical time, Elk Grove's collective past needs to be preserved because it is the roots of its existence that brought the community to its current position. The stories of the past are important to all Elk Grove citizens, and they are essential links to the great story of the state. Knowledge of what happened in this area will help better decisions to be made as a plan for the future of Elk Grove and the south county area is developed.

The incidents in California history described on the next page happened here in Elk Grove and south Sacramento County. These actions are examples of how the people led the way and made important changes that affected not only the way this community functions but how people live in our entire state.

TIMELINE

The Miwok people set the stage for the future city of Elk Grove.

1807: Spanish explorers come through the Cosumnes-Elk Grove area, but they do not stay.

1846: The incident at Murphy's Corral—the first step to California statehood.

1850: Elk Grove Hotel and Stage Stop on the Monterey Trail is founded.

1853: The San Joaquin School is the first public school in Sacramento County.

1868: The Central Pacific Railroad heads south from Sacramento through Elk Grove.

1893: Elk Grove Union High School becomes the first union free high school in California.

1906: Elk Grove is the first in the state to establish a county free library.

1935: Elk Grove Park becomes the first rural park district in the California.

1957: Stockton Road changes to Highway 99 as part of the nationwide freeway system.

1959: The independent school districts of the area vote to become the Elk Grove Unified School District.

July 1, 2000: Elk Grove becomes a city.

Elk Grove once again leads the way as the first new city of the millennium in California. May citizens continue to show the way into the future.

One

Elk Grove
From Stage Stop to City

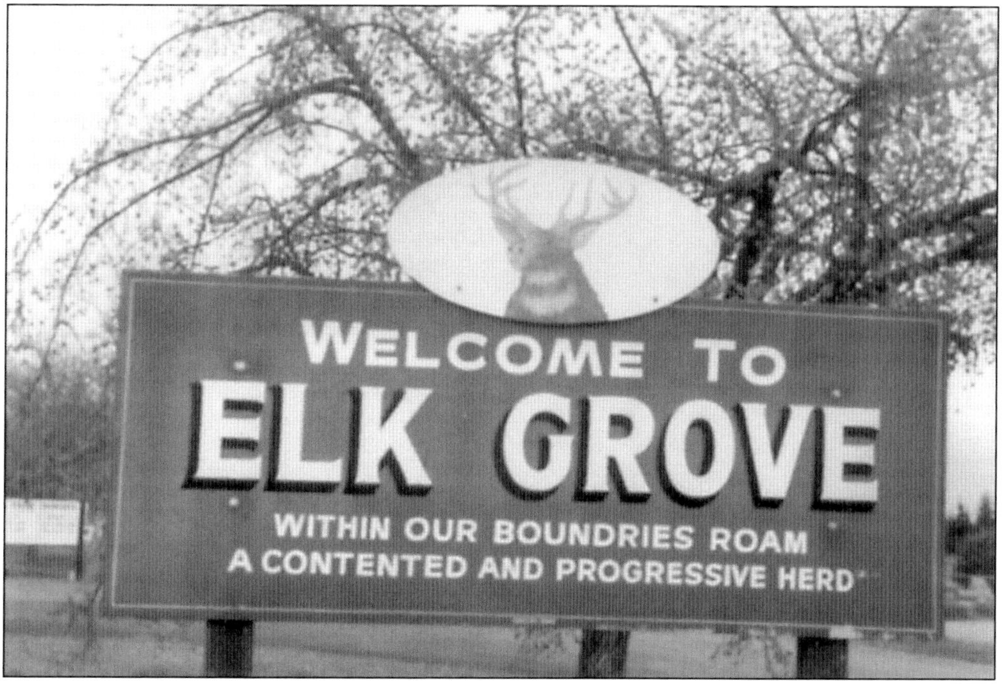

This is the sign that introduced people to Elk Grove long before it became a city. At some time in the late 1950s, two signs were created by a group of local residents and businessmen and placed at the main entry points to Elk Grove. One marked the entrance to Elk Grove from today's Highway 99 on the south side of what is now Elk Grove Boulevard by the cemetery. The other sign was on Elk Grove-Florin Road, south of today's Bond Road on the west just before the creek and the California Fish Hatchery. The reference is to the Elk Grove High School slogan of the Thundering Herd and perhaps to all the cattle that once filled the Elk Grove fields. But the message is as true today as it was a half-century ago, for the people who live in Elk Grove continue to be both contented and progressive.

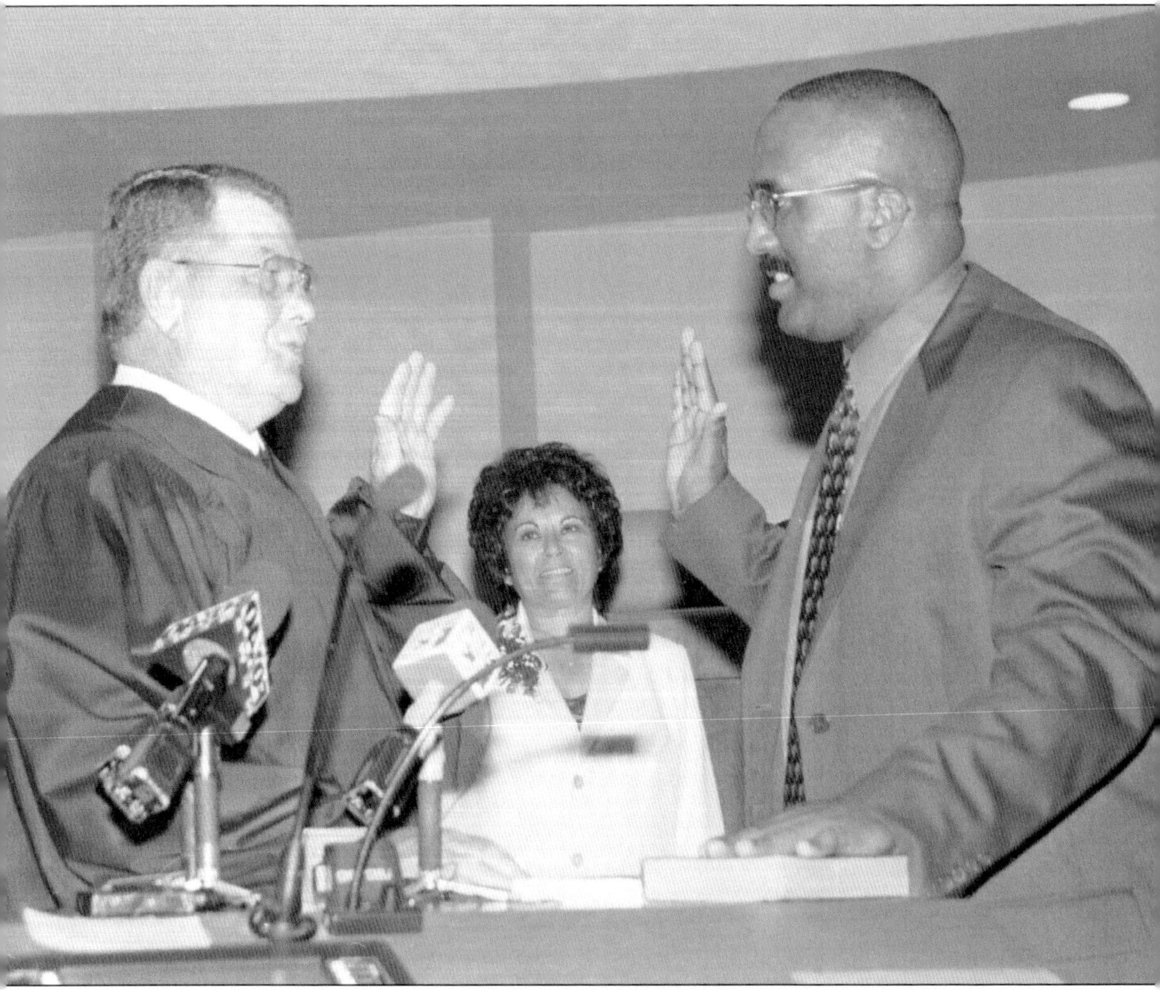

Elk Grove became a city on July 1, 2000. It took several years of community effort to incorporate, and when the decision went to a vote by citizens, cityhood became a reality. The official action to create a common-law city took place in the board room of the Elk Grove Unified School District on Elk Grove-Florin Road. Judge James P. Henke officiated as five new council members took their oaths of office. Sophia Scherman is pictured here watching as Judge Henke administers the oath of office to James Cooper, the first mayor of the City of Elk Grove. Other council members in addition to Scherman were Michael Leary, Richard Soares, and Daniel Briggs. Elk Grove was the first new city of the 21st century in California. The city nearly doubled its population in its first six years and is now over 130,000. (Courtesy of City of Elk Grove.)

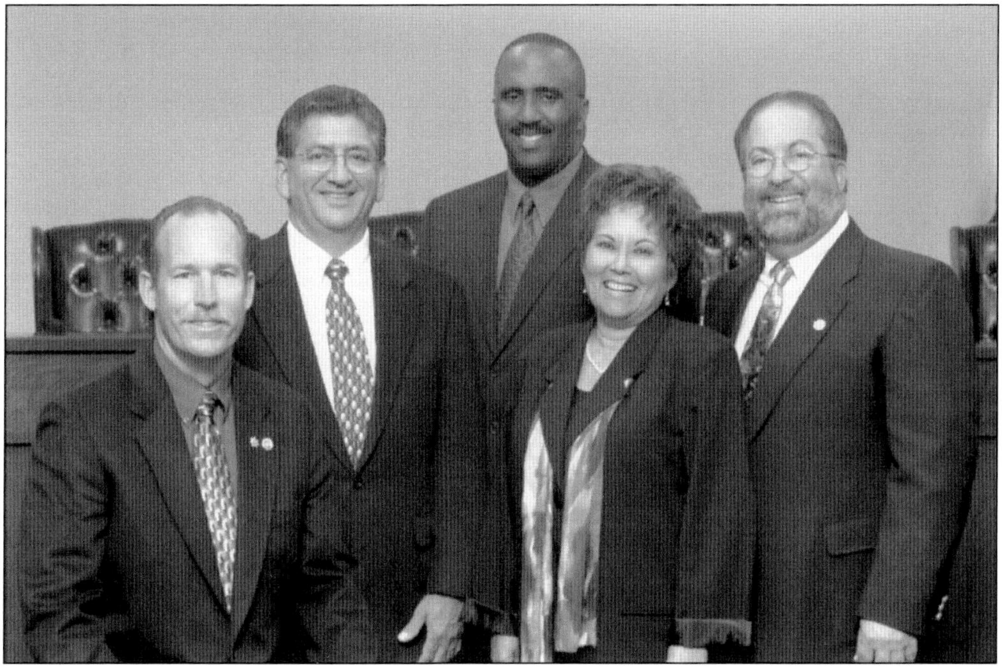

Starting a new city and breaking the long ties to the County of Sacramento were complex proceedings for the new city council. Council members are elected at large but from five specific neighborhoods that are each represented by one council member. Pictured here from left to right are Michael Leary, Daniel Briggs, James Cooper, Sophia Scherman, and Richard Soares. (Courtesy of City of Elk Grove.)

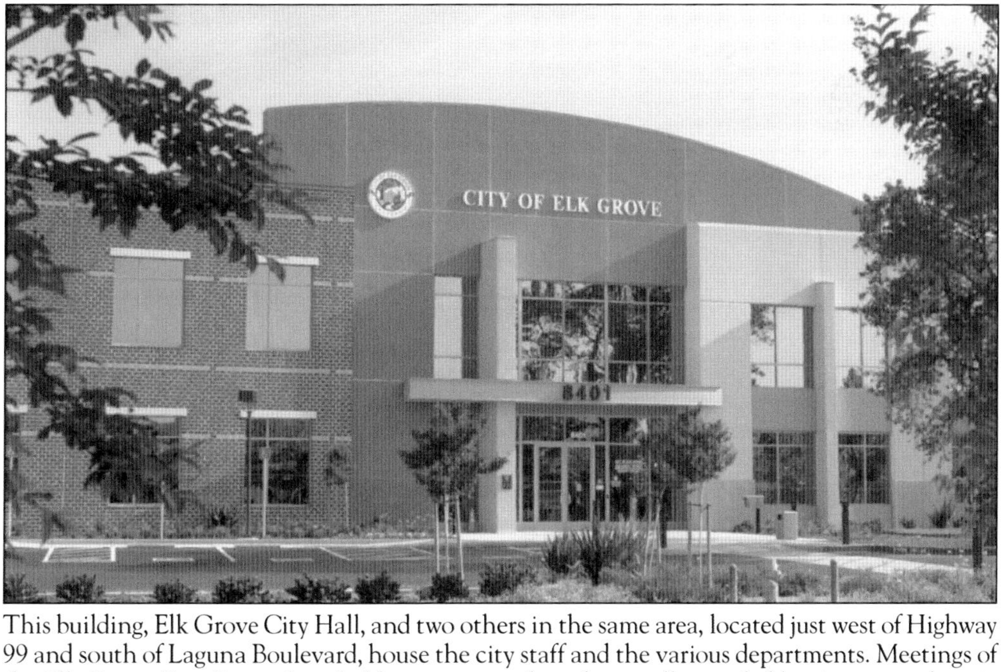

This building, Elk Grove City Hall, and two others in the same area, located just west of Highway 99 and south of Laguna Boulevard, house the city staff and the various departments. Meetings of the Elk Grove City Council are held twice a month and are well attended by citizens as there is a great amount of community involvement in the new city. (Courtesy of City of Elk Grove.)

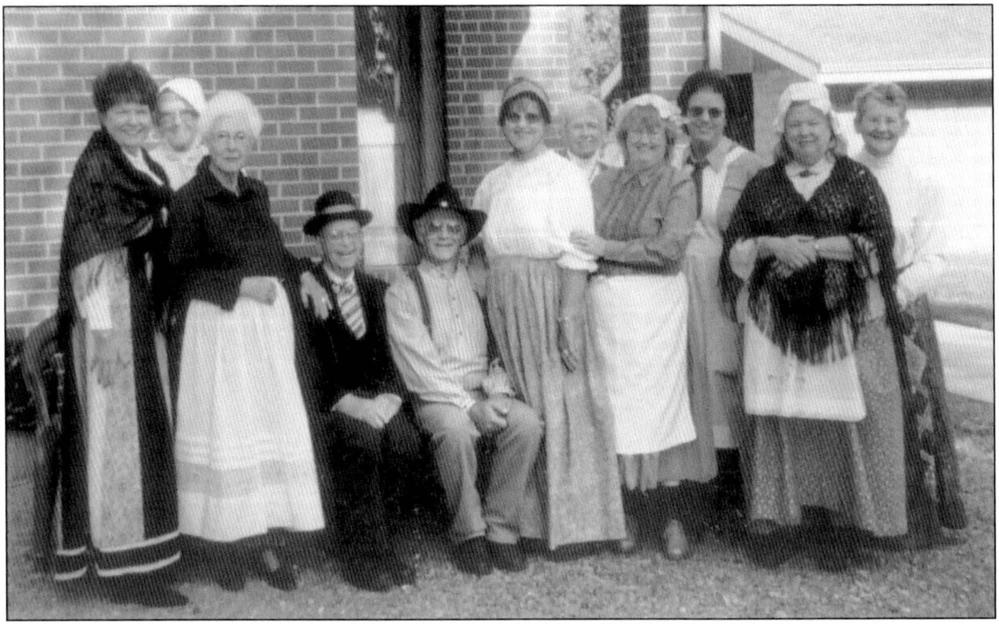

The Elk Grove Historical Society emerged from the Elk Grove Bicentennial Commission of 1975–1976. Citizens across America were encouraged at the time to identify community historical projects to commemorate the 200th anniversary of the United States of America as an independent nation. This photograph was taken at the grand opening of the Elk Grove Hotel and Stage Stop.

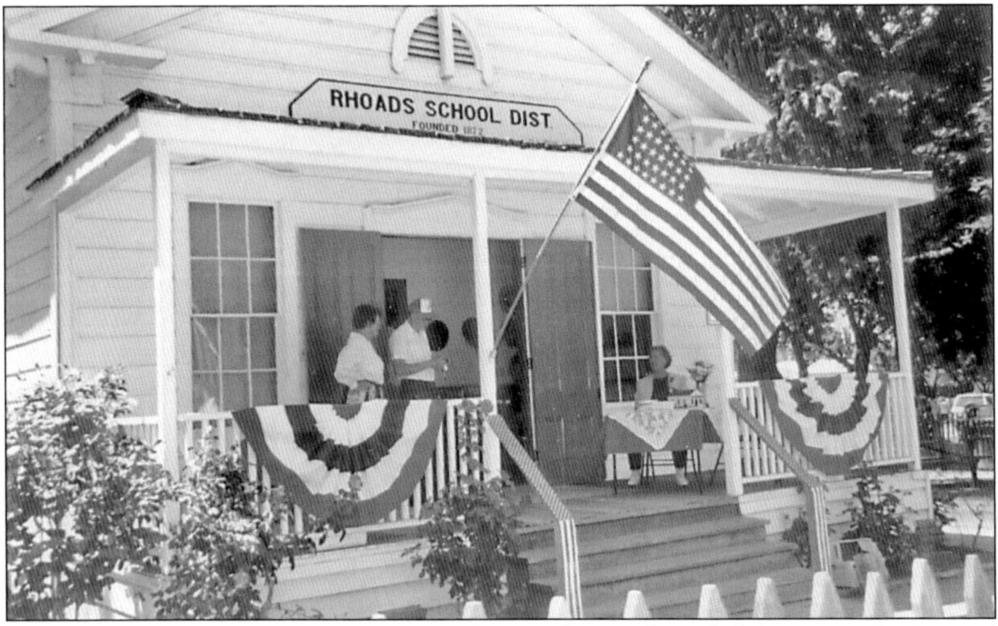

The Bicentennial Commission selected Carl Amundson and Anabel Gage as its leaders and the Rhoads School as a project. The 1872 school, named for John P. Rhoads, a rescuer of the stranded Donner Party of 1847, was moved from Sloughhouse Road to Elk Grove Park. Repaired and refurbished, Rhoads School is a gleaming jewel open to school and community groups. Elk Grove Historical Society volunteers manage and run the programs.

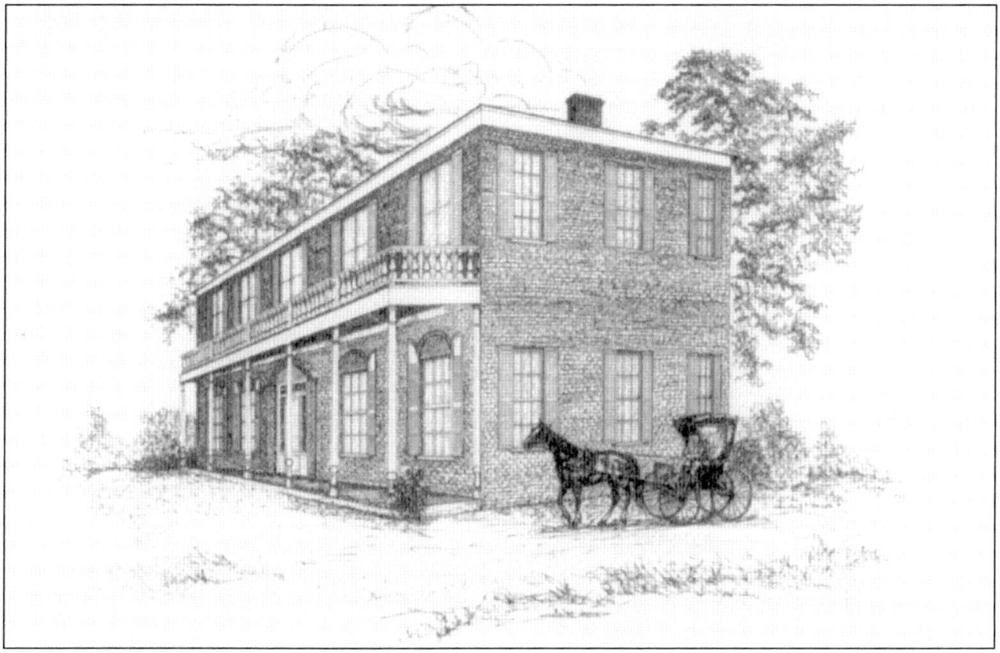

In the 1980s, the Elk Grove Historical Society took on the task of rebuilding the Elk Grove Hotel and Stage Stop of 1850. The building had been torn down in 1957 when Highway 99 was created as part of the nationwide freeway system. Beautifully reconstructed and restored, the stage stop serves as a museum for the community in Elk Grove Park. (Courtesy of Tom Russell.)

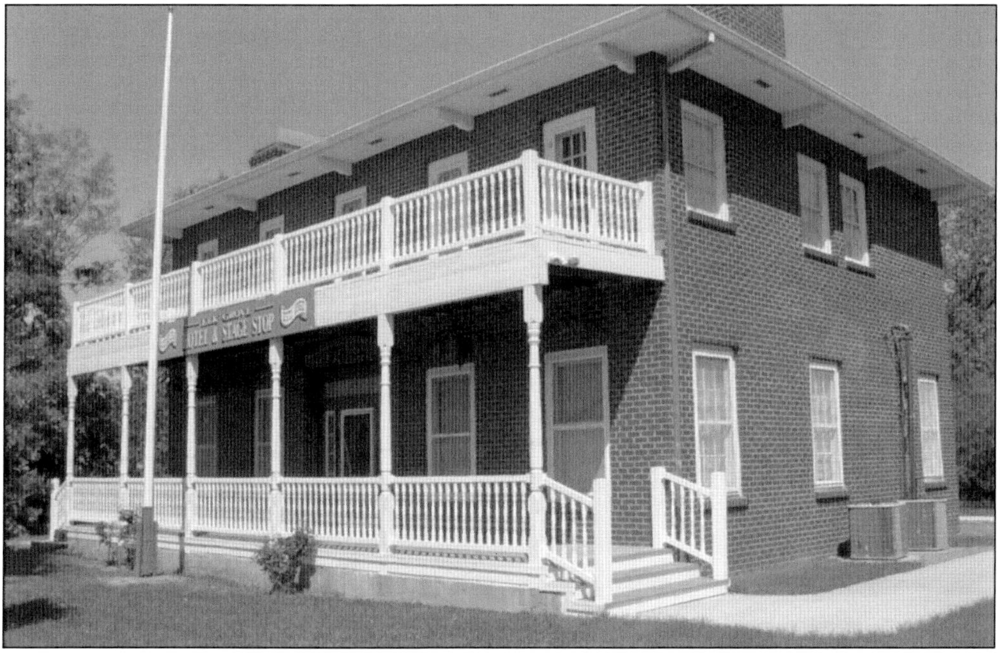

The Elk Grove Historical Society continues to be an active community organization and is always immersed in preservation projects. The city was named a "Preserve America Community" by First Lady Laura Bush in April 2006. This action recognized the longtime efforts of Elk Grove residents and the Elk Grove Historical Society. (Courtesy of Tom Russell.)

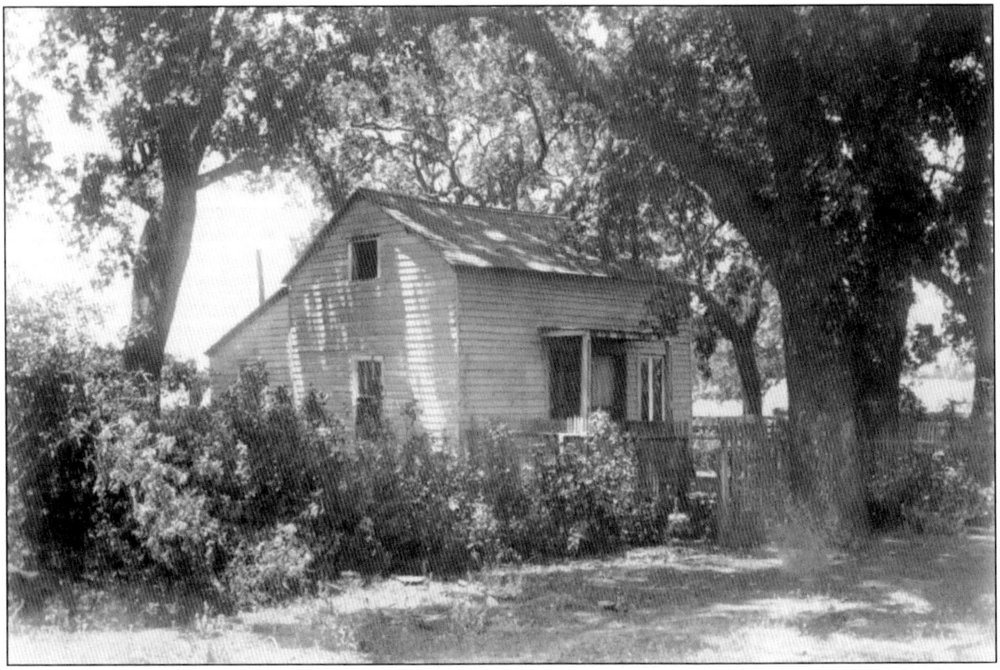

The Elk Grove Historical Society launched two new projects in 2006. The historical buildings pictured on this page have been moved to the museum site at Elk Grove Park where they await restoration. The original Foulks Ranch house of 1853 is shown above, while the original Reese School of 1884 appears in the image below. (Courtesy of Elk Grove Historical Society.)

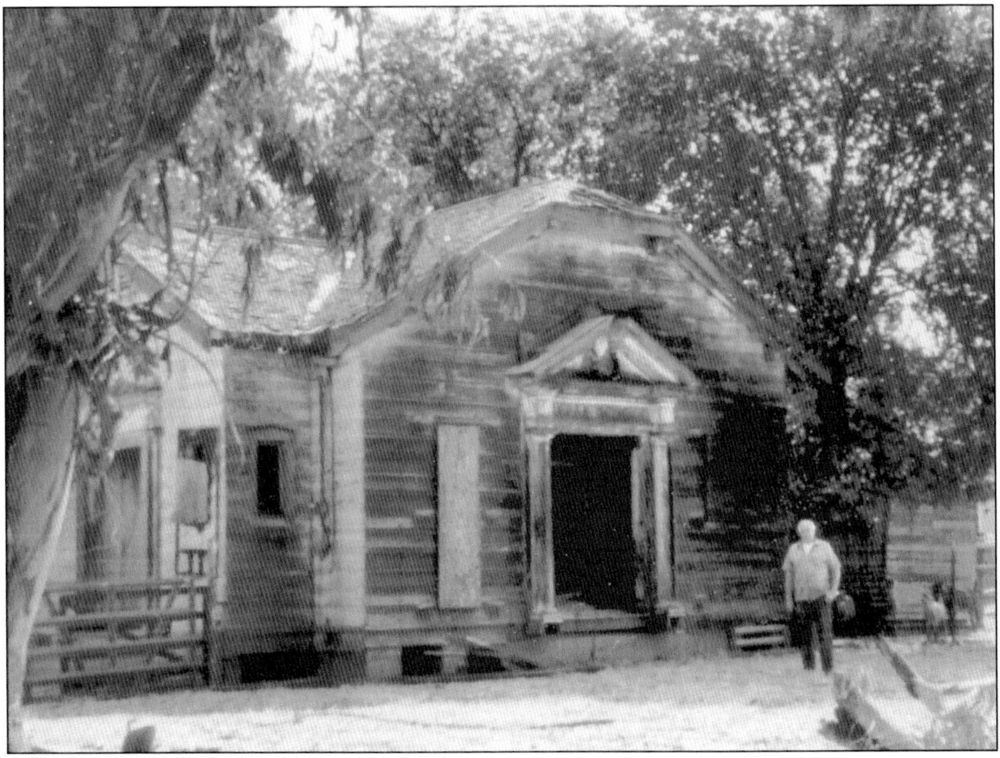

Two

THE BEGINNING

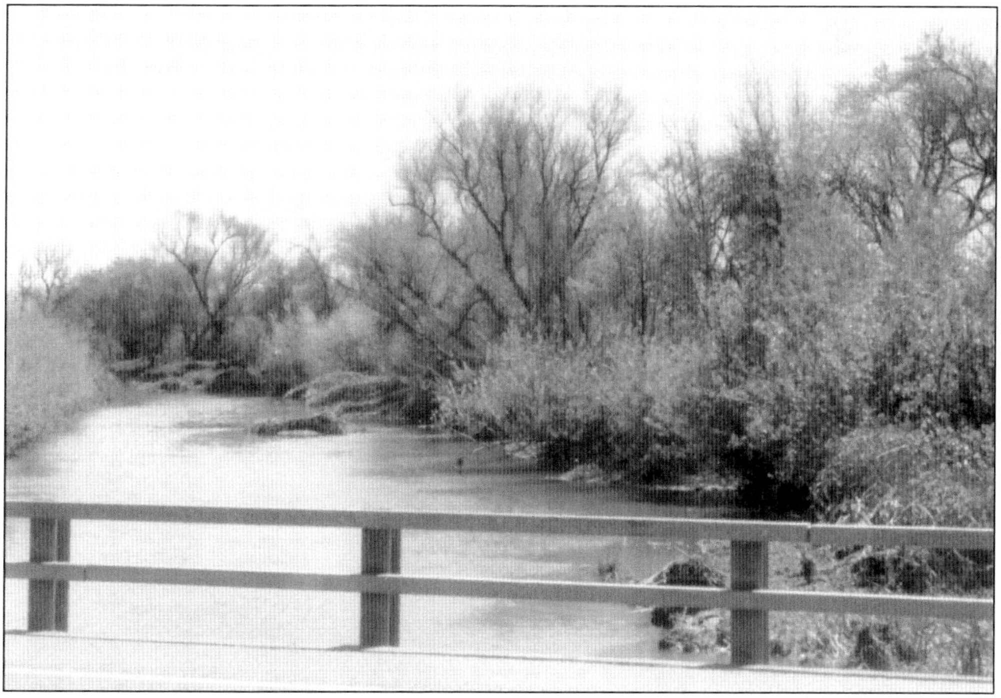

The Cosumnes River is the most striking element of the south Sacramento County geological map. The river gets its name from the Miwok Indians, and it is believed that its source is their word for salmon, *kossum*. The suffix *sumne* means tribe or people. The Miwok people came to the Cosumnes region in search of acorns from the seven varieties of oak trees that thrived along the river. The river itself is wonderfully rich in history and is a treasure trove of old-time tales and lore, including those of gold. Originating in the Sierra Nevada above Plymouth, the river makes its way down through the foothills from Rancho Murieta to Sloughhouse and Wilton before moving toward Franklin, where it joins the Mokelumne River. The two rivers then flow to the San Joaquin River and from there to the Pacific Ocean. The Cosumnes River is one of the last free rivers in the great state of California.

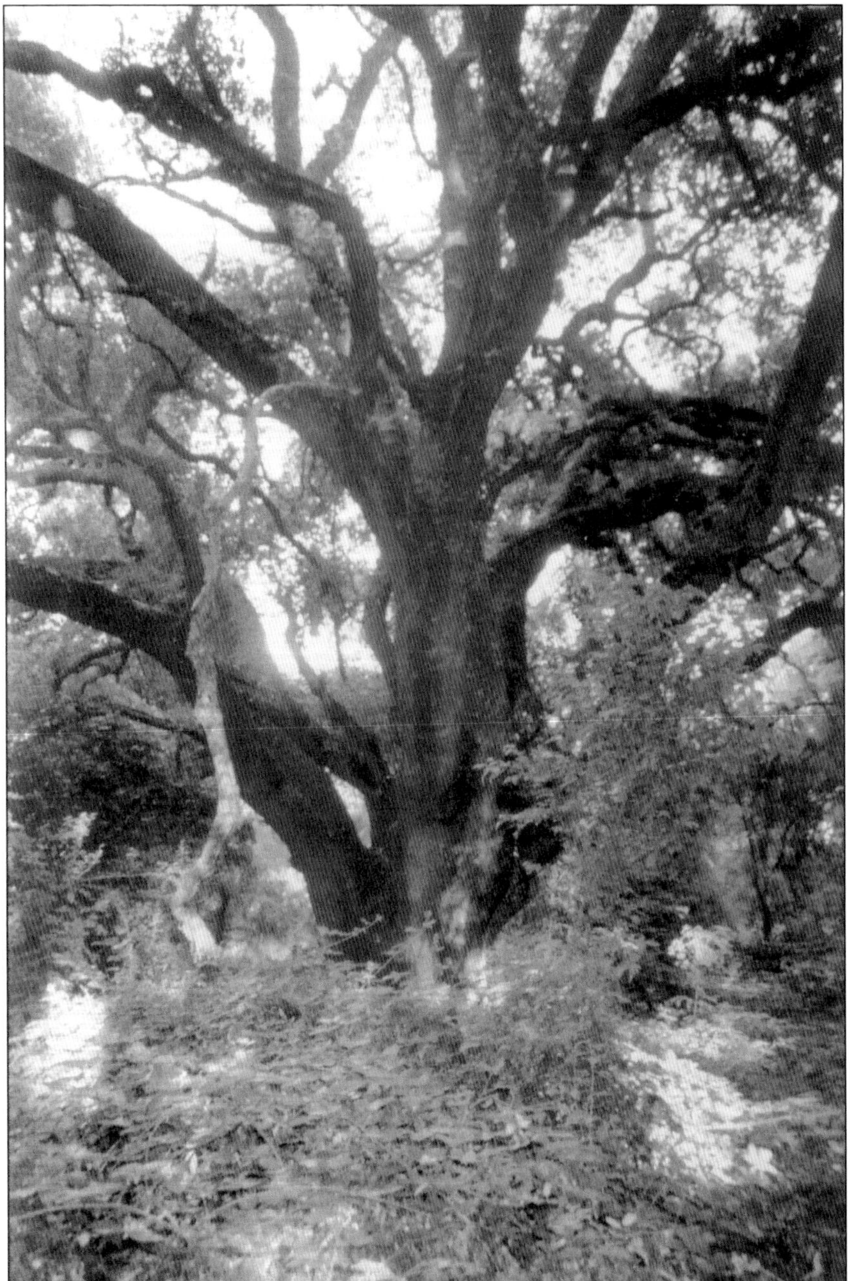

The Cosumnes River queen of oaks is this magnificent tree in the Franklin area. Estimated to be more than 500 years old, it looks like several giant oaks emerging from one trunk. As the tree reaches to the sky, its gigantic branches dip to the ground with their massive weight and then soar wonderfully upward again. This oak is the oldest living thing in the Elk Grove-Cosumnes River area. The Miwok people made good use of the oak trees for food and medical purposes. They also used the many wildflowers for a variety of purposes. Some rolling fields of flowers can still be seen like those that once filled the country. But many fields are being filled with houses, for rapid residential growth is taking the place of the wonderful fields of wildflowers and the oak groves.

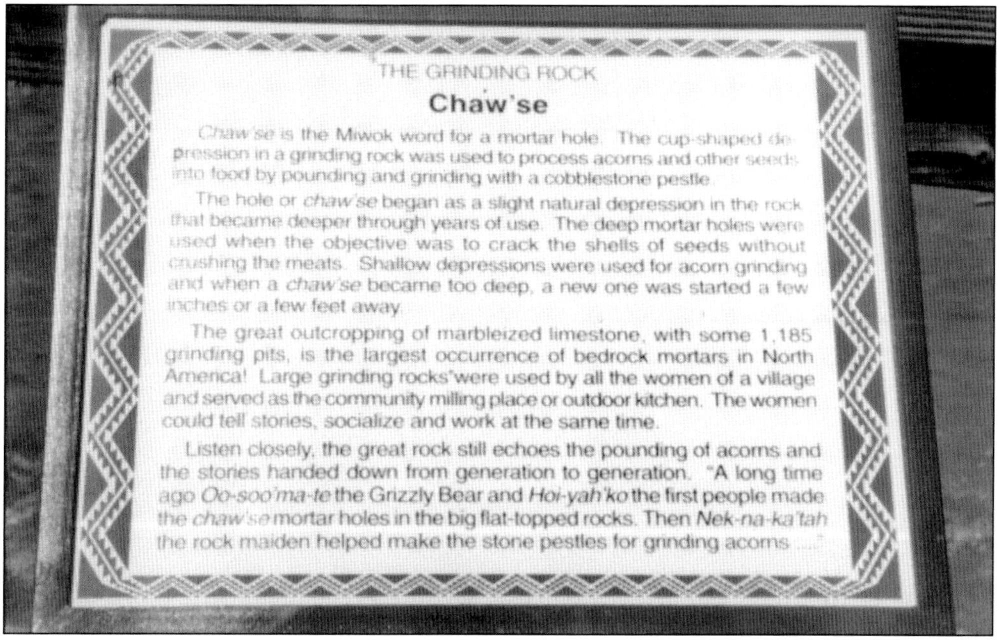

Long before there was an Elk Grove, the Miwok people lived along the Cosumnes River. They had salmon and tule elk, and the many oaks brought them an annual supply of acorns. The Miwok families also traveled south to Yosemite and into the Sierra foothills. The coming of European and American explorers and settlers created conflicts, and the gold rush further threatened the Miwok existence. Families fled to higher elevations, but by the 1850s, their lifestyle and culture was disappearing. As lands became agricultural, it became increasingly difficult for the Miwoks to avoid conflicts with their new, uninvited neighbors.

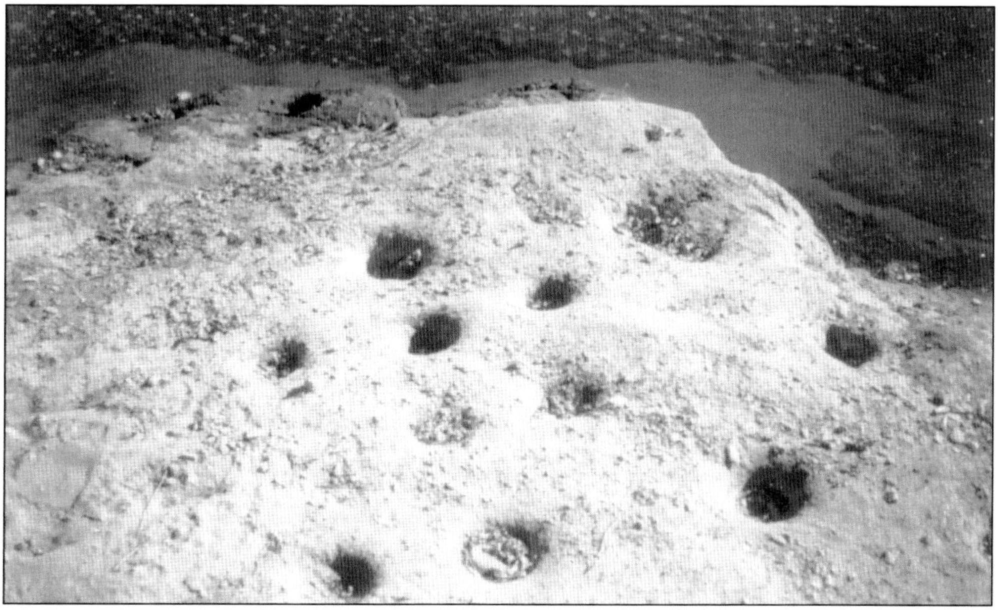

Grinding stones can be found in many areas along the Cosumnes River. It is on these stones that acorns were ground into meal for dietary needs. The grinding rock pictured here was on the Sheldon Ranch on the Cosumnes River. (Courtesy of Ellen Rosa.)

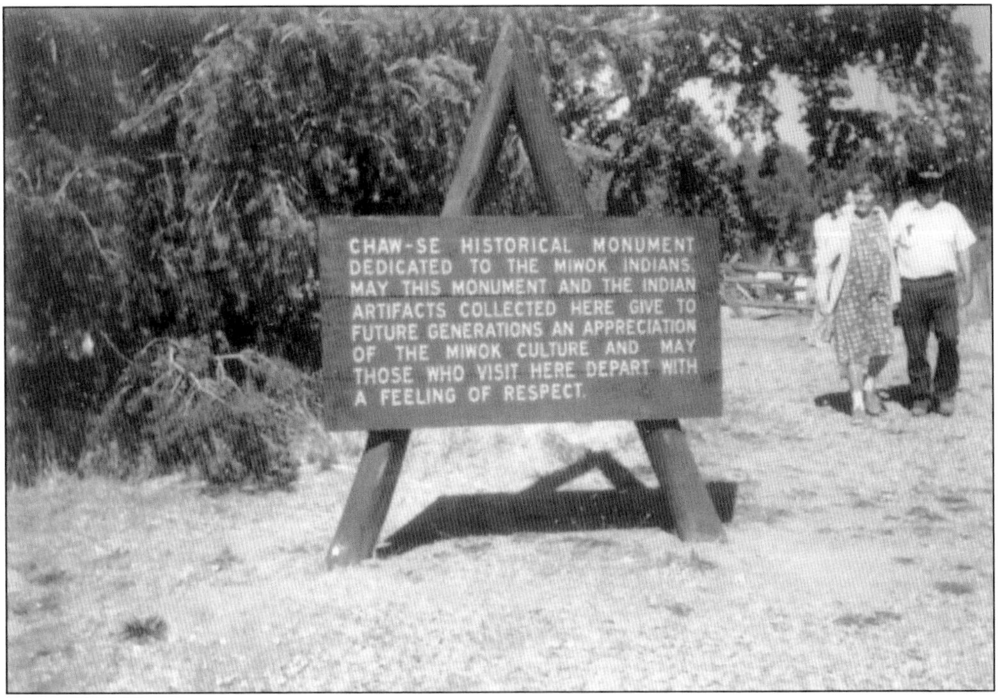

The best examples of Miwok culture are at Chaw'se Indian Grinding Rock State Park in Pine Grove, east of Elk Grove and Sloughhouse. The grinding rock (that's what Chaw'se means in Miwok) is a huge, natural outcropping of limestone. Today the local Miwok groups are referred to by their federally recognized names, the Wilton Rancheria Miwok and the Ione Band of Miwoks.

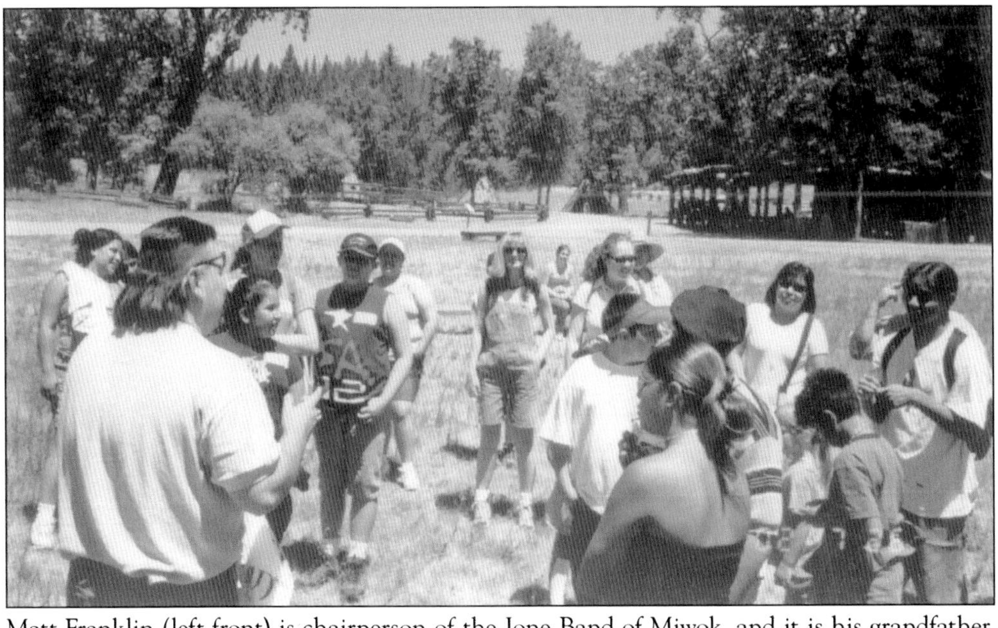

Matt Franklin (left front) is chairperson of the Ione Band of Miwok, and it is his grandfather, Elder William Franklin, who played a large role in the development of Chaw'se. Matt, who works for the Elk Grove School District, was recognized by President Clinton in 1999 for his work. This is a fine tribute to the first people who lived in the Elk Grove area.

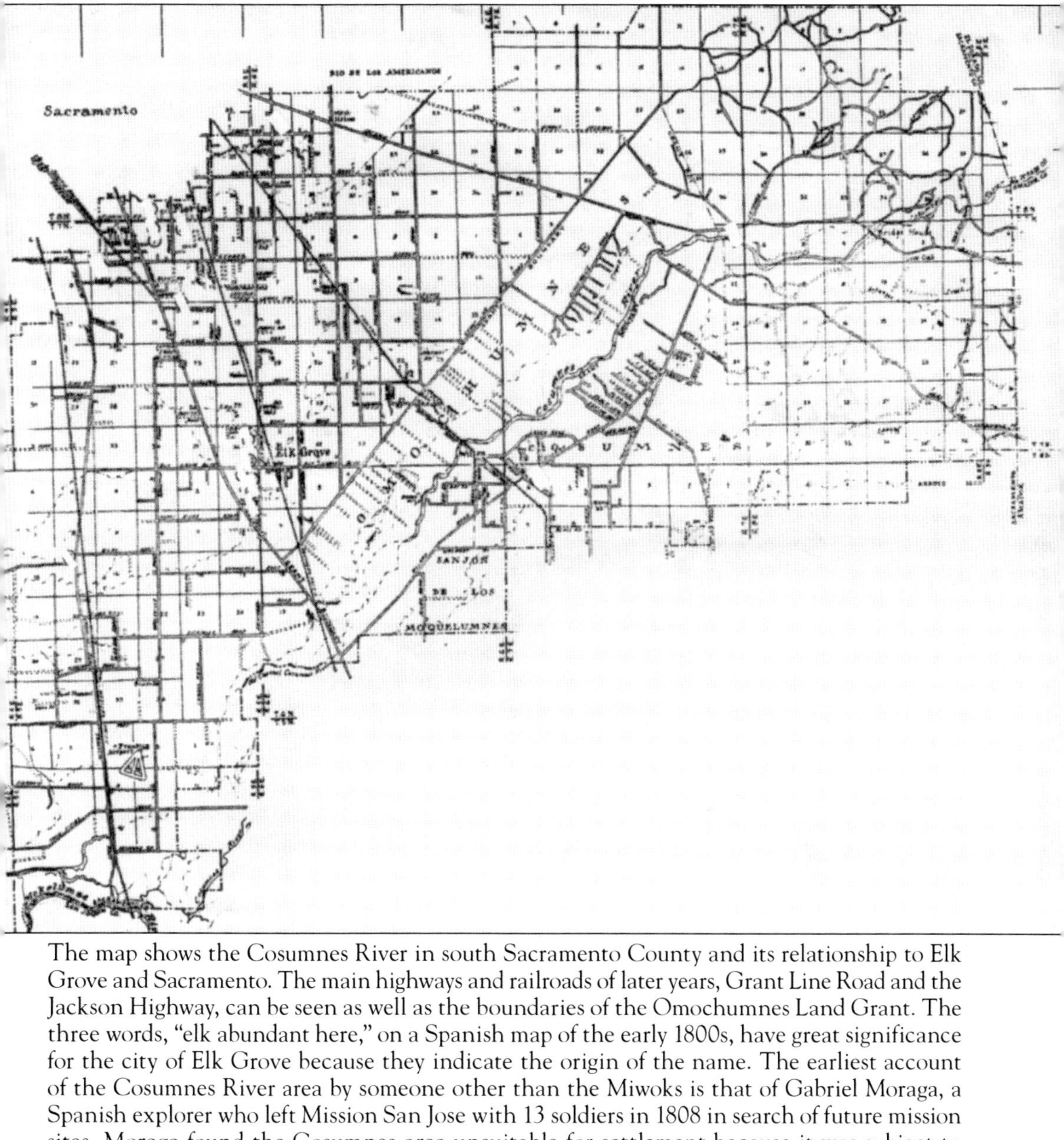

The map shows the Cosumnes River in south Sacramento County and its relationship to Elk Grove and Sacramento. The main highways and railroads of later years, Grant Line Road and the Jackson Highway, can be seen as well as the boundaries of the Omochumnes Land Grant. The three words, "elk abundant here," on a Spanish map of the early 1800s, have great significance for the city of Elk Grove because they indicate the origin of the name. The earliest account of the Cosumnes River area by someone other than the Miwoks is that of Gabriel Moraga, a Spanish explorer who left Mission San Jose with 13 soldiers in 1808 in search of future mission sites. Moraga found the Cosumnes area unsuitable for settlement because it was subject to flooding. His report stated that it was too wet and marshy and filled with *lagunas* (lagoons). The tules were an obstacle, and there was no stone for building foundations. Moraga named the river Rio de Cosumnes, which is what it is still called today. Other names on the map are "prairie land" in the Valley Hi area and *flora* where Florin is today.

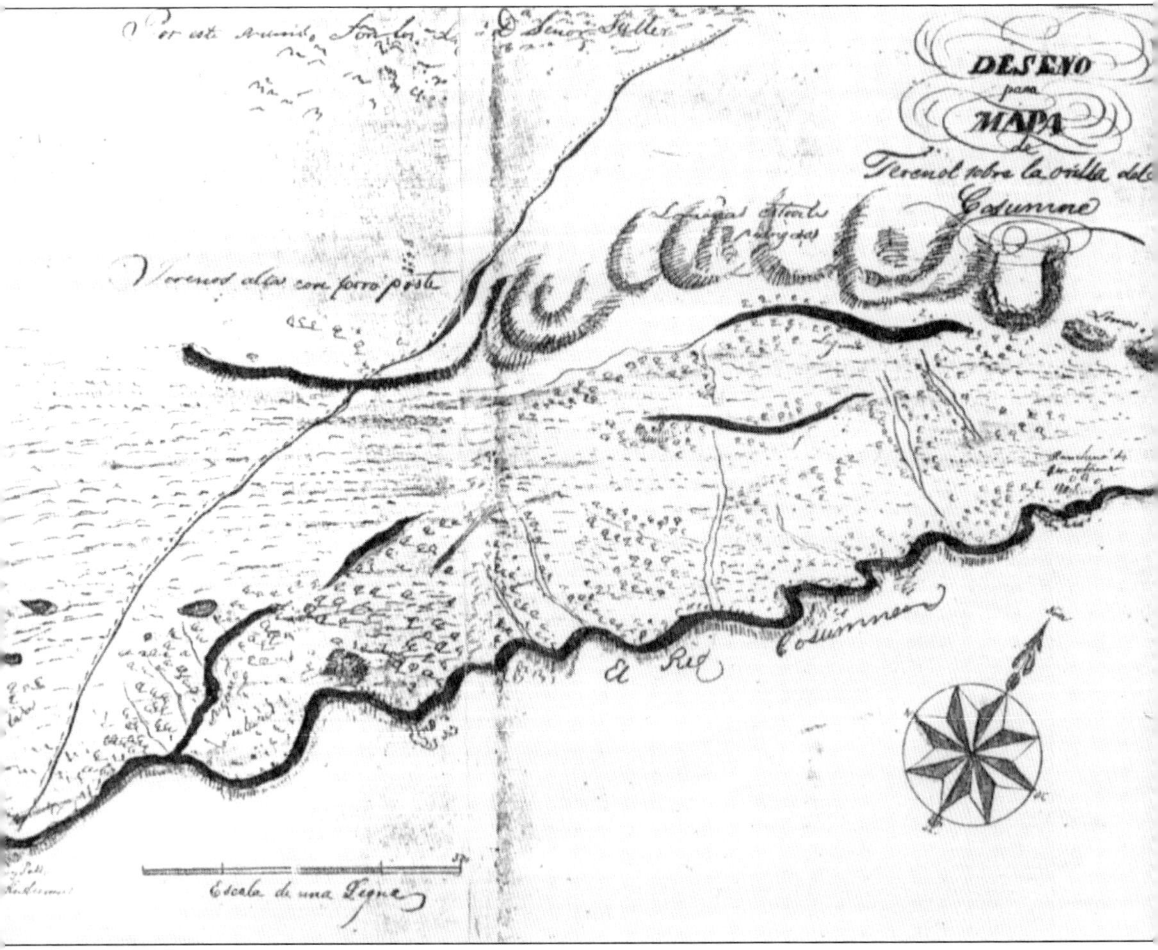

The Omochumnes Land Grant of 18,551 acres was awarded to Jared Dixon Sheldon in 1844 by the Mexican government of California for having built the custom house in Monterey. Grant Line Road will forever be a reminder of California's Mexican days. With its aim on Mount Diablo, many miles away, the road was the boundary of the Rancho Omochumnes on the Rio de Cosumnes. The grant's surveyor was William Tecumseh Sherman, a U. S. Army lieutenant who became well known later as a Civil War general. Sheldon and his partner, William Daylor, divided the grant into three parcels—the Upper Daylor Ranch, Sheldon's Ranch, and the Lower Daylor Ranch. Mexican ranchos were all over California in the 1840s, and the hide and tallow trade was booming. Huge herds of cattle roamed at will in much of Mexican California, making Monterey a busy port with ships filled with California products bound for the rest of the world. Sheldon and Daylor anticipated being part of that busy market. (Courtesy of Ellen Rosa.)

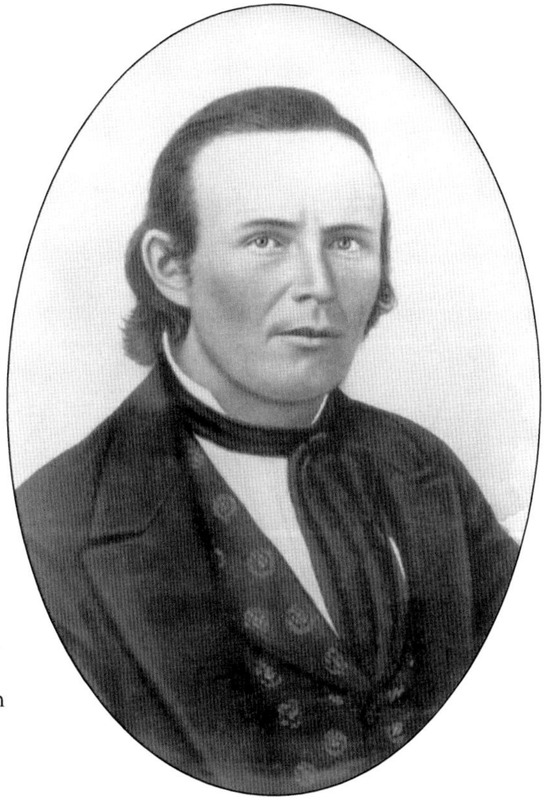

The partners, Jared Sheldon and William Daylor, married the daughters of Thomas and Elizabeth Rhoads, who had come to California in 1846. Sarah was 16 and Catherine only 14, but Daylor and Sheldon courted them shortly after the family arrived. Daylor married Sarah, and Sheldon married Catherine, and these weddings in the spring of 1847 were the first recorded at Sutter's Fort. Sheldon had his bachelor cabin, a house made of sawed boards from the Sacramento port. The house was on a slough, and that is how the name Slough House (later spelled as one word) came to be known. It was near Sheldon's gristmill, the first one in Northern California, on the Cosumnes River. Daylor and Sarah settled at what later became known as Daylor's Place, with the post office of Cosumne. (Courtesy of Ellen Rosa.)

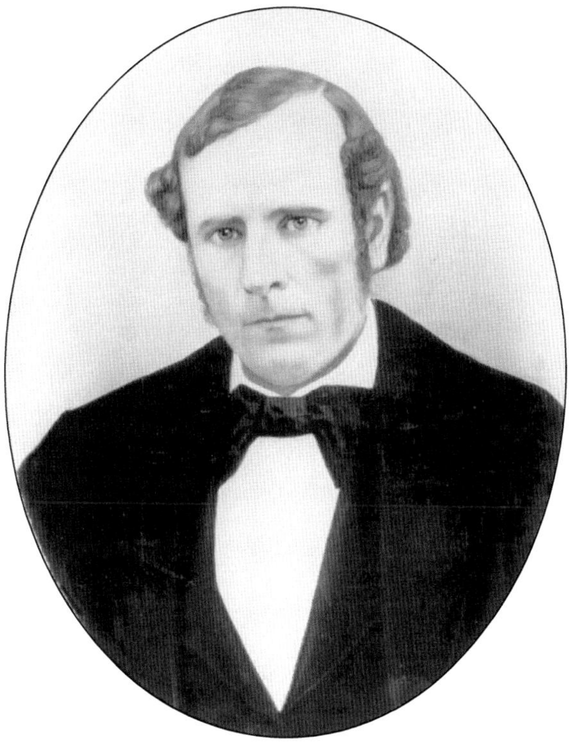

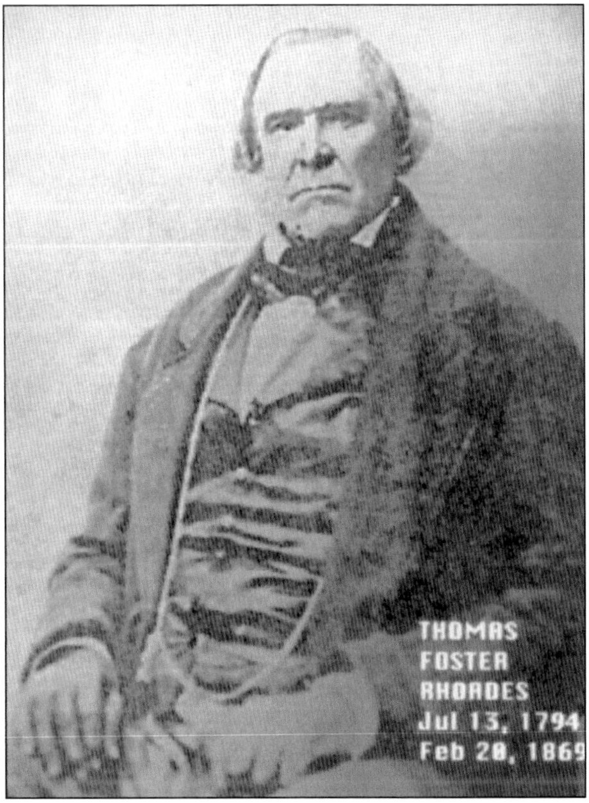

Thomas Rhoads, a friend of Brigham Young, brought 51 family members to California in 1846. The first Mormons to come overland to California, they came in search of religious freedom as they had endured harassment of Latter Day Saints in the Midwest. The Rhoads group traveled with the Donners but took the Oregon Trail instead of the Sierra crossing. Sutter allowed them to camp at Dry Creek, south of the Cosumnes River.

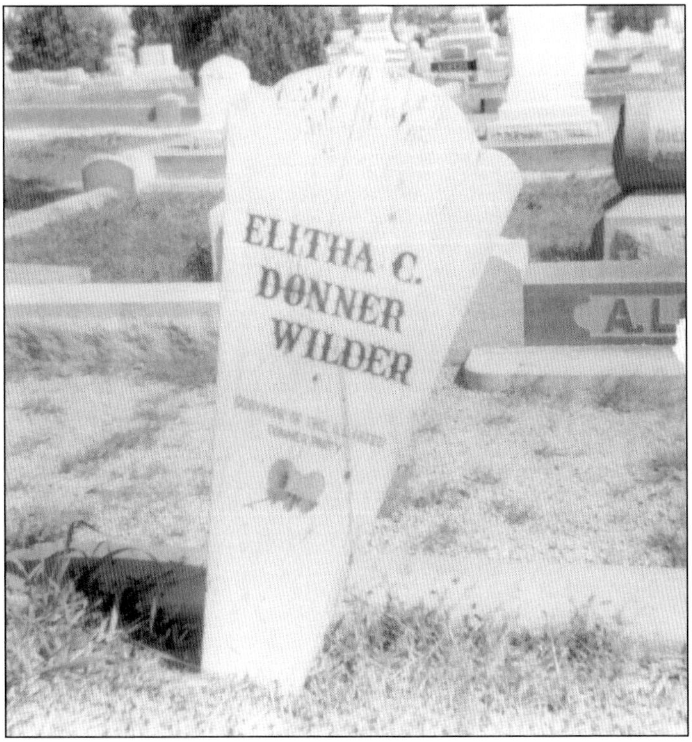

Elitha Donner, buried in the Elk Grove Cemetery, was 12 years old when the Donner Party was stranded in the Sierra Nevada in the winter of 1846–1847. Elitha, her two sisters, and others were rescued by John and Dan Rhoads, sons of Thomas and Elizabeth Rhoads. The Rhoads School in Elk Grove Park (originally on Sloughhouse Road) was named for John P. Rhoads.

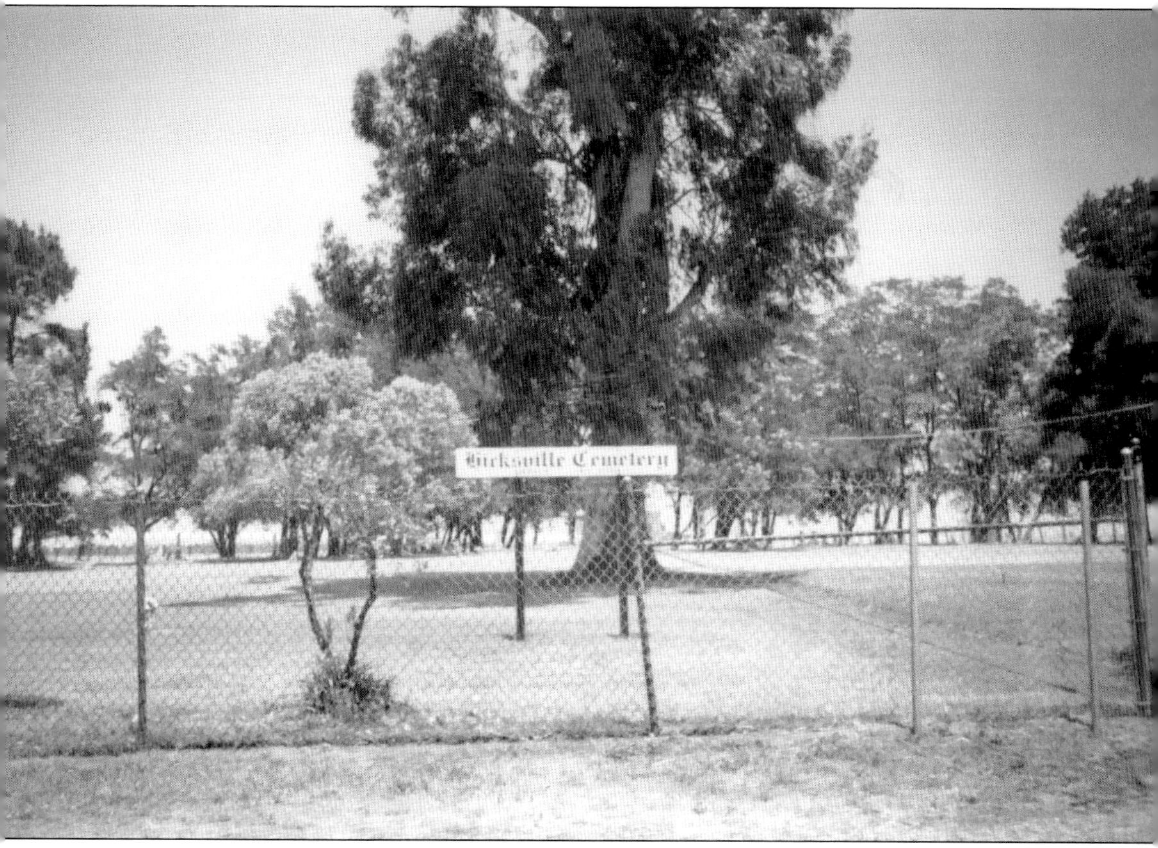

All that is left of the town of Hicksville south of the Cosumnes River is the cemetery, but it is a place filled with stories. Here are a just a few: the fascinating tales of Billy Hicks, an early day California cattle baron; the adventures of the McCauley family and their entourage of slaves traveling to California to avoid the Civil War; Hicksville's McCauley, the very successful manager of San Quentin Prison who got caught up in numerous financial scandals; the famous race track at Hicksville, known later as Arno, with the finest racing horses in America; a courtroom controversy over the ownership of the Chabolla, one of California's most tangled properties; the romance of an honest to goodness Italian count, Pio Valensin, and Alice McCauley, the girl who sang "Dixie" in San Francisco and was almost arrested for such a treasonous action; and the final chapter, the storybook Valensin Ranch, once more than 50,000 acres but now one of the finest natural preserves of the Cosumnes area.

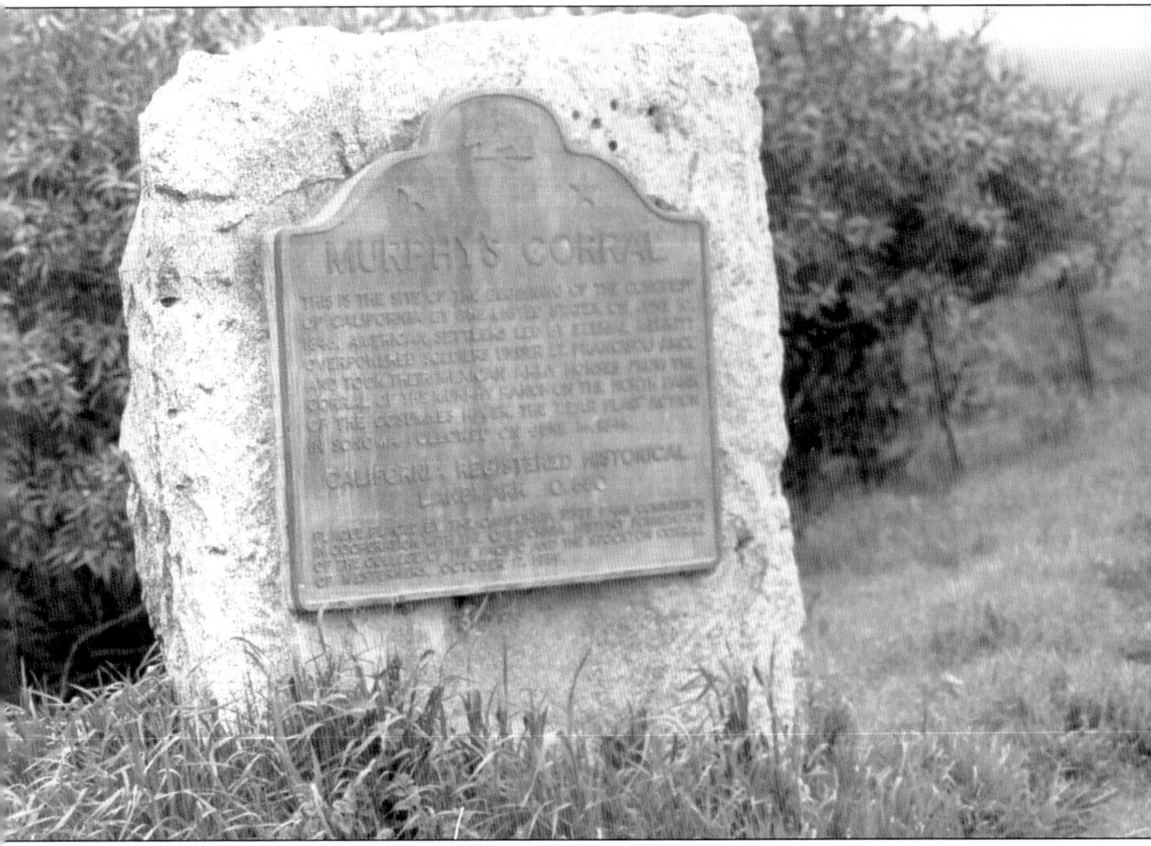

Martin Murphy Jr. owned Rancho Cazaderos, north of the Cosumnes River, on the west side of today's Highway 99, known then as the Monterey Trail. The Murphy family earned a place in California history for opening the wagon trail across the Sierra Nevada. The Stevens/Murphy/Miller party crossed the mountains in 1844 and followed the Yuba and Bear Rivers to the valley. Years later, this became the route taken by the Central Pacific for the transcontinental railroad. At Martin's corral, just a few miles south of Elk Grove, an important event occurred on June 10, 1846, that resulted in statehood for California. This incident is described as the first overt act in the conquest of California by the Americans, and it happened four days before the Bear Flag Uprising in Sonoma. Mexican soldiers moved a large number of horses from San Rafael to San Jose, spending the night at Murphy's place. American settlers, led by Ezekial Merritt, released the horses from the corral. This act set the stage for what was to come—independence for California and eventual statehood. (Courtesy of Tom Russell.)

Three

THE SEARCH FOR GOLD

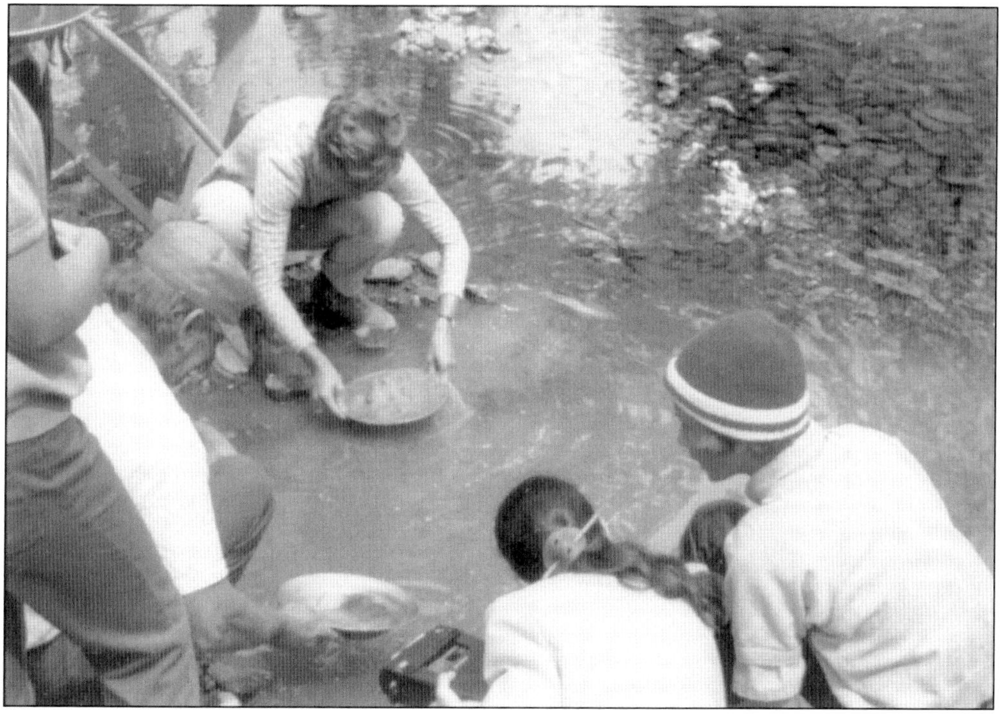

Gold was discovered in May 1847 by Elizabeth Rhoads and Jemima Powell just south of Elk Grove and Galt and the Cosumnes River area. The two women were washing clothes in Dry Creek when they saw the glittery pieces. When their husbands came home from working in the woods for John Sutter, the men decided that the pebbles could be gold. They set off for Sutter's Fort in the morning, an all-day journey. Sutter verified that it was gold, and he told them to mine it only at night. The precious metal was taken to San Francisco without disclosing its source, and the secret mining of the gold continued. After Elizabeth died, Thomas journeyed to Salt Lake to join his friend, Brigham Young. He took with him $17,000 in gold from Dry Creek and the Cosumnes River. In this photograph, students step back into the past to pan for gold.

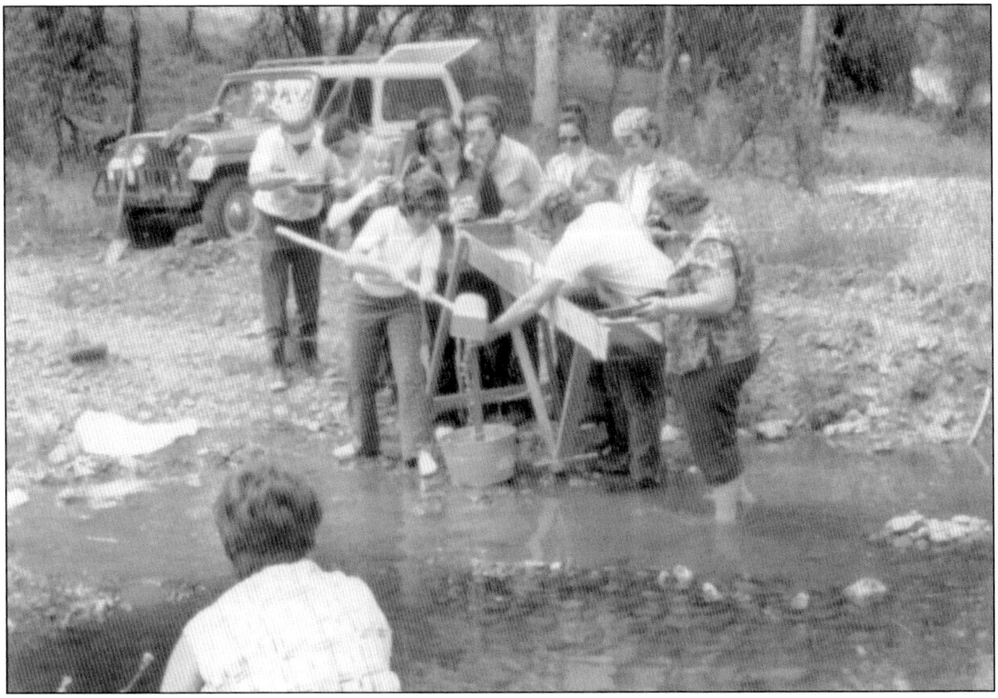

Joseph Kerr students and teachers try gold mining in 1973. They were hoping they would be as lucky as Elizabeth Rhoads was in finding some nuggets.

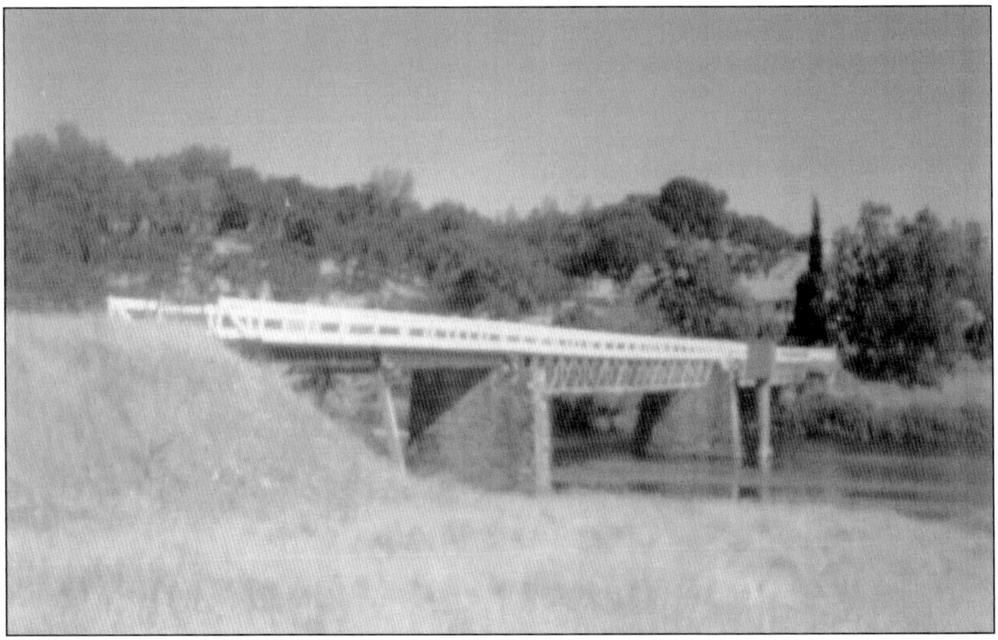

Gold mining was very profitable on the Cosumnes, but being able to cross the river was a necessity for gold miners. Samuel Putnam became a rich man after he built a toll bridge at Michigan Bar, the route from Weber's Place (Stockton) to Hangtown (Placerville). Instant city/towns were created overnight—Live Oak, Sebastopol, Bridge House, Michigan Bar, Katesville, Cook's Bar, Wilson's Exchange, Cosumne, and Slough House.

As many as 2,000 people lived in each of the overnight towns that had post offices, hotels, livery stables, and blacksmith shops. They all hoped to make their fortunes with a lucky strike or two. By 1970, only one family, the Rumans, lived at Michigan Bar, and all the little towns were gone. But in 2006, the area is home to hundreds of families in the growing community of Rancho Murieta. The Rumans are pictured here in the 1970s.

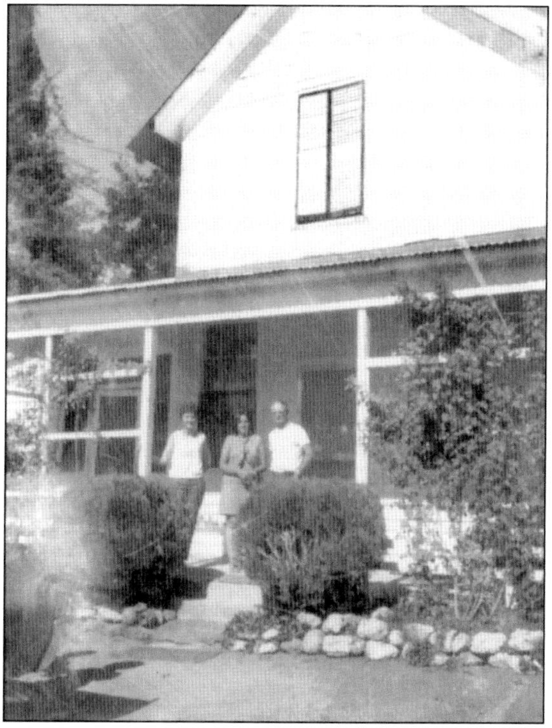

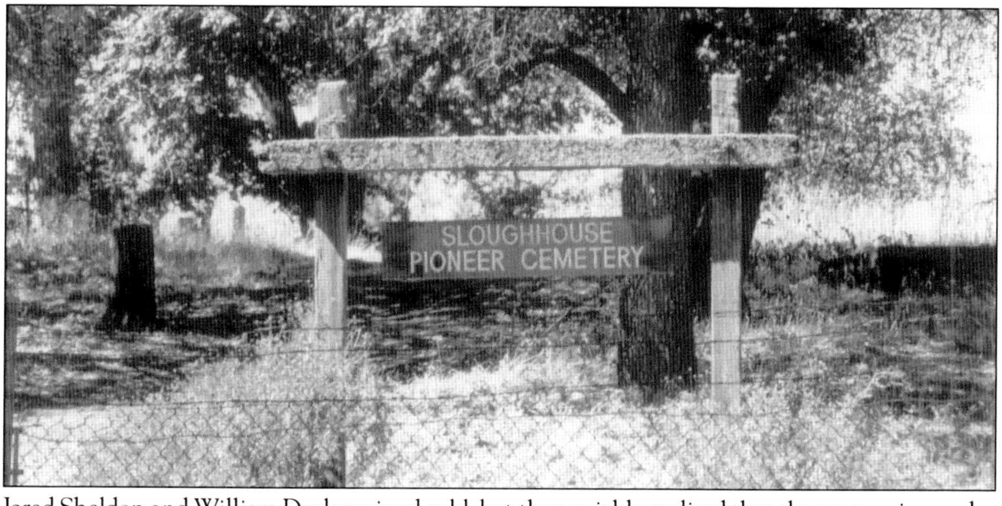

Jared Sheldon and William Daylor mined gold, but they quickly realized that the many miners who came to the Cosumnes River needed services, and they set out to provide them. In a short time though, both men were dead, and neither was able to carry out the vision of what the Cosumnes River Valley and the Omochumnes Grant could have been. Daylor's death resulted from the terrible cholera epidemic of 1850. He had gone to Sutter's Fort for supplies for his store, and when he tended to a dying man, he fell victim to the quick-acting disease. By the time he rode his horse back to his Cosumnes home, he was near death. William Daylor was the first person to be buried on the hill that is known as the Sloughhouse Cemetery. The cemetery, off Meiss Road and close to the Sloughhouse Inn, is one of the oldest in northern California. The land was deeded to the Daughters of the Utah Pioneers in 1972 by Percy Westerberg, a descendant of Catherine Rhoads Sheldon Mahone Dalton.

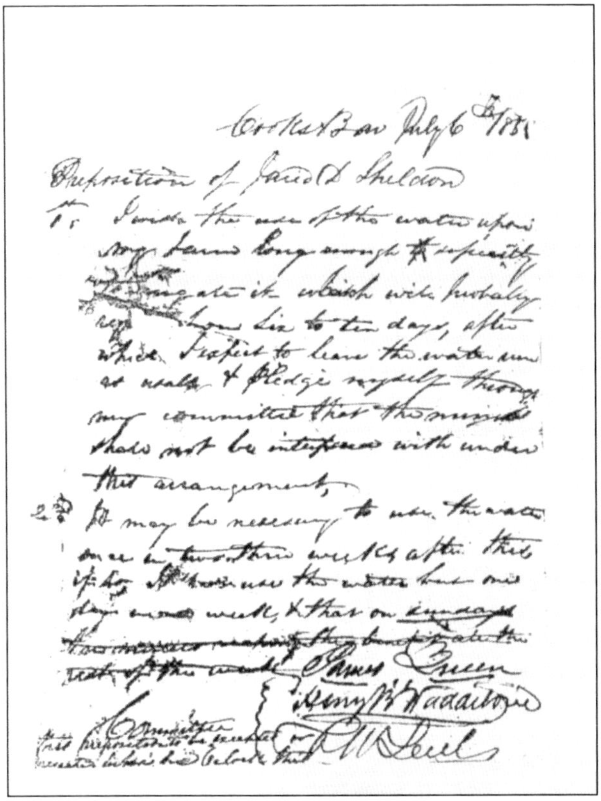

Cooks Bar July 6th 1851

Proposition of Jared D Sheldon

1st I wish the use of the water upon my dam long enough to [illegible] irrigate it which will probably [illegible] from six to ten days, after which I expect to leave the water run as usual & pledge myself through my committee that the miners shall not be interfered with under that arrangement,

2d It may be necessary to use the water once in two or three weeks after this if so I [illegible] use the water but one day each week, & that on [illegible]

[illegible]

James Green

Henry W Waddington

Committee

[illegible]

R W Steel

Jared Sheldon left mining to raise vegetables for the many gold miners who were camped on his property. These miners became angry because the dam Sheldon built to irrigate his crops was flooding their claims. An agreement was made that Sheldon would only water on Sundays, but the miners confronted Sheldon on a July morning in 1851. Sheldon and two others were shot in what became known as the tragedy of the Cosumnes. (Courtesy of Ellen Rosa.)

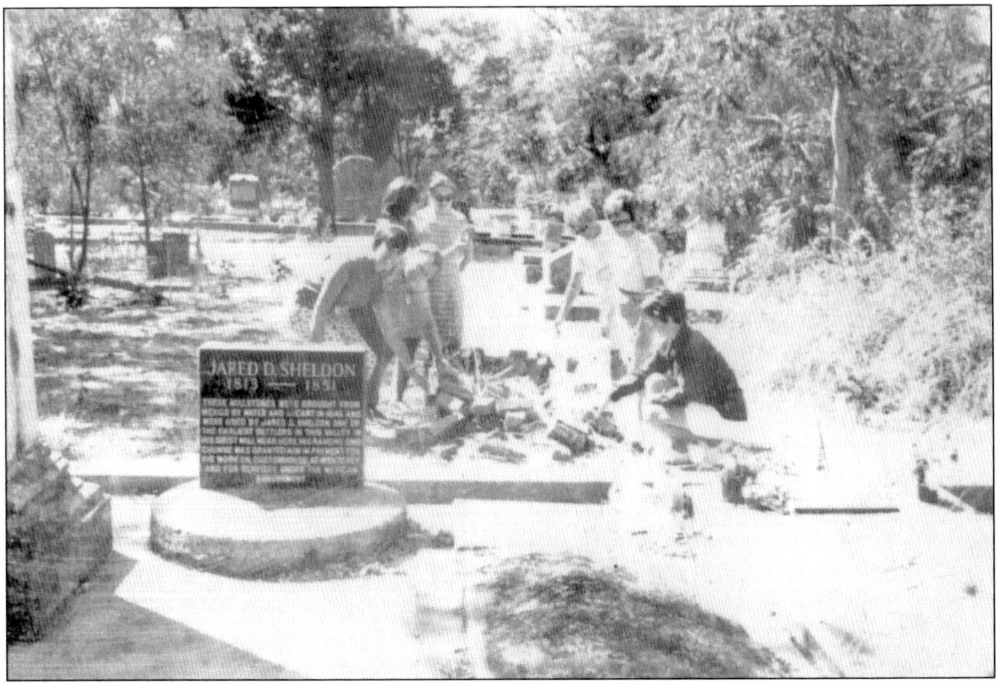

One of the wheels from Sheldon's gristmill is seen in this 1970 photograph of the Sloughhouse Cemetery. The wheel was later stolen from the cemetery.

Catherine Rhoads Sheldon was widowed at the age of 18 in 1851 when her husband, Jared, was murdered by the miners. Left with three small children, she persevered and continued the Slough House stage stop and store. Marrying two more times, Catherine Rhoads Sheldon Mahone Dalton was clearly the matriarch of the Sheldon family. (Courtesy of Ellen Rosa.)

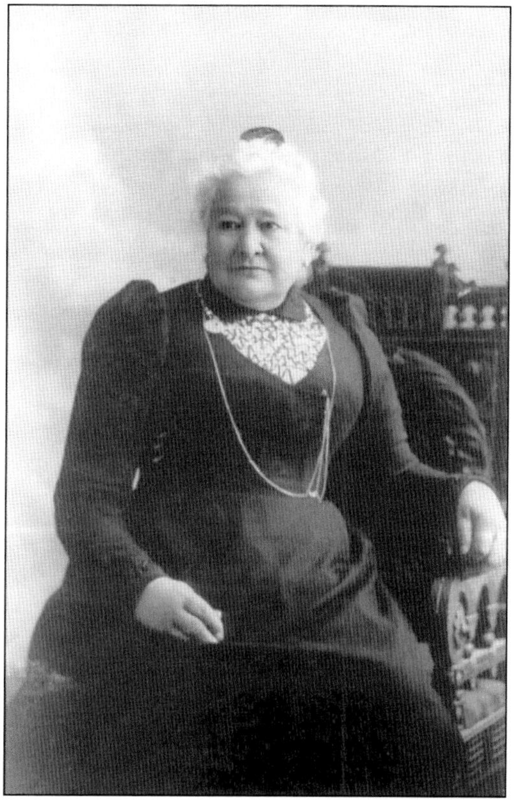

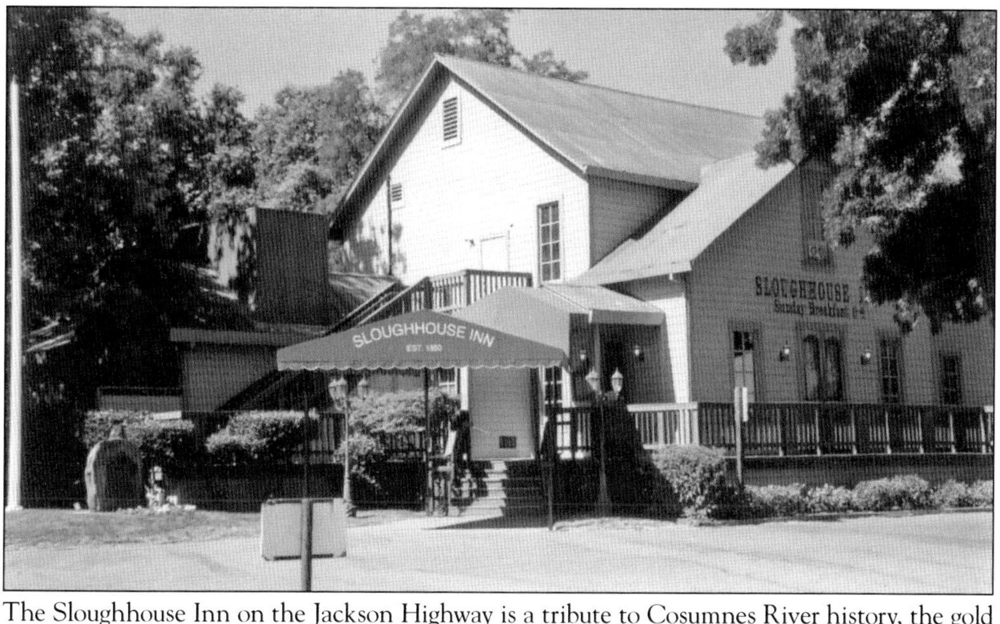

The Sloughhouse Inn on the Jackson Highway is a tribute to Cosumnes River history, the gold days, and the beginnings of agriculture. The historical marker is just to the left of the entrance. Catherine's sister Sarah married William Robinson Grimshaw after William Daylor's death, and they continued the store at Cosumne. The descendants of Sarah and Catherine—the Grimshaws, Sheldons, and Westerbergs—have played important roles in Sloughhouse.

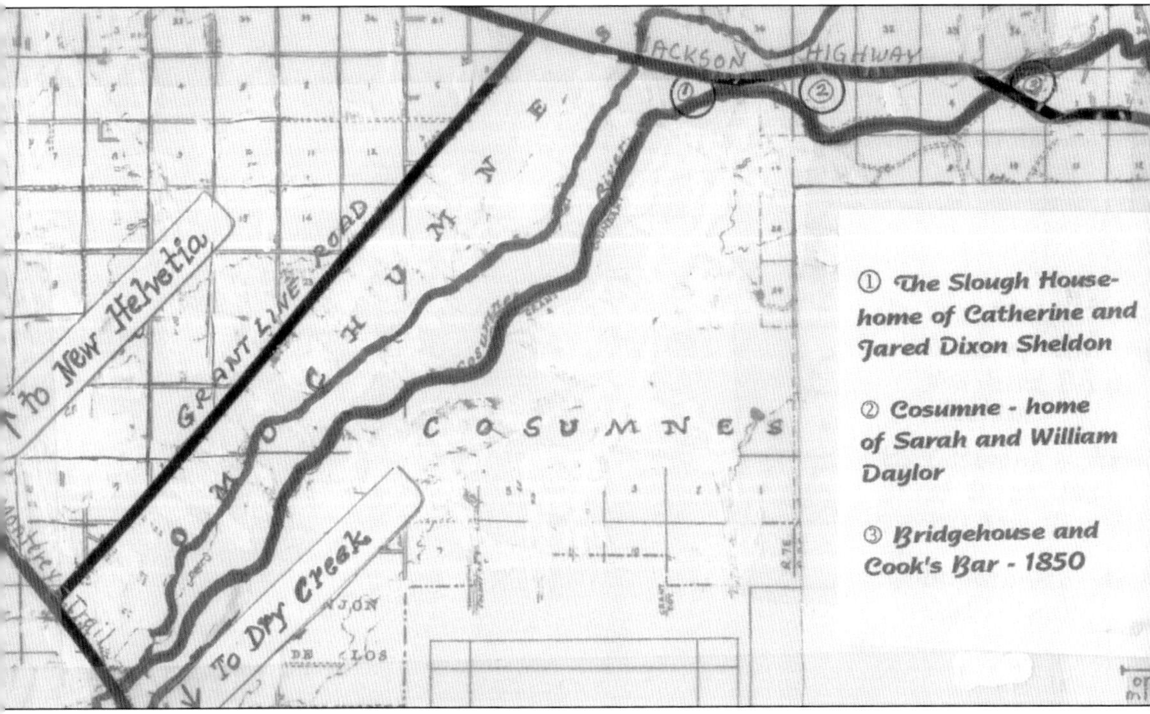

The Cosumnes River defined the early transportation systems of south Sacramento County. The Monterey Trail paralleled the Sacramento River and ran from New Helvetia (Sutter's Fort) to Monterey, the capital of Mexican California. The entire area flooded in the winter, so travelers took the higher ground to the east for their route. In the gold days, these two trails became known as the Lower and Upper Stockton Roads. Today they are Franklin Boulevard and Highway 99. Grant Line Road, the marker of the Omochumnes Grant, connected Upper Stockton Road with the Jackson Highway. Another route to Michigan Bar and Placerville was Bandeen Road on the south side of the river. It is known today as Dillard Road.

James W. Hall built a hotel/stage stop, the Elk Grove House, on Upper Stockton Road. It was near a grove of oak trees that is now Elk Grove Park. Hall opened a post office and was justice of the peace, and he provided travelers with places to sleep and eat, pick up mail, and take care of business.

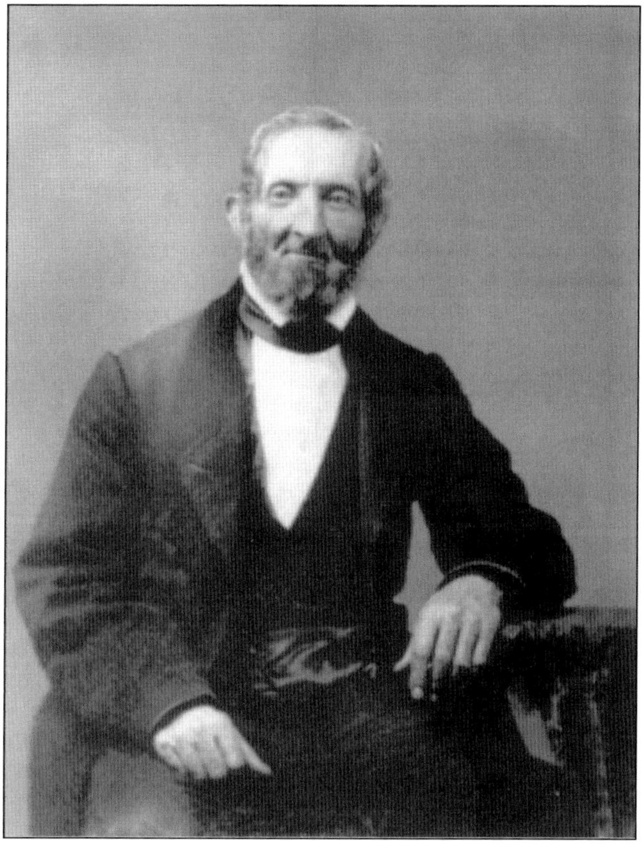

Hall created the name for what is now the growing city of Elk Grove perhaps because of the tule elk that wandered through the oak grove on their way to the Cosumnes River. Another story is that Hall saw a rack of elk horns hung in a tree, and yet another is that Hall knew of a place called Elk Grove in Missouri. Perhaps all three contributed to the name of Elk Grove. (Courtesy of Dave Morse.)

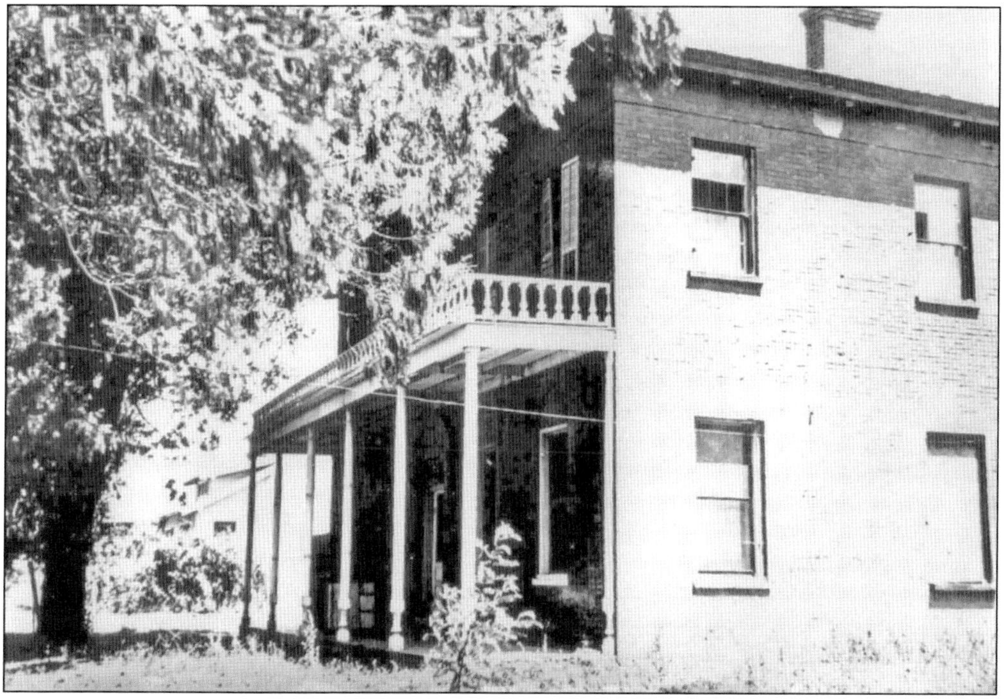

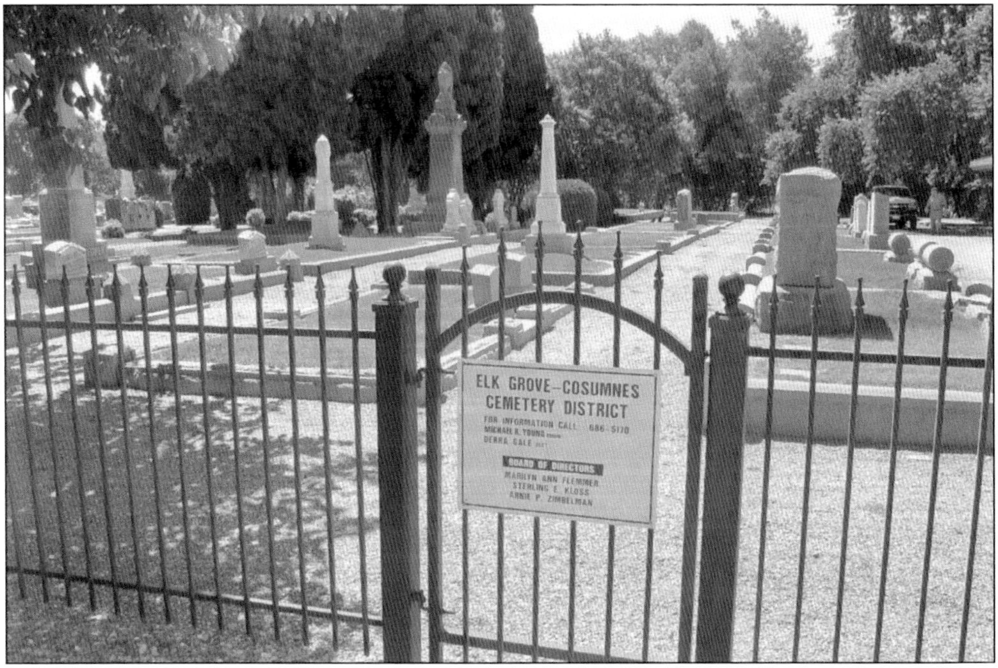

The cemetery at Highway 99 and Elk Grove Boulevard is all that is left of the second site of Elk Grove, called Buckner. In 1853, James Buckner built a hotel on the northwest corner to compete with Hall's establishment. Stockton Road at that time was covered with clouds of dust all summer as stages pulled over to rest their weary loads, and in the winter the adobe clay soil created many problems for horses and wagons. Buckner may have been the one who put the road (later Main Street and Elk Grove Boulevard) through to Grant Line to catch the traffic of the gold mines. (Courtesy of Tom Russell.)

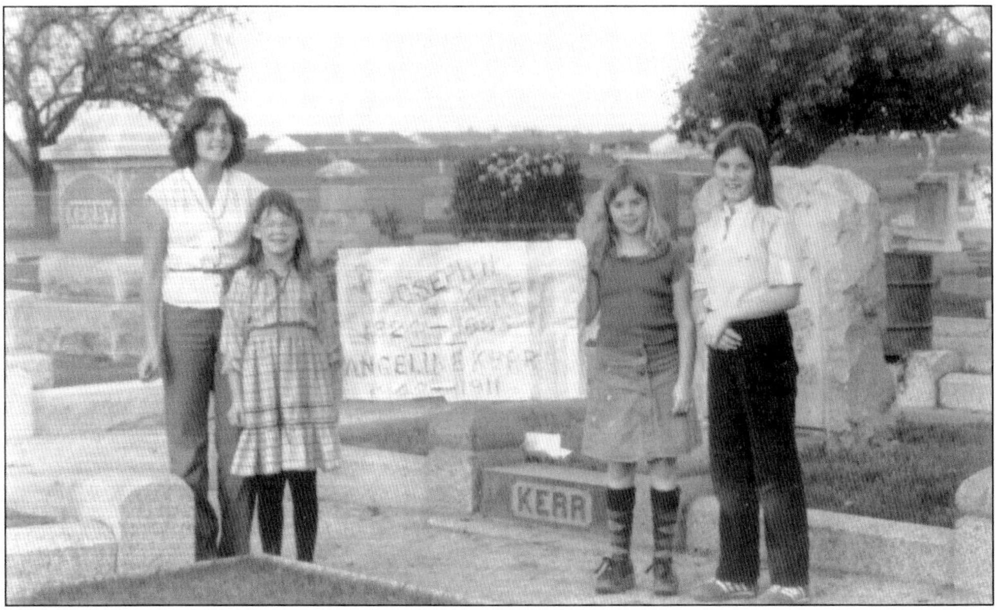

Students create rubbings of the tombstones in the cemetery during the 1970s as they study about Elk Grove's pioneers.

Four

THE FARMERS

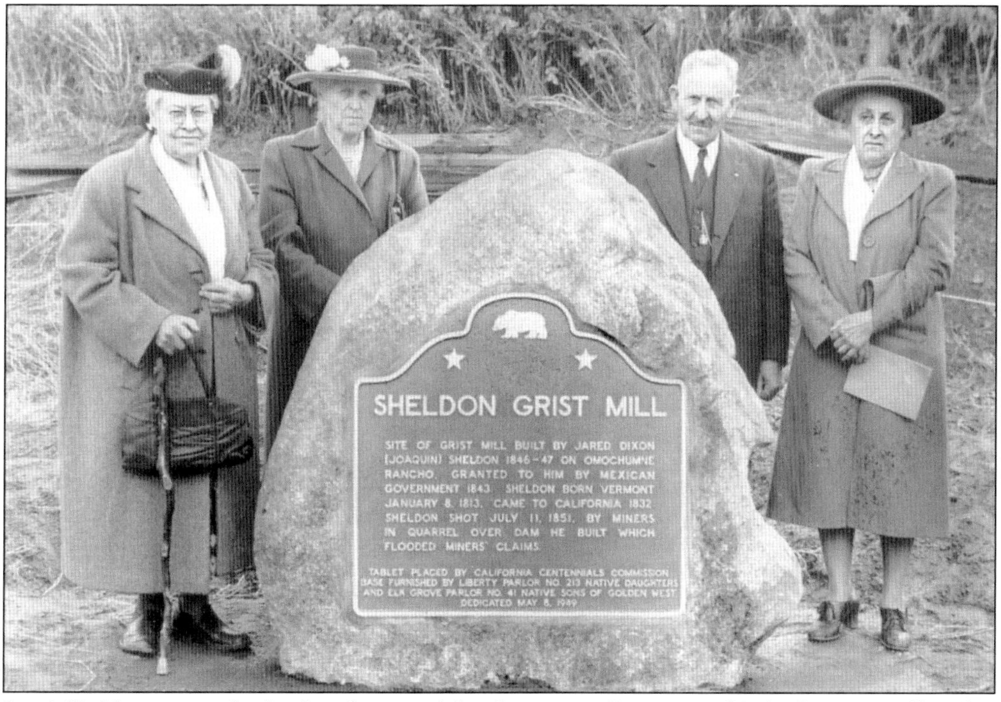

Jared Sheldon was truly the first farmer of the Cosumnes River area. He built a gristmill on his Omochumnes Rancho in 1846, and the Elk Grove Parlor of the Native Sons and Daughters of the Golden West dedicated the Sheldon Mill site on May 8, 1949. The historical marker is located near the Sloughhouse Inn on Deer Creek. Pictured here from left to right are Catherine (Polly) Sheldon Granlees, Jessie Grimshaw, Jared William Sheldon, and Kittie Sheldon Cothrin, the mother of Ellen Rosa. From this agricultural beginning at Sloughhouse there have been several eras of farming, including cattle, grain, orchards, vineyards, hops, dairies, and chickens. Davis corn is renowned throughout the region, and it is sold at the site of the former town of Cosumne, also known as Daylor's Place. The 1990s saw a return to vineyards, which are beginning to cover many fields and rolling hills. (Courtesy of Ellen Rosa.)

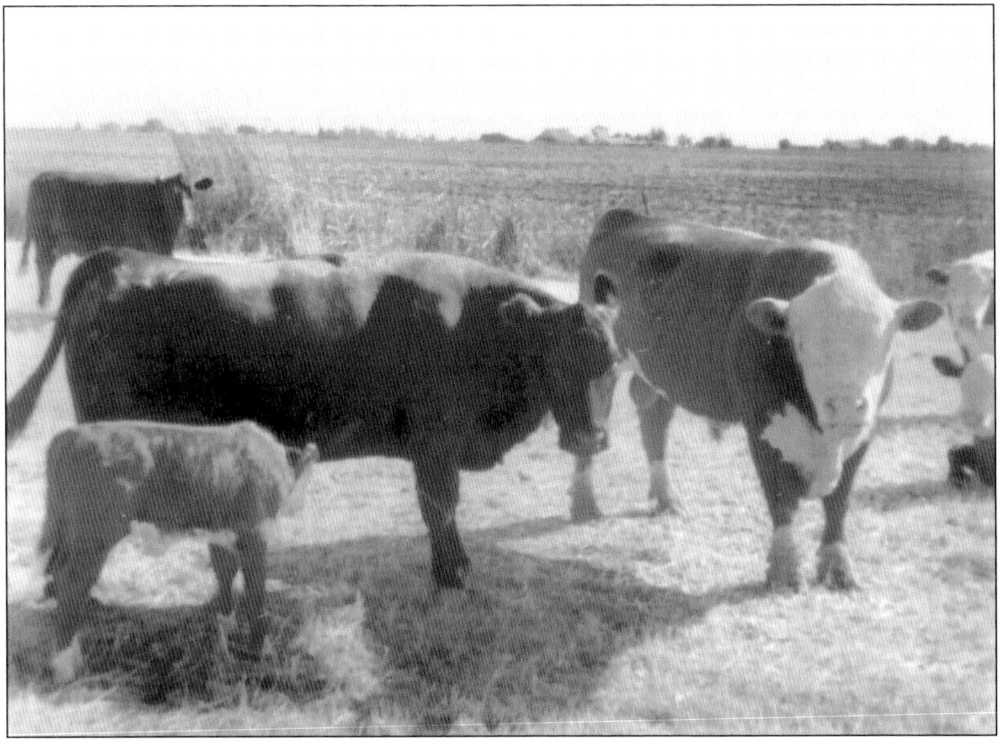

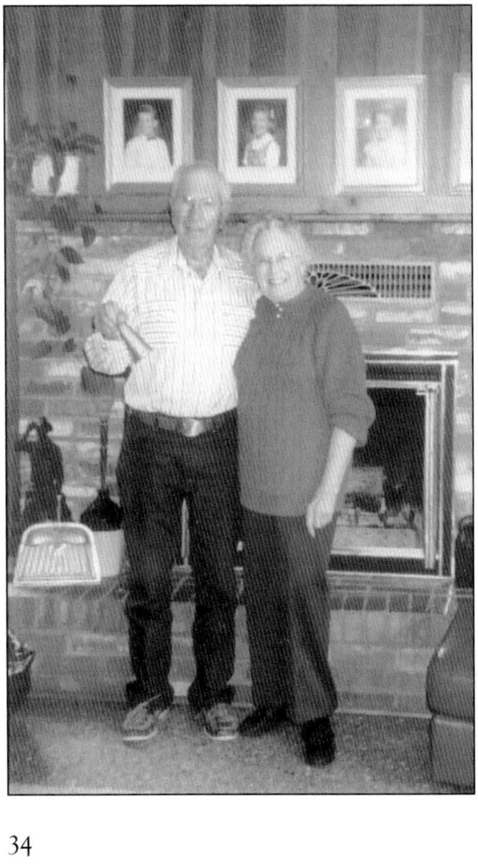

Jared Sheldon and William Daylor brought cattle to the Omochumnes Grant in the 1840s. The hide and tallow trade was flourishing in Mexican California, and if it had not been for the discovery of gold, the Cosumnes-Elk Grove area might have become famous as cattle country. In 1855, land grants and government lands were put up for sale in California, and the early farmers focused on cattle and sheep.

The cowbell reminded Gordon and Verna Van Vleck of their cattle-ranching days. The Van Vlecks of Michigan Bar and the Sierra foothills continued the family tradition of taking cattle to mountain pastures for the hot summer months. Gordon was president of the National Cattlemen's Association and the California Cattlemen's Association. He served for eight years as California's secretary of resources under Governor Deukmajian.

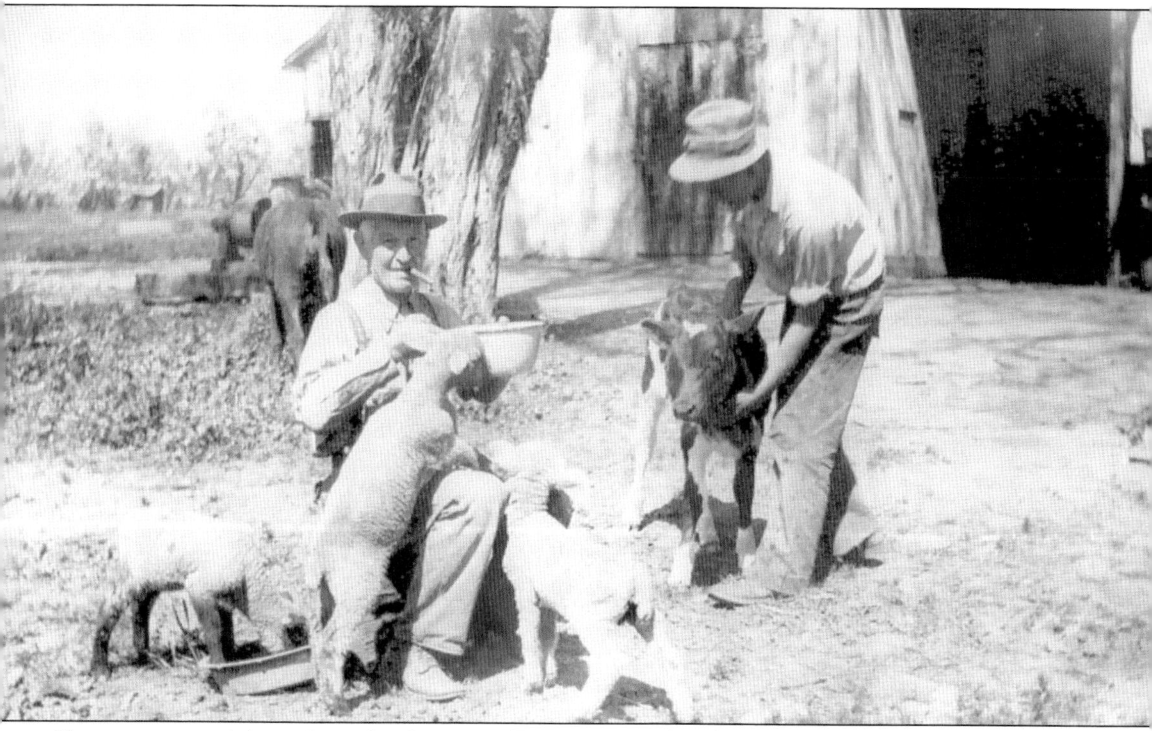

Sheep were raised throughout the Cosumnes River area. In this photograph, Frederick Grimshaw, and his son, also named Frederick, feed the lamb and the calf. One of the first large-scale sheep men was John Ehrhardt, who with his son John brought 7,000 sheep across the plains and mountains to Sheldon in 1852. Gold ruled the Cosumnes River, but there was not enough food for the miners, so extravagant prices were paid for anything edible. The Ehrhardts made a fine profit on their sheep venture, and young John decided to stay in the area. The next sheep men were the McConnell brothers on the Murphy place. They focused on wool, shearing 12,000 sheep one year and shipping 100,000 pounds of wool to Boston. The Wackmans in Elk Grove were sheep ranchers, and so were the Waegells on Eagle's Nest-Sunrise. From 50,000 sheep in Sacramento County in the 1920s, there were only 9,400 in 1985, and 2,500 of those belonged to the Waegells. The decline was attributed to people eating less meat, synthetic fibers preferred to woolen clothing, and sheep falling prey to growing numbers of coyotes. (Courtesy of Ellen Rosa.)

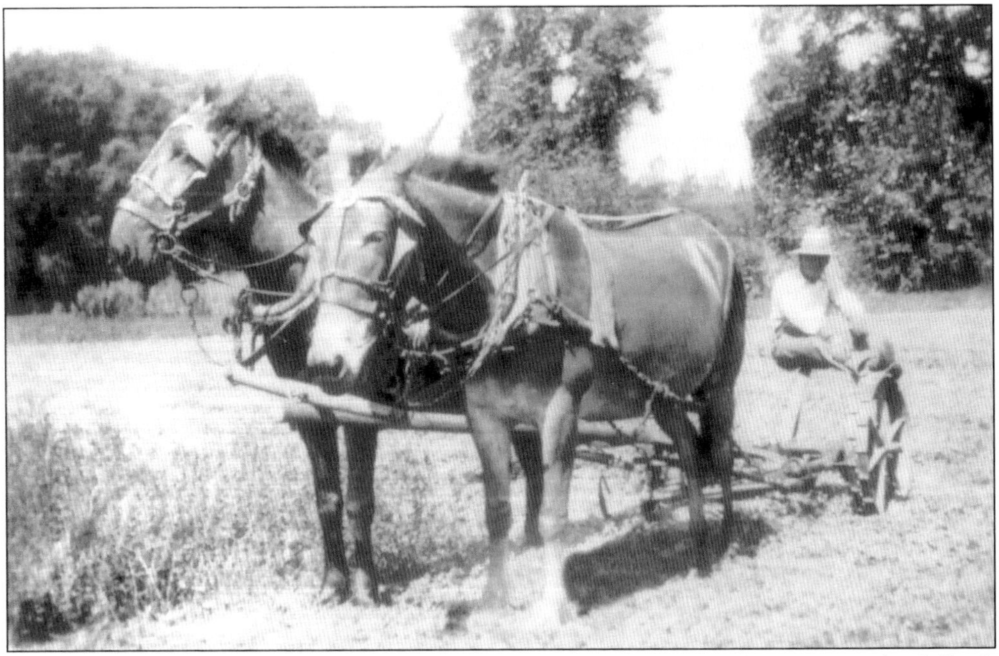

The first farmers to cultivate the fields around the Cosumnes River had to conquer the difficult soils. They became clever in fashioning extensive plows and other necessary machinery. Wheat was a major crop in the flat lands—even in clay and adobe soils. The hot summers created extremely dry wheat kernels that were able to withstand the long ocean trip to European markets. (Courtesy of Ellen Rosa.)

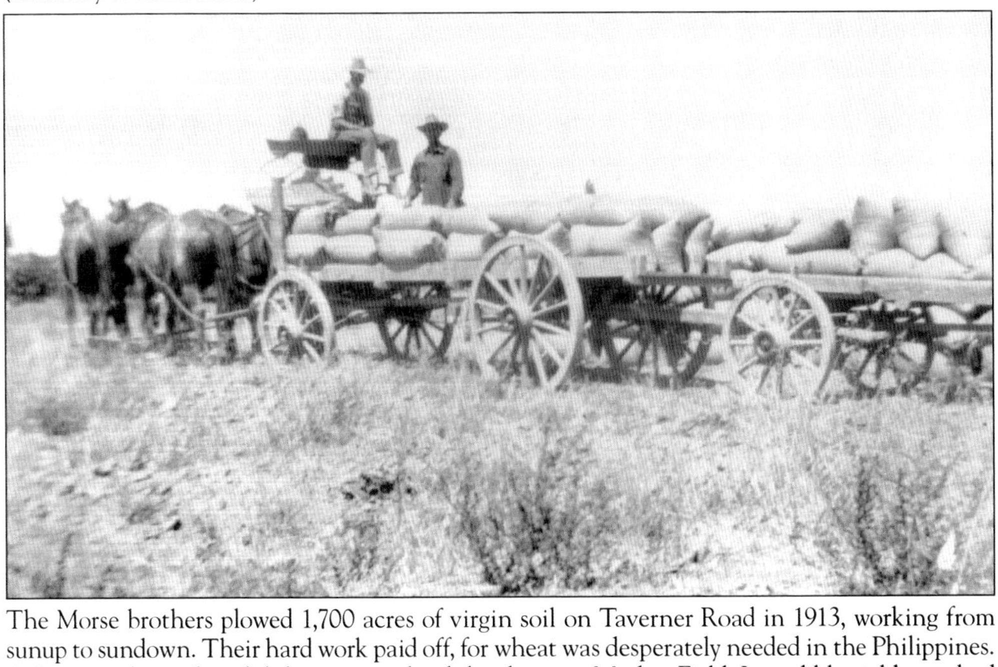

The Morse brothers plowed 1,700 acres of virgin soil on Taverner Road in 1913, working from sunup to sundown. Their hard work paid off, for wheat was desperately needed in the Philippines. A few years later, they did the same on land that became Mather Field. Incredible yields resulted from planting wheat on soil that had never been cultivated, making the hard work extremely productive. (Courtesy of Dave Morse.)

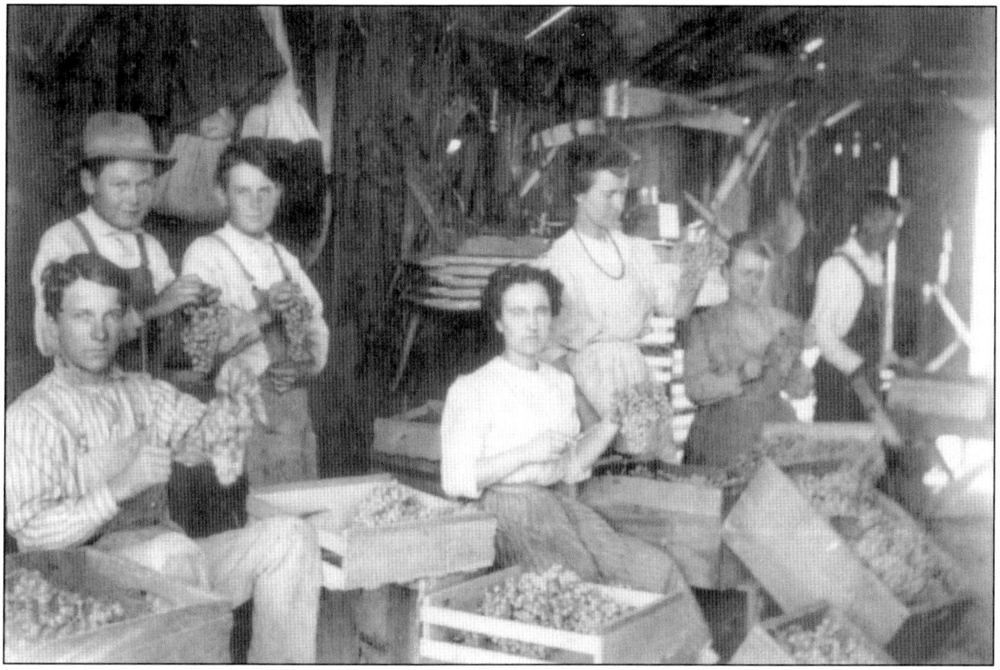

When the Central Pacific Railroad came through Elk Grove in 1868, farmers were able to turn their grain fields into orchards and vineyards. Getting grapes ready for market at the Rusby Packing Shed in 1910 are members of the Bond family.

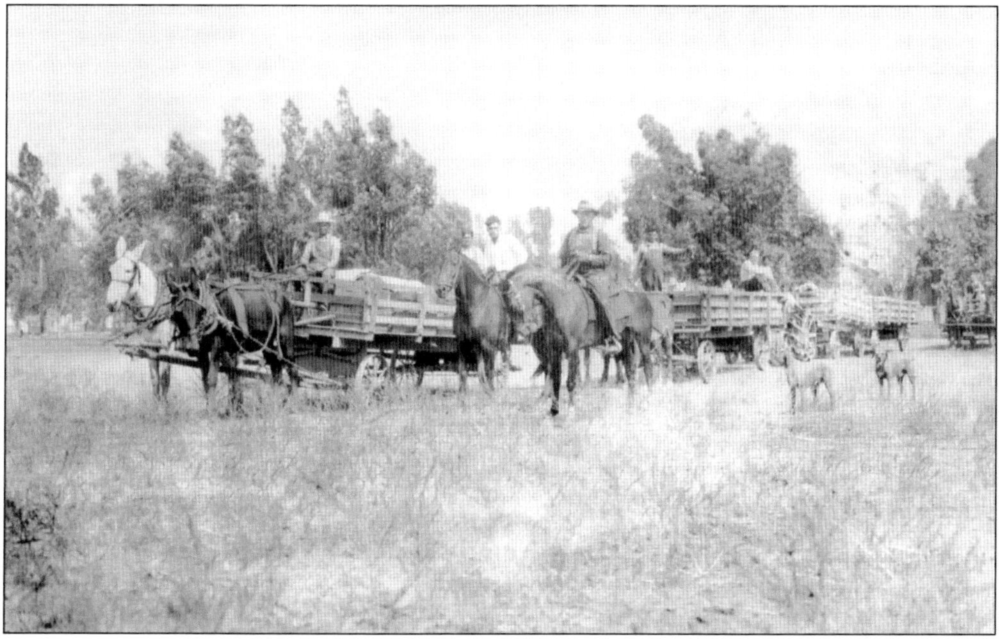

Workers head to the California Vineyard Company east of Bradshaw Road. Hundreds of acres of grapes were raised there and shipped out by the California Traction Line Railroad. The company had 1,400 acres in Tokay grapes in 1912 and was said to be the largest vineyard in the world. The road that led to the company is known today as Calvine Road, from the name of the company—the California Vineyard Company.

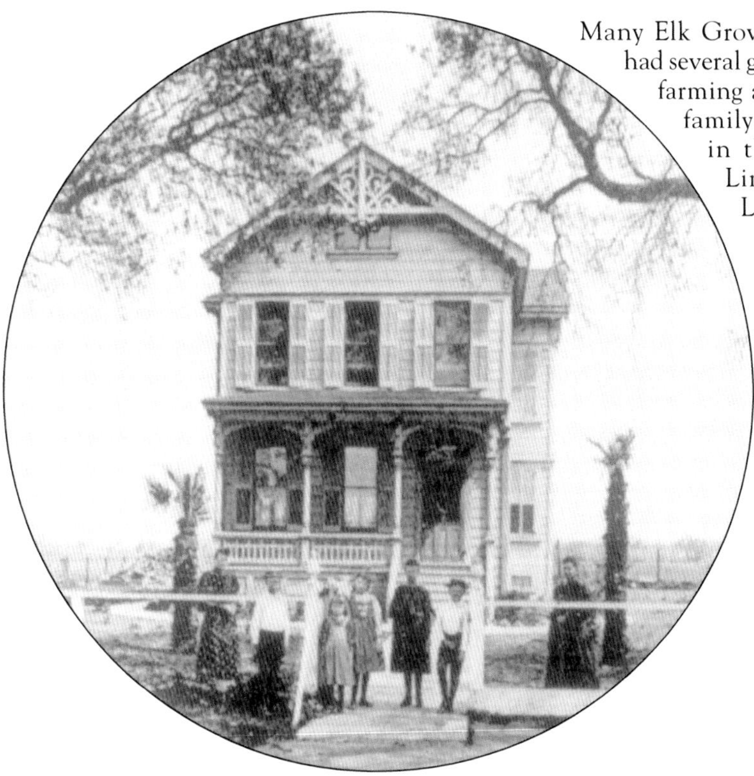

Many Elk Grove area families have had several generations involved in farming and ranching. Mahon family members have lived in this house on Grant Line Road since 1882. Lester Mahon spent all of his 94 years on the ranch. The ranch went through various stages with almond and fruit orchards and growing hops, but mostly cattle were raised, which is still a practice today. (Courtesy of Ellen Rosa.)

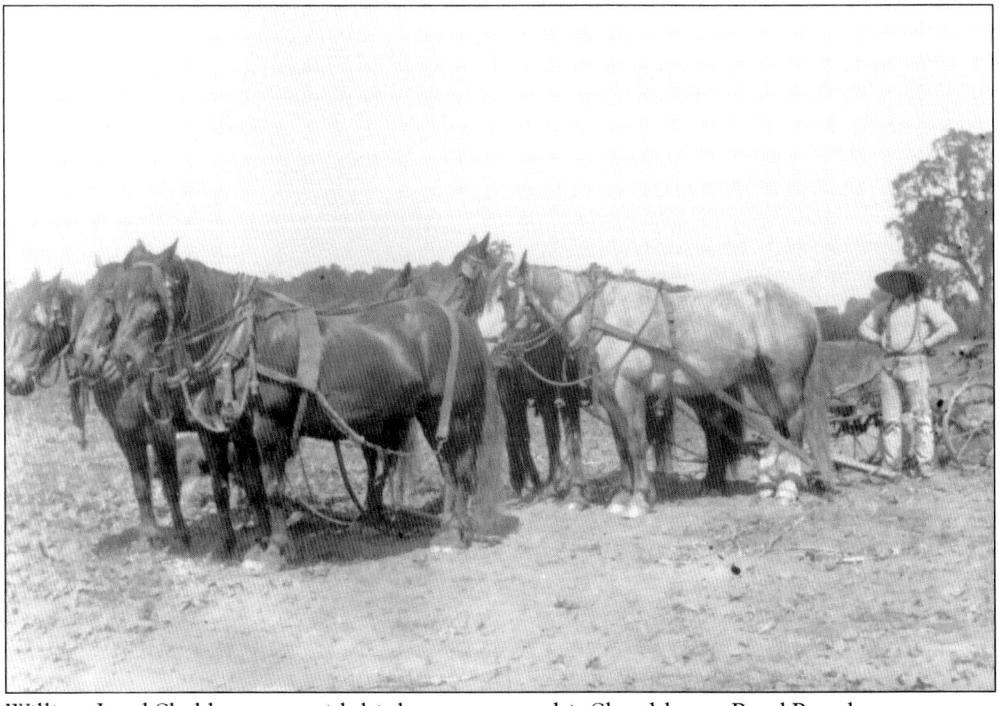

William Jared Sheldon poses with his horse team on his Sloughhouse Road Ranch.

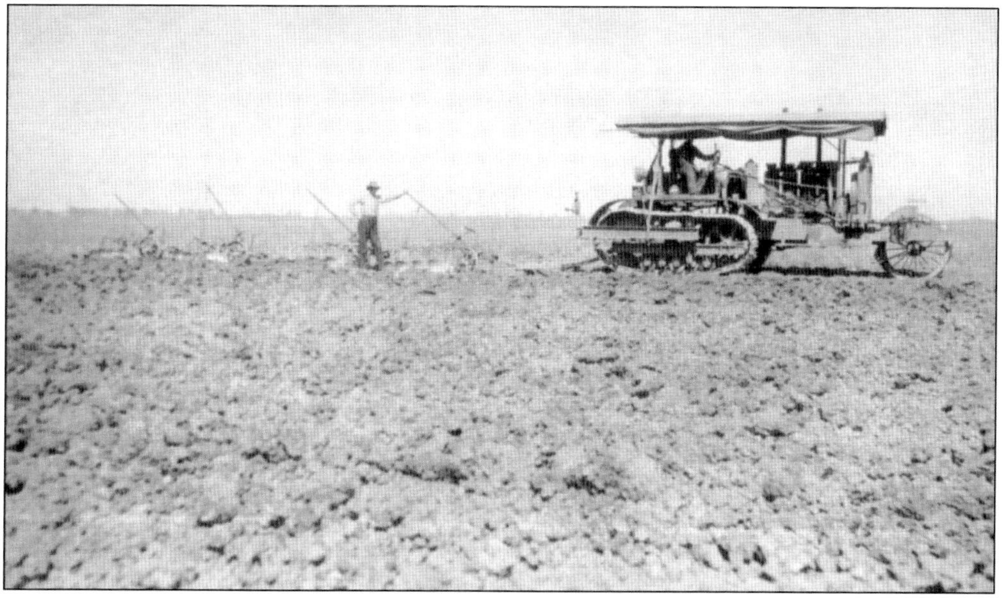

The Morses purchased a Caterpillar in 1917 from Benjamin Holt's small Stockton company. They were the first in the area to use the new technology, and the machine worked well on the heavy clay soil of Bruceville. Arch Morse is pictured here with the new machine. The Holt Company became one of the great developers of farm machinery. (Courtesy of Dave Morse.)

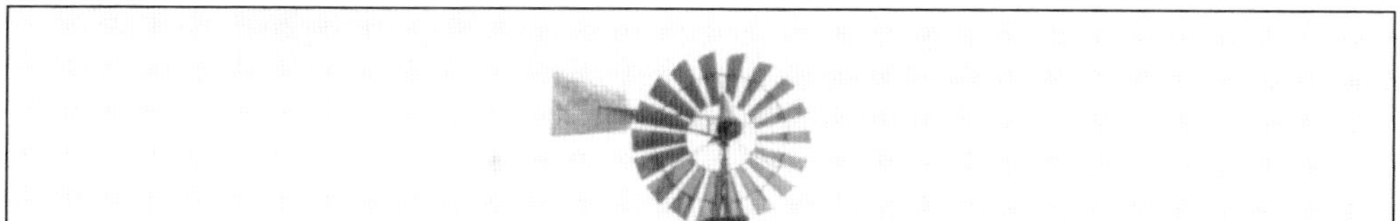

Water levels were at 10 feet in most Elk Grove areas. Farmers had windmills on every knoll to fill their tank houses with water. Mallet Jackson invented a unique small windmill in 1879. Called the Jackson Windmill, it was widely used in the Florin area for irrigating strawberries and grapes. Jessie Cumpston Baker climbed this type of windmill to look for fire in the fields on Bruceville Road. Some windmills can still be seen today.

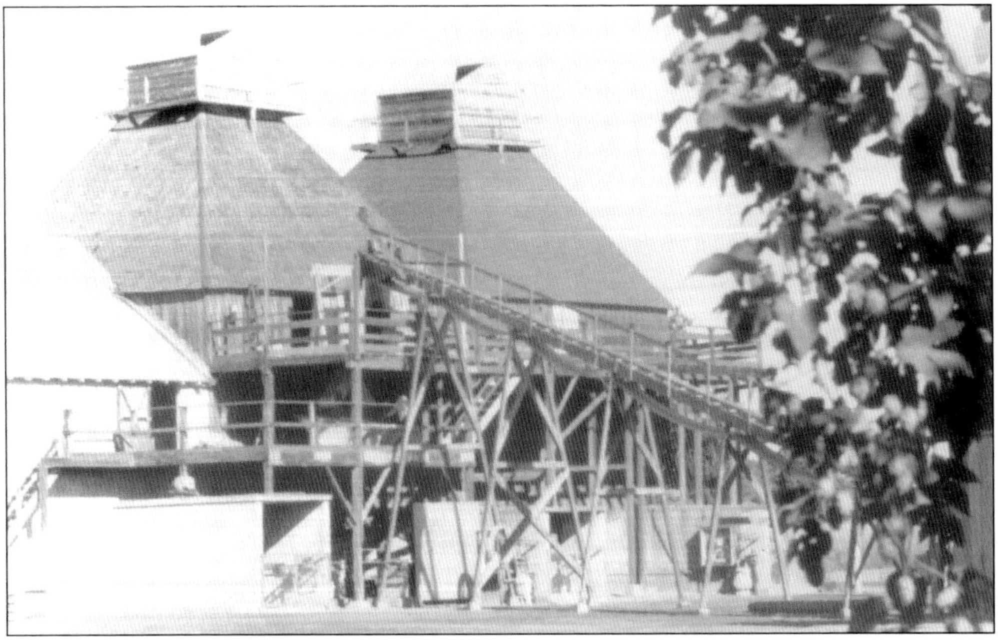

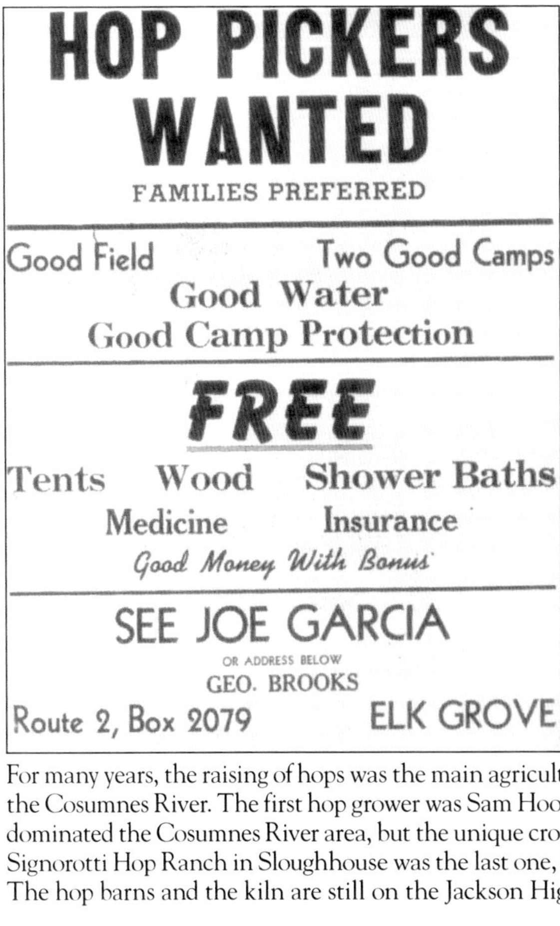

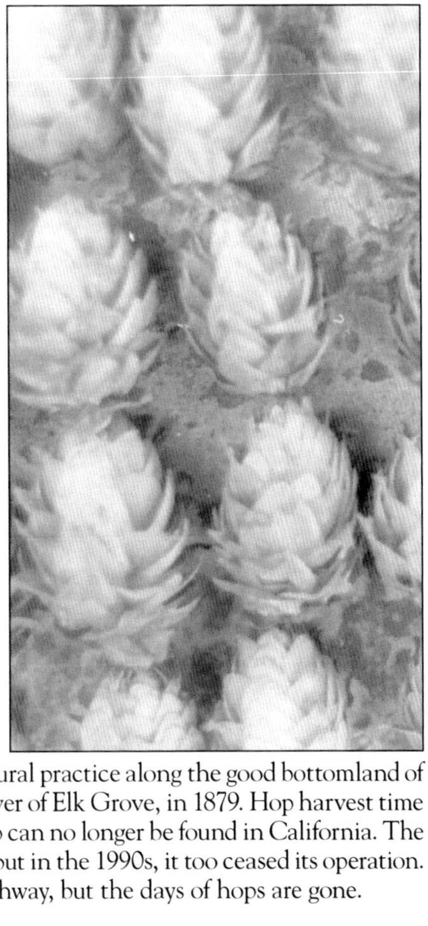

For many years, the raising of hops was the main agricultural practice along the good bottomland of the Cosumnes River. The first hop grower was Sam Hoover of Elk Grove, in 1879. Hop harvest time dominated the Cosumnes River area, but the unique crop can no longer be found in California. The Signorotti Hop Ranch in Sloughhouse was the last one, but in the 1990s, it too ceased its operation. The hop barns and the kiln are still on the Jackson Highway, but the days of hops are gone.

Avelino Signorotti came to Sloughhouse as a young boy in 1910. He worked on the Sheldon Ranch until he was able to acquire his own hop ranch. Pictured here just before harvest are Avelino's grandson Paul (left) and son George. Behind them are the hop vines stretched out on the trellis and reaching to the sky.

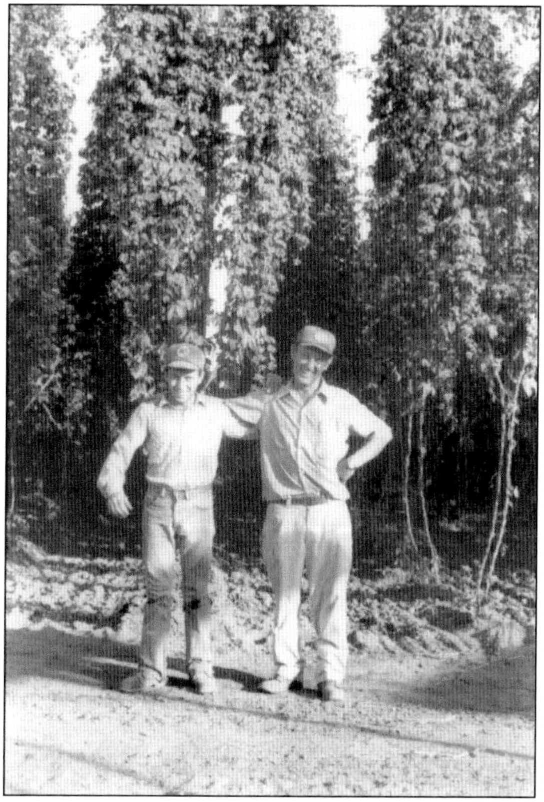

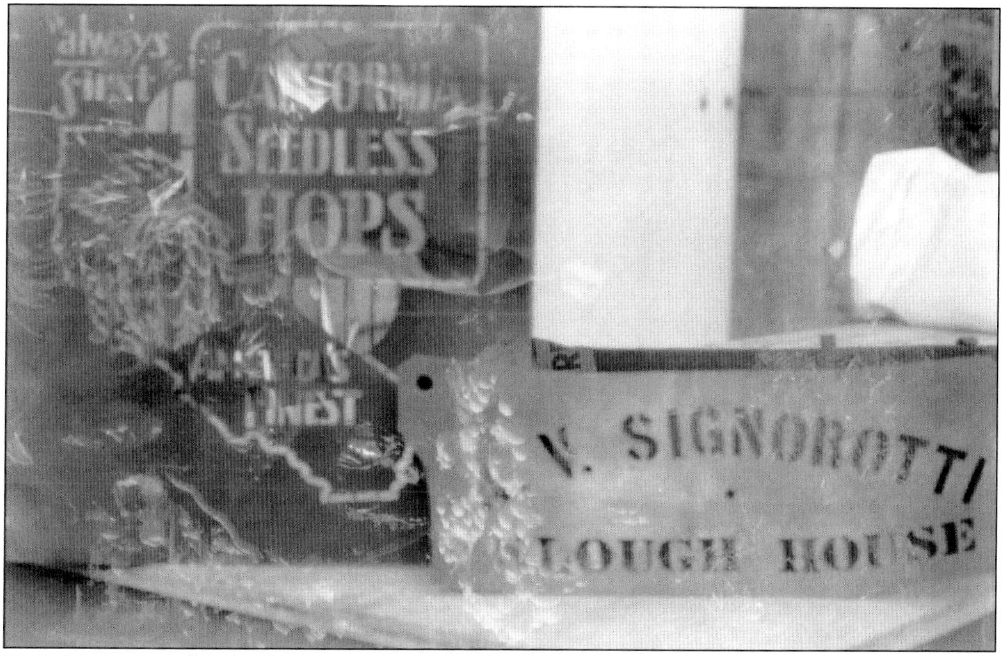

Paul Signorotti, the third generation to farm hops, is a vice president of S. S. Steiner Inc. in Spokane, one of the largest hop companies in the country. Gone, but not forgotten, is the Signorotti Slough House Hops.

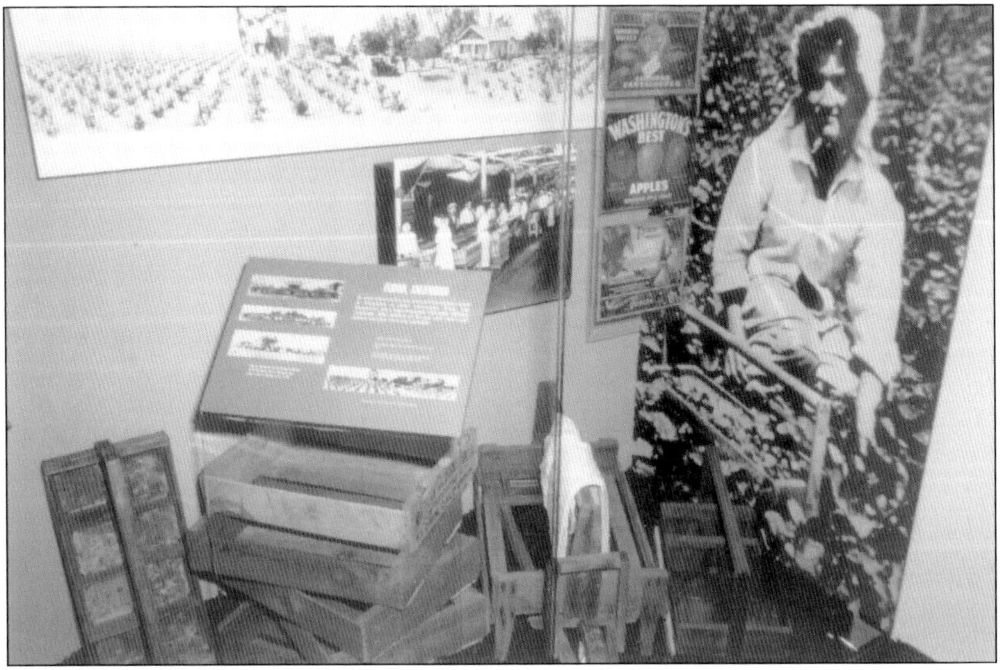

Grapes and strawberries covered most of the land from today's Highway 99 to what became Mather Air Force Base. Acres and acres of strawberry fields and vineyards made Florin the strawberry capital of California, and the busy workdays of the 1920s and 1930s put Florin on America's map. This photograph portraying Florin's agricultural past is on display in the Smithsonian Institution in Washington, D.C. The woman to the right is Mary Tsukamoto's mother, Mrs. Dakuzaku.

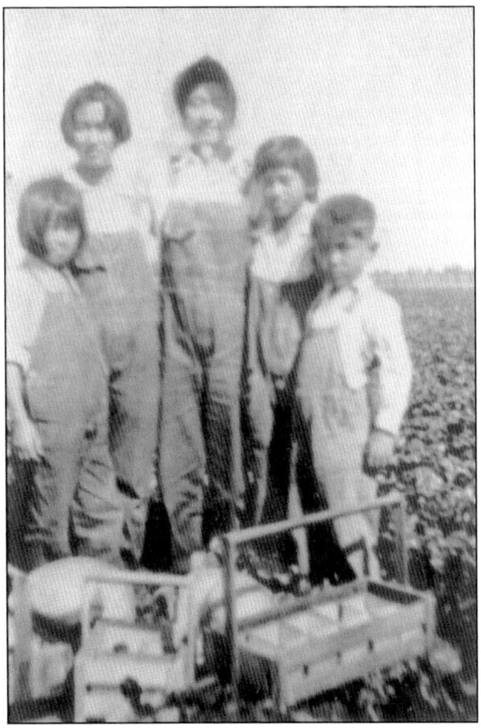

Japanese immigrants began to arrive in Florin and Elk Grove before 1900. The families had grapes and strawberries as joint crops. Pictured here are the Dakuzaku children in the 1920s. The berry and grape era had ended in May of 1942 when all Japanese families were sent to internment camps at the beginning of World War II. (Courtesy of Mary Tsukamoto.)

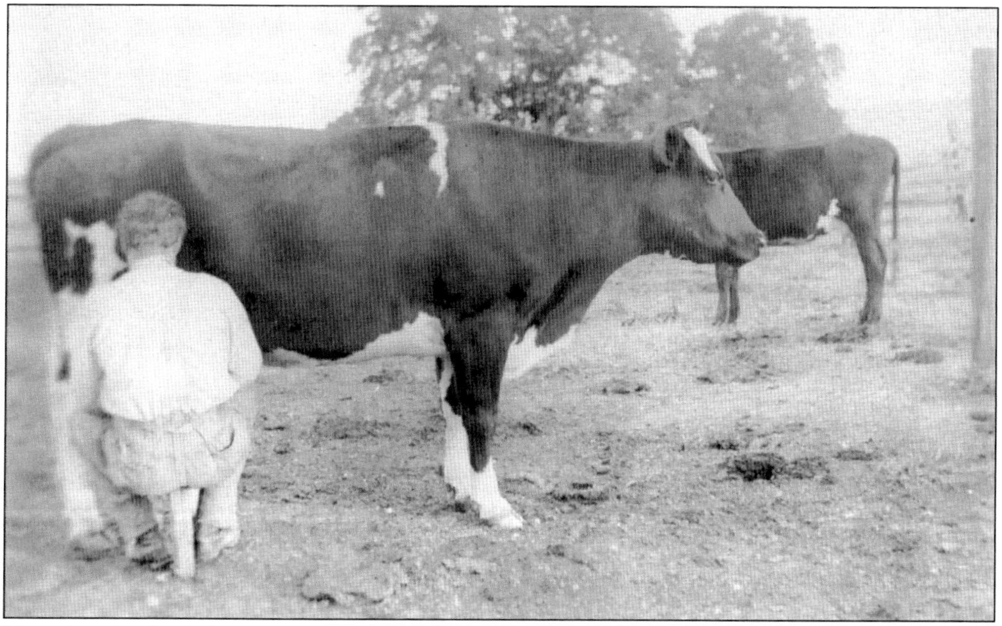

Most families had their own cows for milk and beef. But when the railroads came through the Cosumnes River area, small farm dairies and chicken ranches developed throughout the south county. The California Traction Line was called the "Milk Train" because it carried fresh milk and eggs to the growing cities of Sacramento and Stockton. Here Lauren Sheldon milks one of the family cows. (Courtesy of Ellen Rosa.)

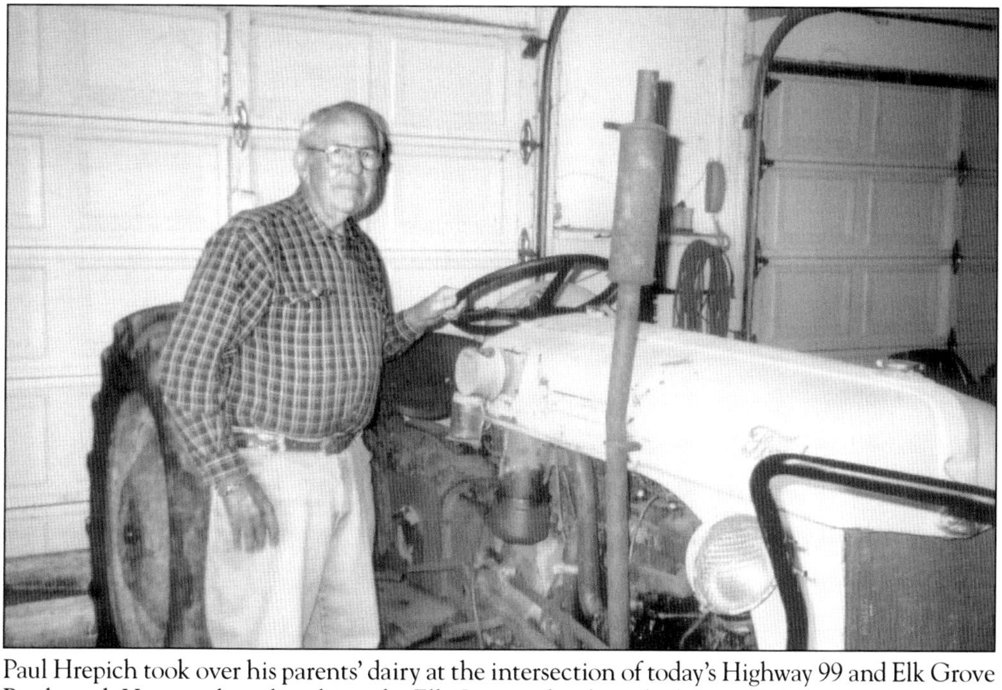

Paul Hrepich took over his parents' dairy at the intersection of today's Highway 99 and Elk Grove Boulevard. He was also a bus driver for Elk Grove schools and, along with his wife, Dorothy, an active volunteer at the Rhoads School. He is pictured here with a restored tractor, one of his many interests.

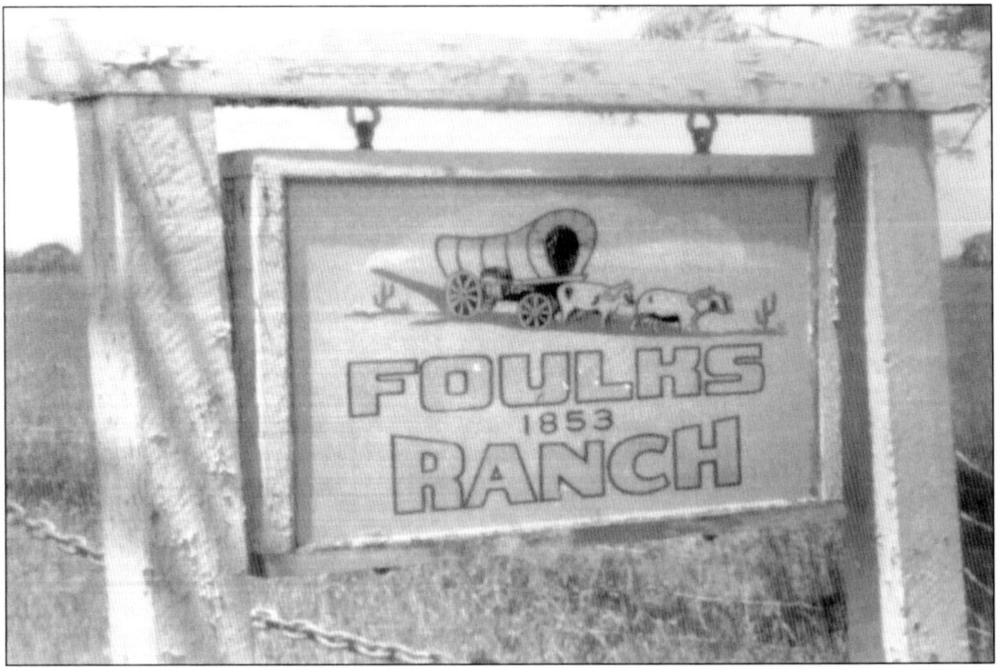

Fields of wildflowers were turned into farms in the Elk Grove area over the years. Many farms, including the well-known Foulks Ranch, are being taken over for a variety of land uses for residential and business purposes.

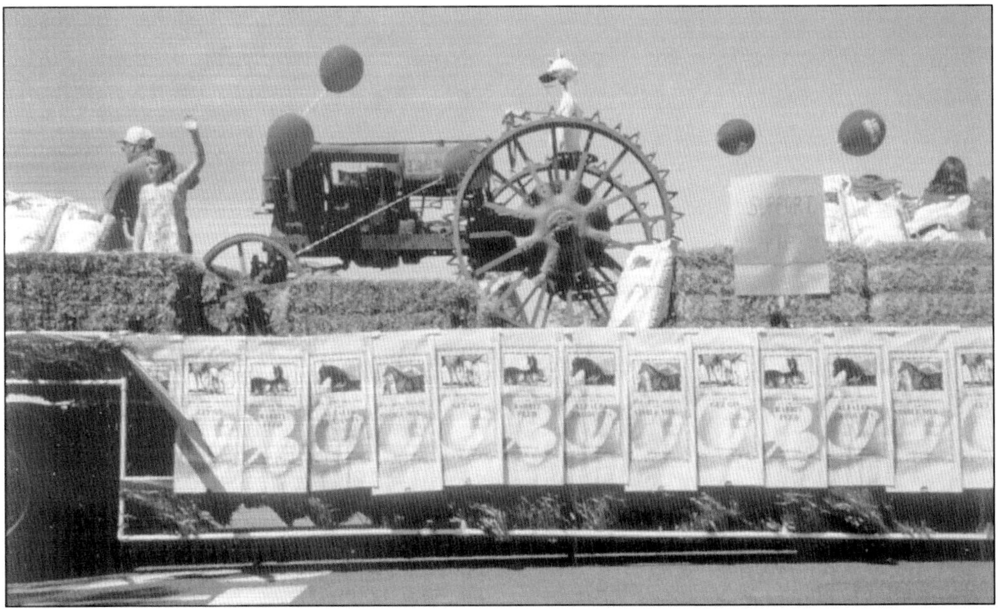

Young people continue to be active in 4-H community groups, building on the strong agricultural foundation of the past. Some newcomers are duplicating successes of previous years. Southeast Asian families are raising strawberries and selling them from roadside stands. Horse stables and riding academies are replacing the sheep and cattle of the past. The grain fields are gone, but wine grapes are taking their place. The new vineyards are waiting out the time before they too become the backyards of new residents.

Five

THE SCHOOLS

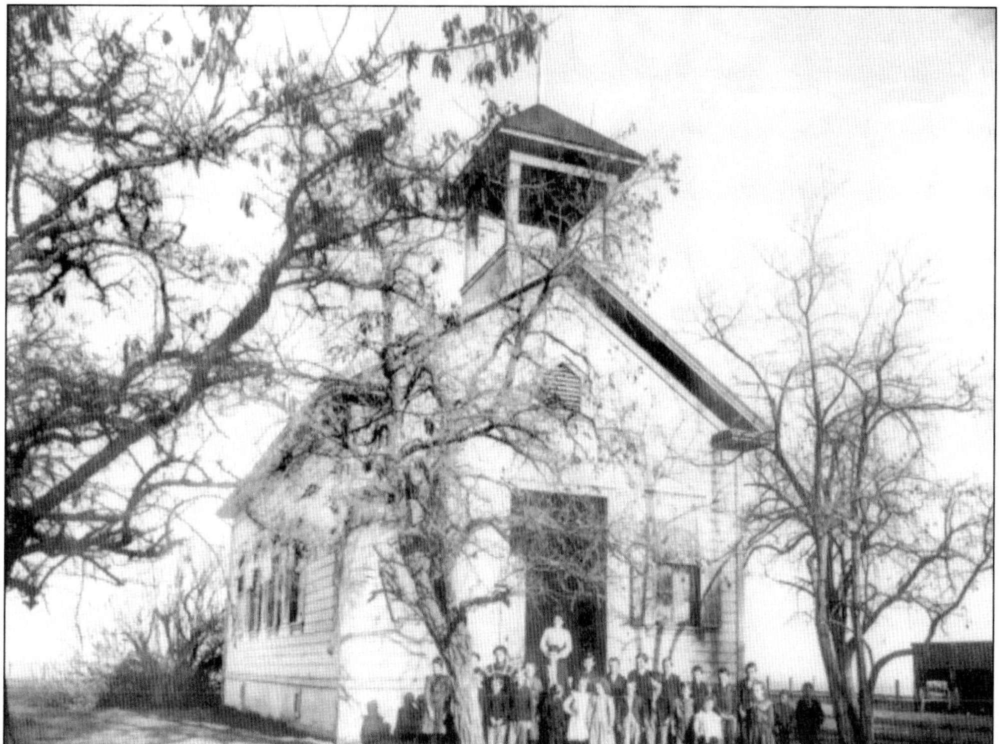

The San Joaquin School (1853) was the first official public school in Sacramento County. It was established by the first settlers in the area around the Murphy ranch. The name came from the San Joaquin Township, one of the original townships in Sacramento County that included all of Elk Grove and Florin. The school was located at today's Grant Line Road and Highway 99. In 1928, the school was closed and merged with the Elk Grove Grammar School. The only reminder of the San Joaquin name today is the little cemetery at Sheldon Road and Highway 99.

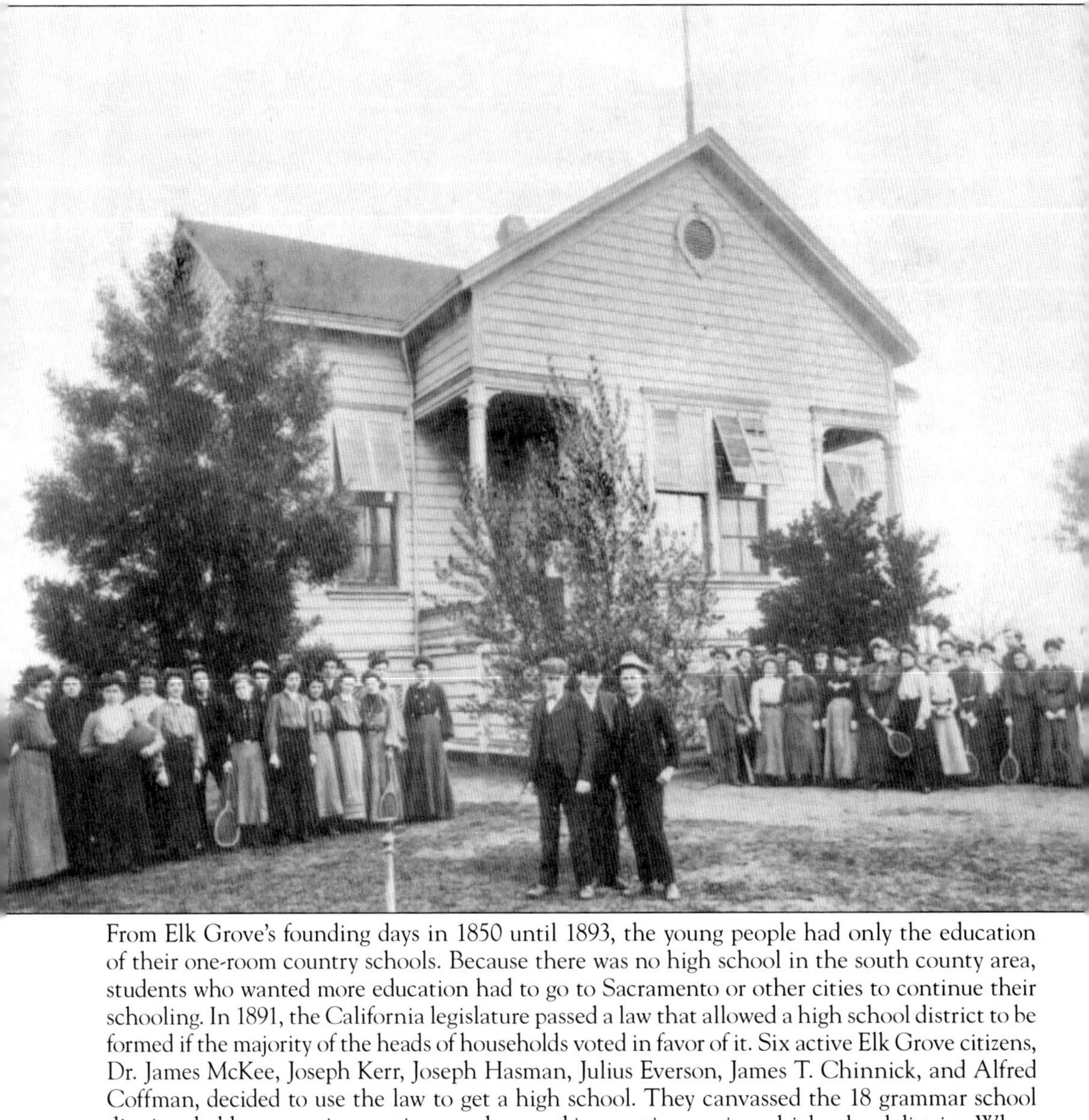

From Elk Grove's founding days in 1850 until 1893, the young people had only the education of their one-room country schools. Because there was no high school in the south county area, students who wanted more education had to go to Sacramento or other cities to continue their schooling. In 1891, the California legislature passed a law that allowed a high school district to be formed if the majority of the heads of households voted in favor of it. Six active Elk Grove citizens, Dr. James McKee, Joseph Kerr, Joseph Hasman, Julius Everson, James T. Chinnick, and Alfred Coffman, decided to use the law to get a high school. They canvassed the 18 grammar school districts, held community meetings, and spurred interest in creating a high school district. When the election was held, 16 districts voted to form the Elk Grove Union High School District. This was the first time that elementary districts formed a high school district in the state of California. The first high school opened in 1893 at a site on Main Street that was donated by Joseph Kerr.

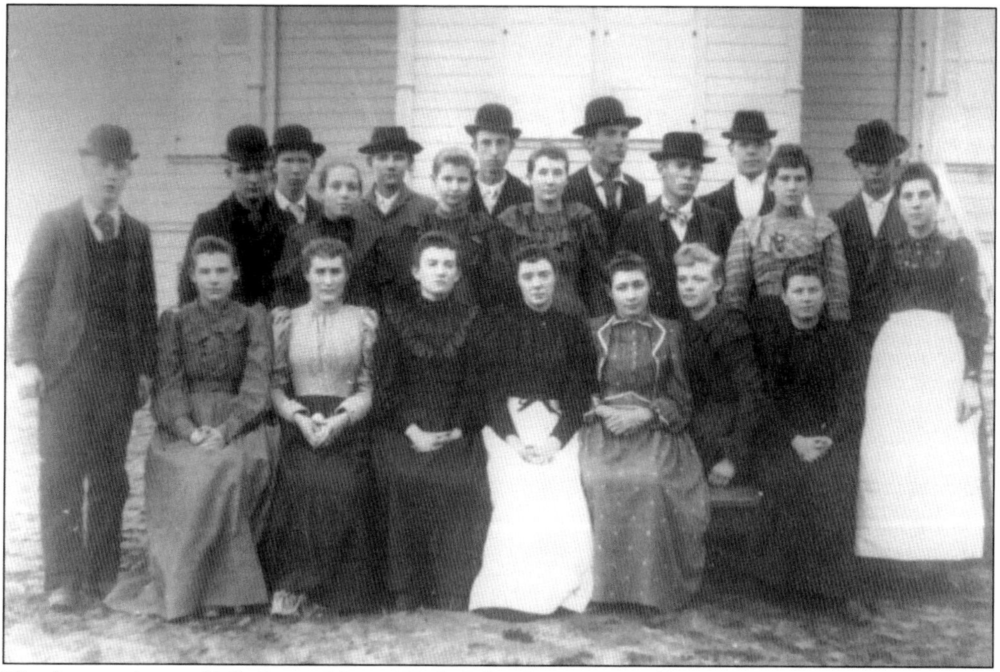

The first students of Elk Grove Union High School are pictured here. The first principal/teacher was Robertson McKissick from San Francisco. He is in the back row, wearing the white cravat. The first students to graduate in 1898 were Mary Duffy, L. T. Everson, S. R. Gage, Leila Hunt, Eva Kerr, Clinton Kirby, Fred Schelmeyer, and M. A. Jenkins.

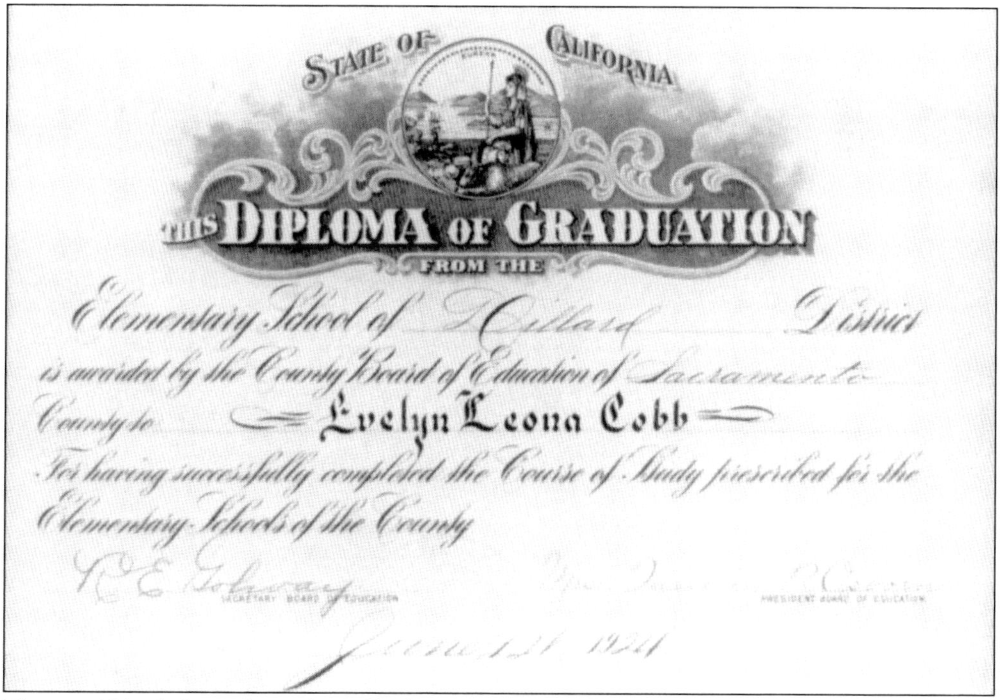

State of California

This Diploma of Graduation from the

Elementary School of Dillard District

is awarded by the County Board of Education of Sacramento

County to Evelyn Leona Cobb

For having successfully completed the Course of Study prescribed for the Elementary Schools of the County

Secretary Board of Education

President Board of Education

This is a 1924 diploma from the Dillard School in Wilton. Evelyn Cobb Cornelius was a teacher in Elk Grove schools for many years.

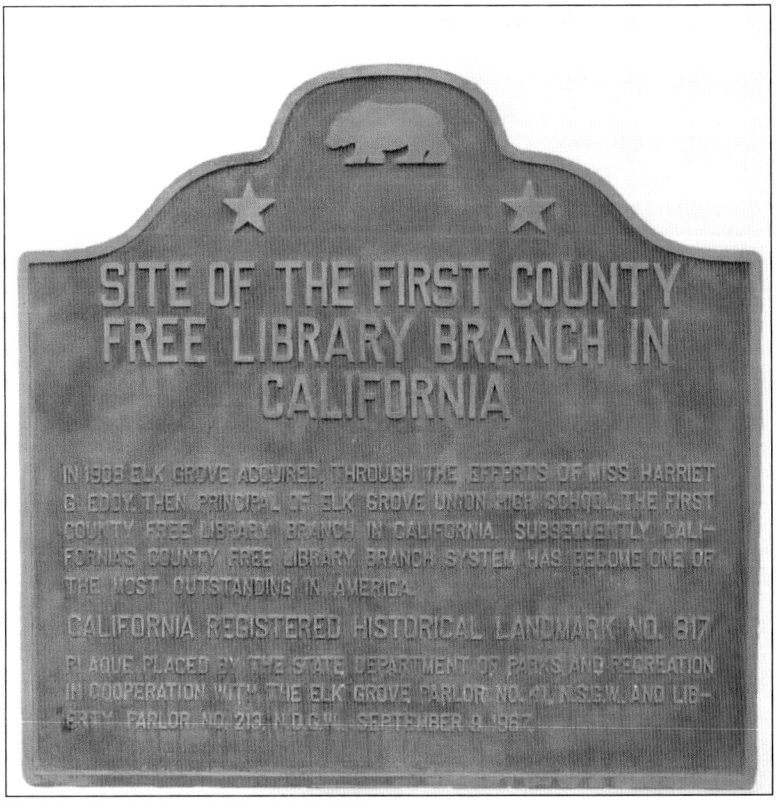

Elk Grove not only had the first union-free high school in California, but the town also was the site of the first county free library in the state. The original library was established in 1908 by principal Harriet G. Eddy in order to gain accreditation for the high school.

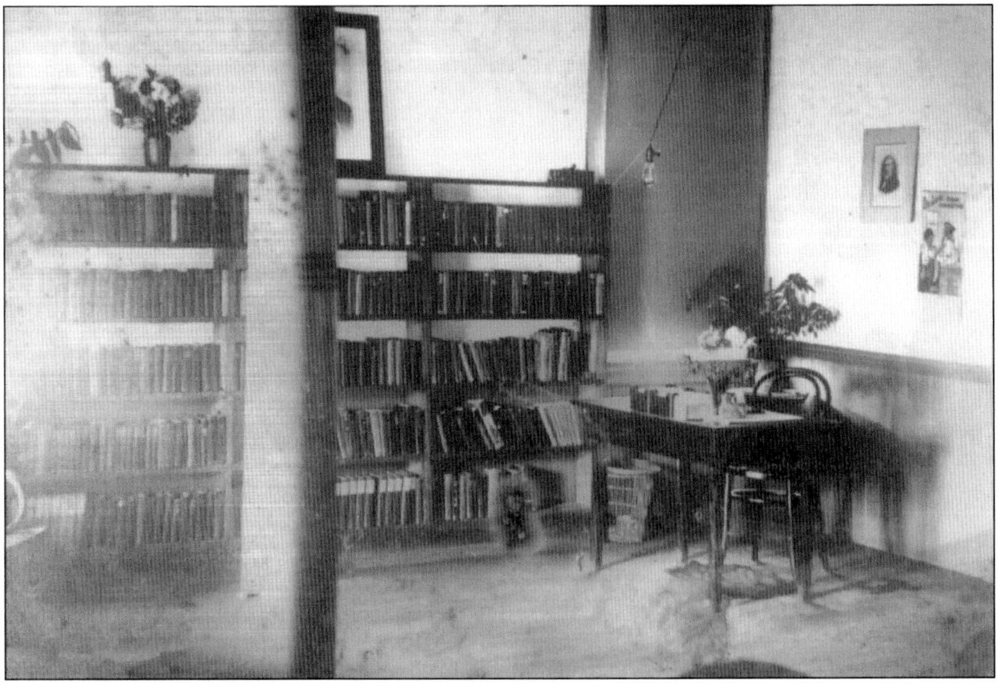

Miss Eddy created the library in the WCTU (Women's Christian Temperance Union) building, next door to the high school. The building is now the Elk Grove Grange Hall on Main Street.

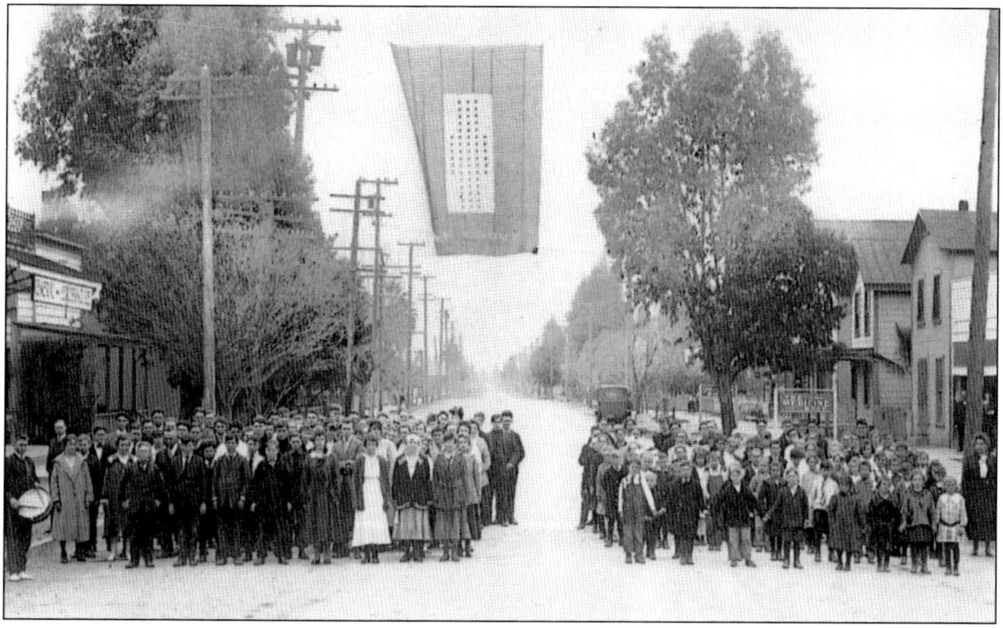

Pictured here on Elk Grove's Main Street are students of Elk Grove Union High School on the left and Victory School children on the right. It was believed that the celebration was somehow related to World War I or the armistice. The banner says "Elk Grove" and has what appears to be 55 stars. However, it was recently found that the date of the photograph may have been as early as 1910, but the reason for the demonstration is unknown.

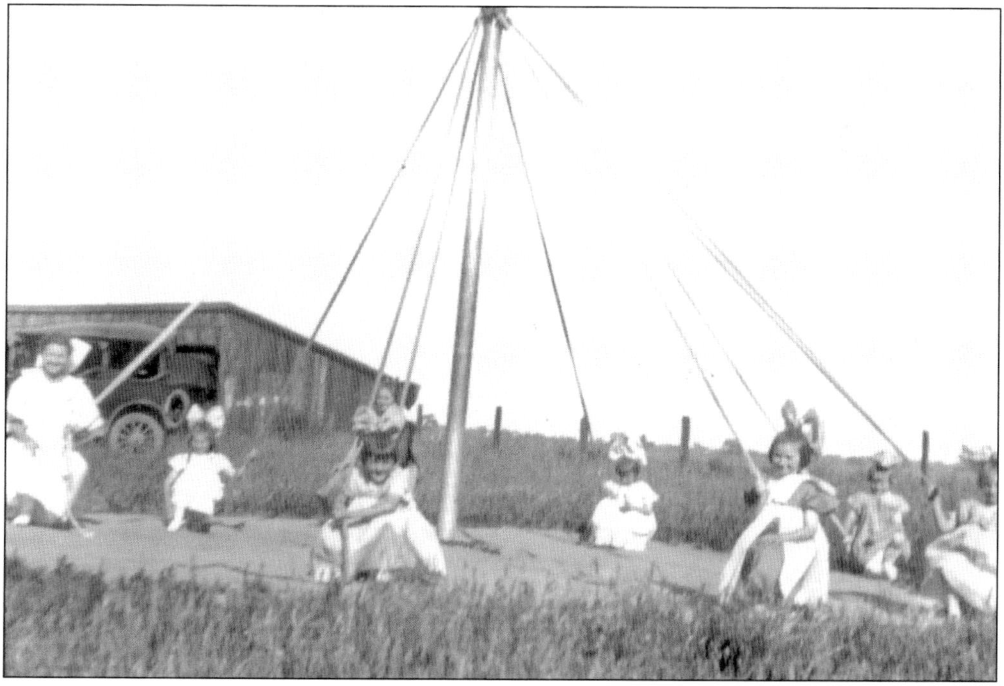

Children swing at the San Joaquin School for what could be a May Day celebration. The teacher looks on at the left. Her car is behind her in front of the barn where the children kept their horses while they were at school.

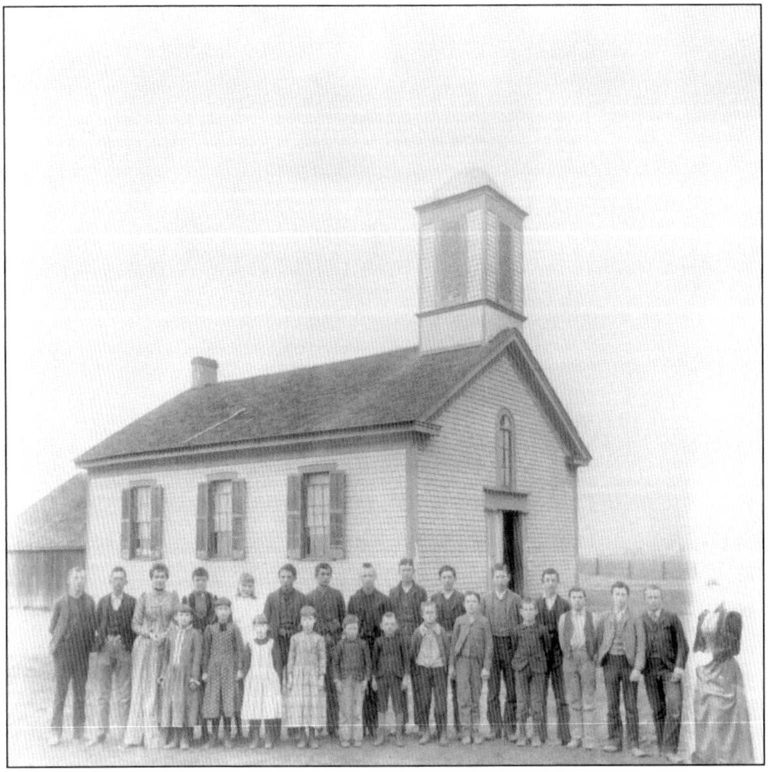

The Elk Grove Grammar School on Upper Stockton Road was built in 1860 as the third school in San Joaquin Township, but it was replaced in the 1880s. The old school was moved to the Foulks Ranch and was torn down in 2006. The second school is still on Stockton Boulevard as is the brick building on Main Street that was built in 1921.

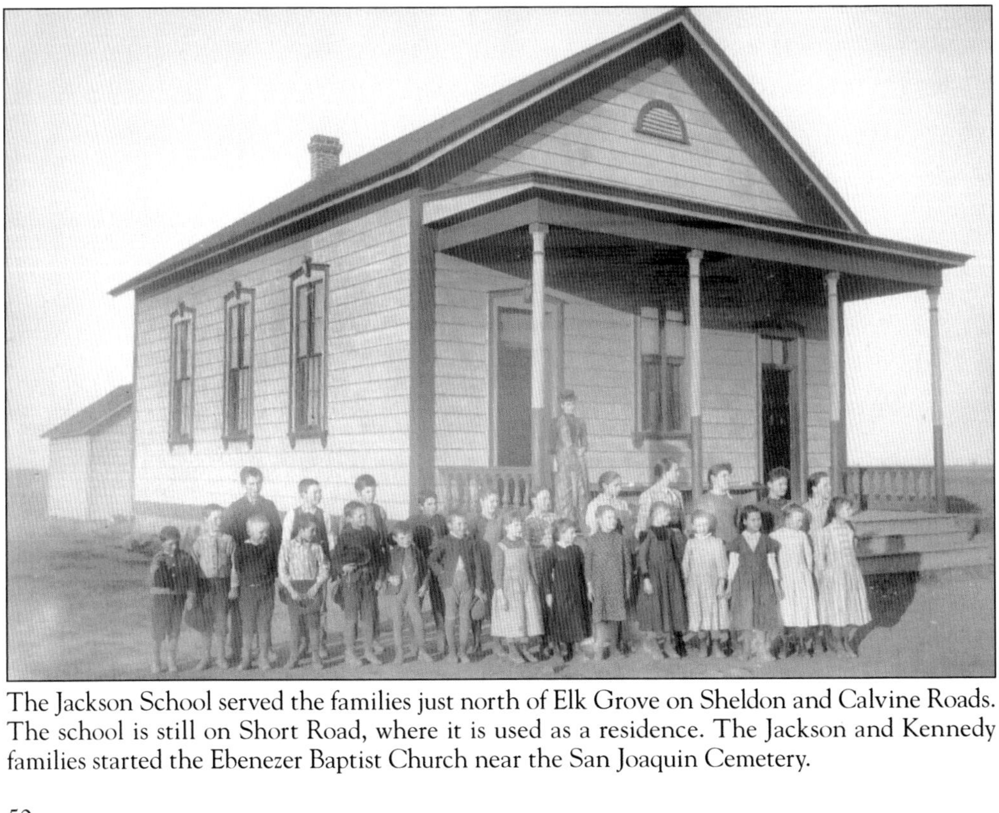

The Jackson School served the families just north of Elk Grove on Sheldon and Calvine Roads. The school is still on Short Road, where it is used as a residence. The Jackson and Kennedy families started the Ebenezer Baptist Church near the San Joaquin Cemetery.

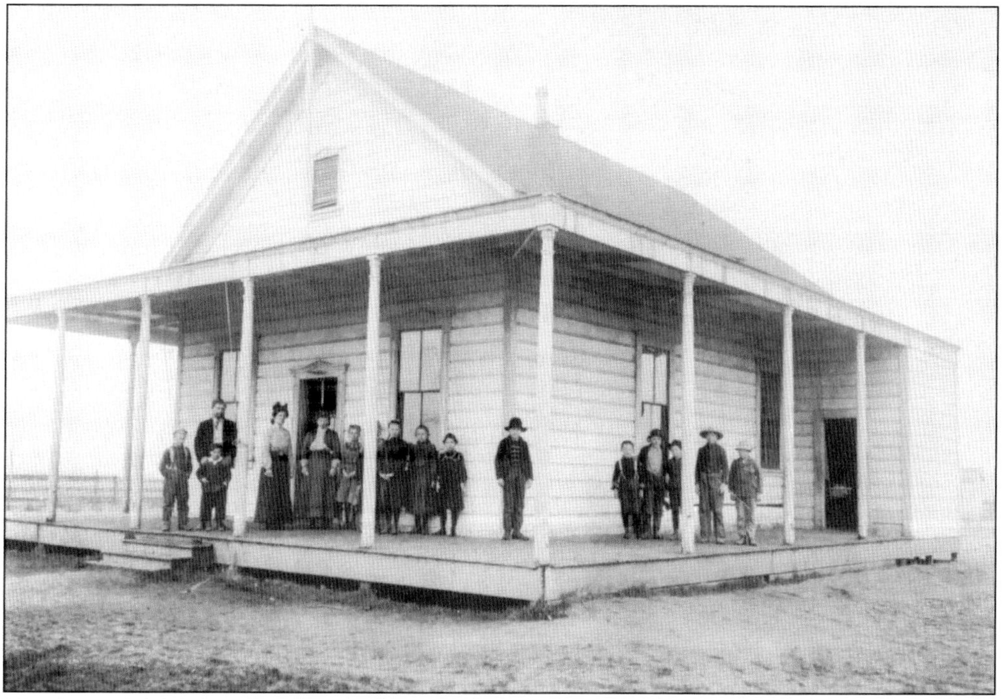

The Carroll School on Lambert and Bruceville Roads was built in 1877, but it was too small by the 1920s and was replaced by a new and modern school. However, the new school burned down in 1959, and the students were transported to the Elk Grove Grammar School.

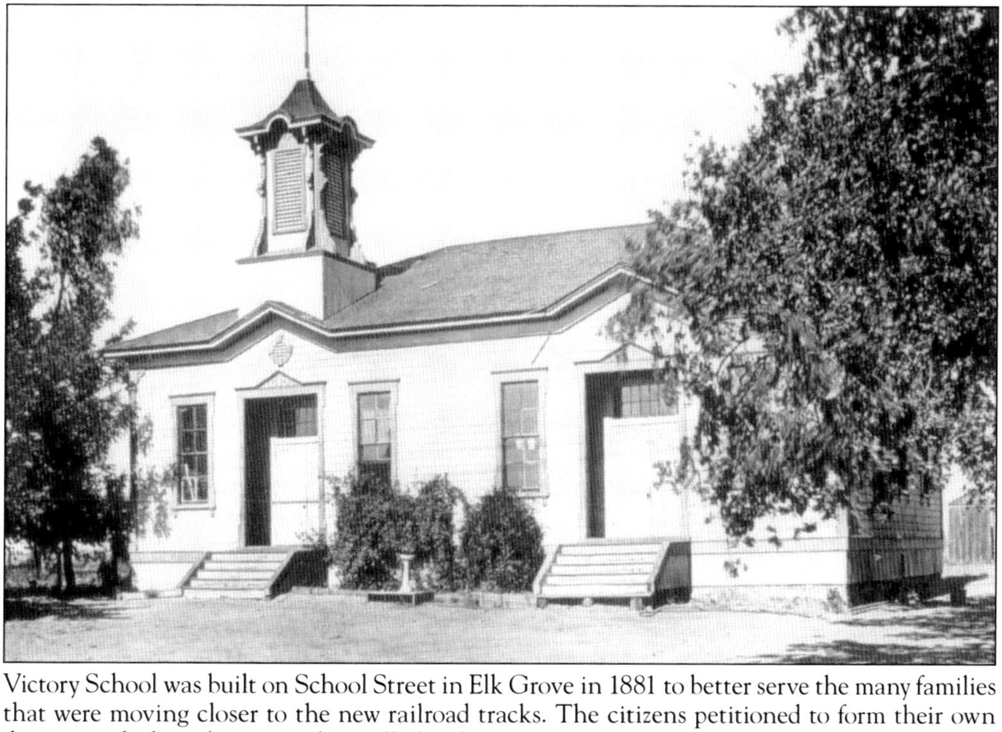

Victory School was built on School Street in Elk Grove in 1881 to better serve the many families that were moving closer to the new railroad tracks. The citizens petitioned to form their own district, and when they won, they called it the Victory School and District.

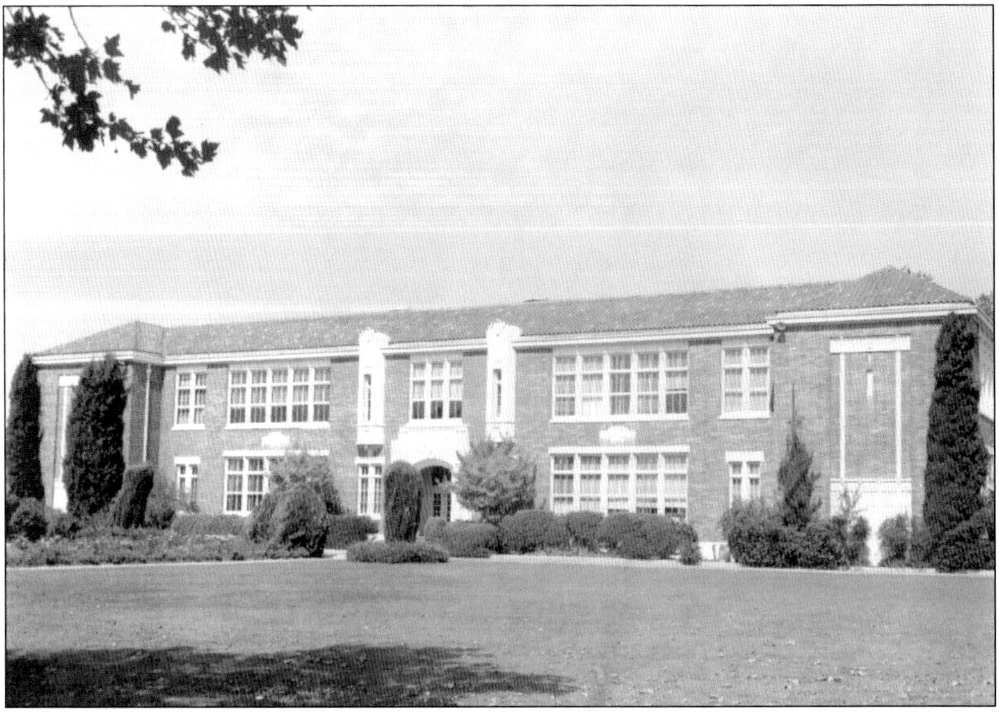

From its humble start in the 1890s, with barely enough students to open the school, Elk Grove Union High School persevered and flourished. In 1923, this impressive brick building was erected on Main Street and Elk Grove-Florin Road. A new high school was constructed in 1964, and this building was demolished in 1967 because it was not earthquake-proof. (Courtesy of Elk Grove Historical Society.)

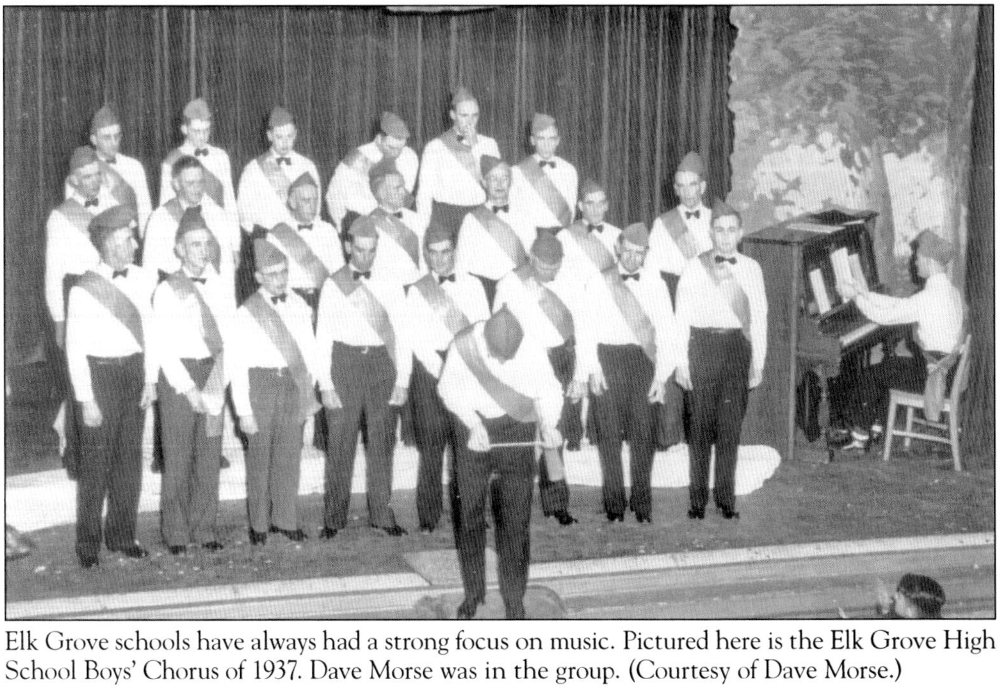

Elk Grove schools have always had a strong focus on music. Pictured here is the Elk Grove High School Boys' Chorus of 1937. Dave Morse was in the group. (Courtesy of Dave Morse.)

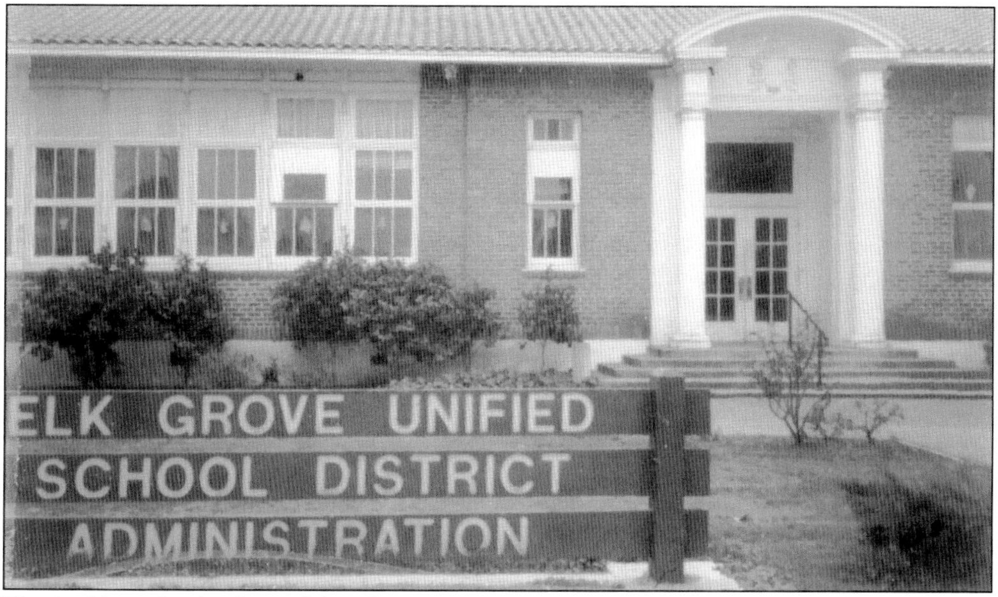

This building, the third site of the Elk Grove Grammar School on Elk Grove Boulevard, served as the school district office until 1994. The building is now the home of the Elk Grove Community Services District.

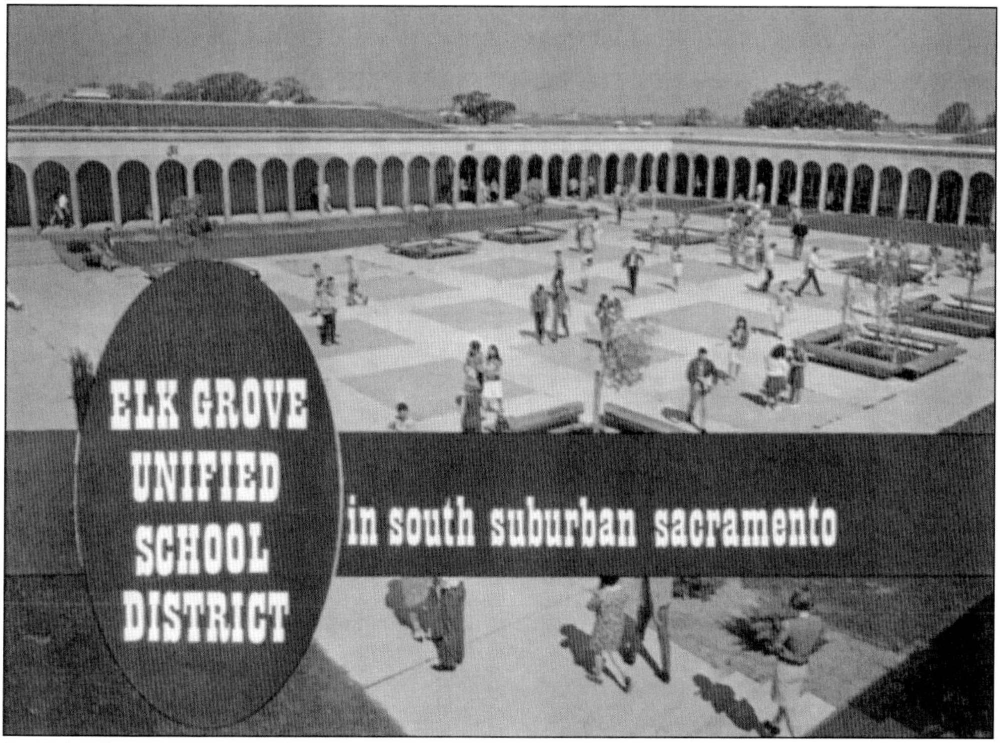

In 1964, the district opened a new Elk Grove High School next to Elk Grove Park, and the old building became Joseph Kerr Junior High School. From 1893 to 1977, the district had only one high school. Valley High was built in 1977, and in 2006, there are eight high schools with a ninth under construction.

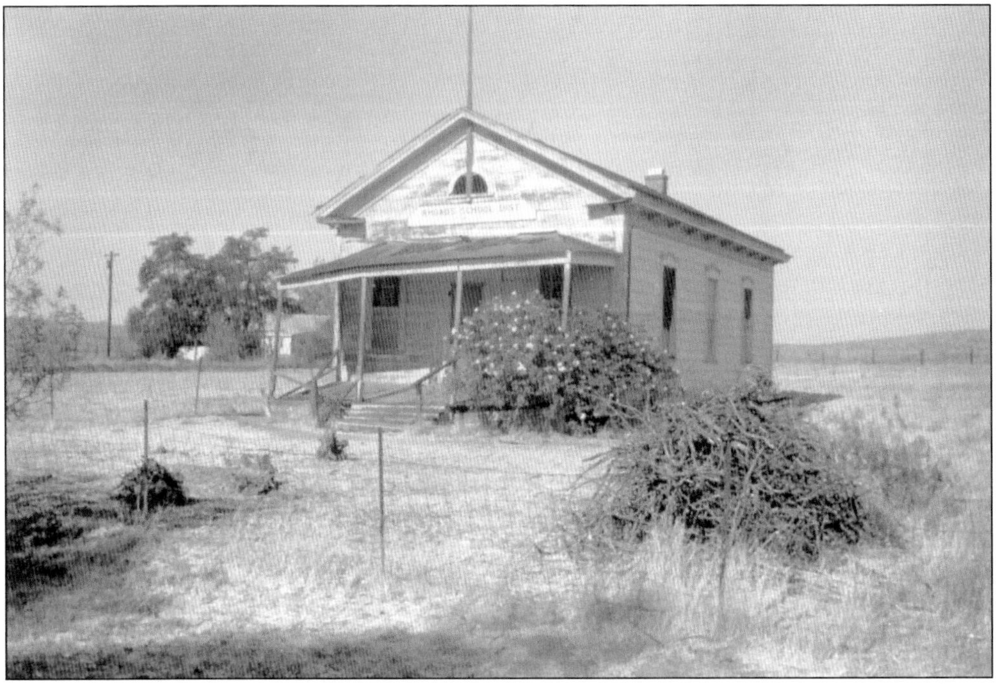

This is what the Rhoads School looked like on Sloughhouse Road in 1975. Named for John P. Rhoads, a rescuer of the Donner Party, the little school served its community from 1872 to 1949. (Courtesy of Tom Russell.)

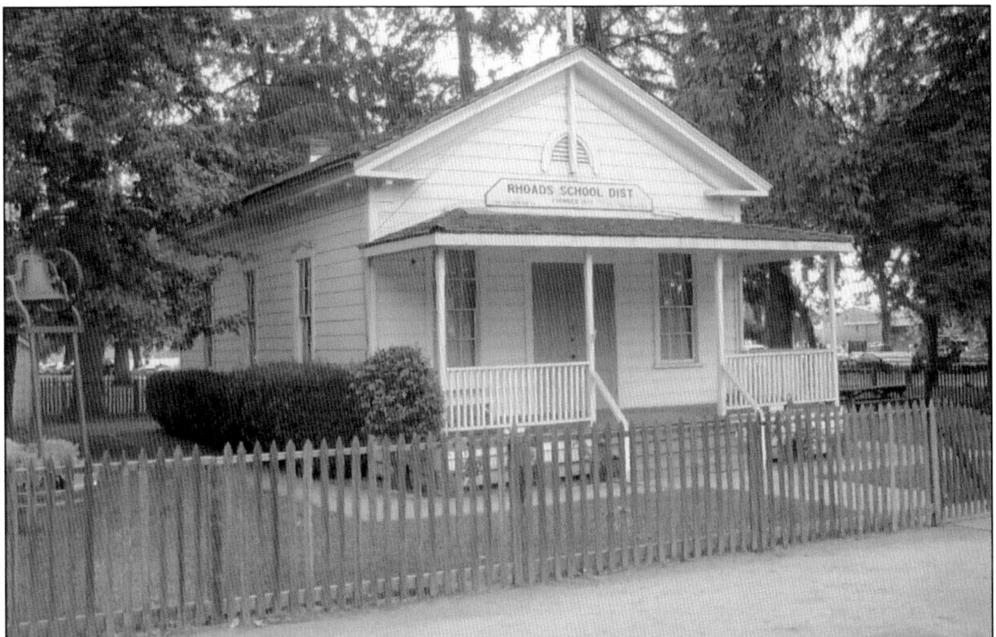

The Elk Grove Bicentennial Commission, the predecessor of the Elk Grove Historical Society, moved the school to Elk Grove Park and restored it to its 1900-era greatness in 1975. The bell from the Wilson School at Sloughhouse is on the left. The Rhoads School is available for the use of school and community groups. (Courtesy of Tom Russell.)

Six

Main Street and Business

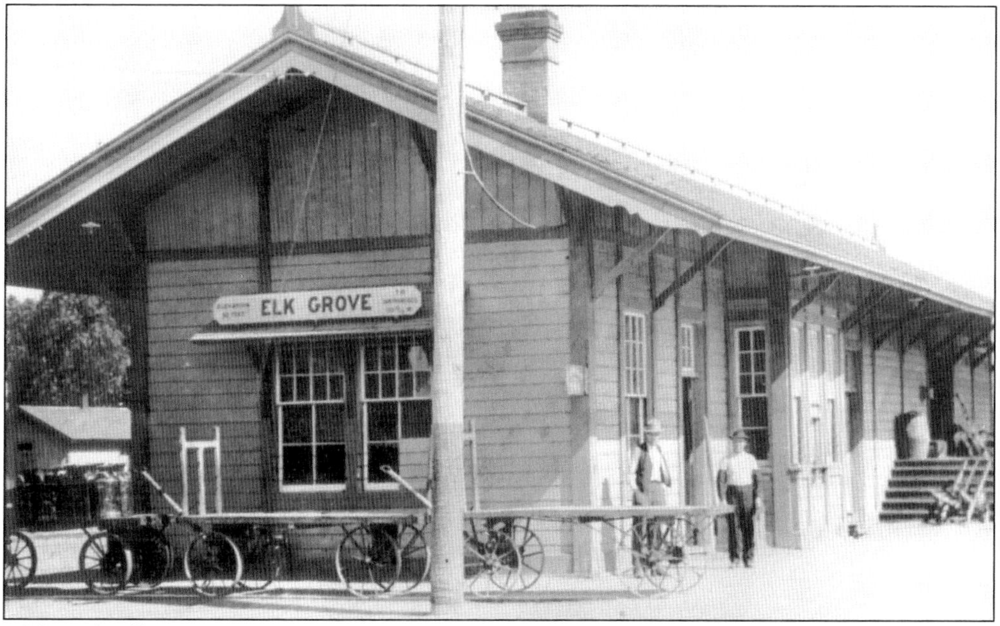

Although Elk Grove officially had its beginning in 1850, when stage lines flourished in the Sacramento and Stockton areas, it was an 1868 event that established Elk Grove's destiny. In that year, the Central Pacific Railroad finished its line from Sacramento to Stockton and on to San Francisco. Unfortunately, whether by design or by neglect, the shiny new tracks missed the little settlement of Elk Grove that was then north of its original location at the intersection of today's Elk Grove Boulevard and Highway 99. The railroad didn't miss Elk Grove by much, but a mile is a mile, and there was no way that having tracks a mile away was going to make a town the picture of prosperity. The little town struggled to survive and serve the growing agricultural community, but some folks had visions of the prosperity that could occur if the town were closer to the railroad. In 1876, the town of Elk Grove began to move to the new railroad tracks. The railroad truly brought Elk Grove into the 20th century—just as cityhood brought Elk Grove into the 21st century.

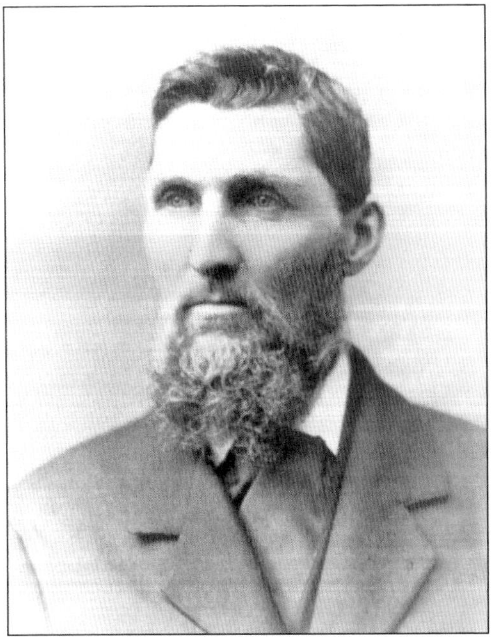

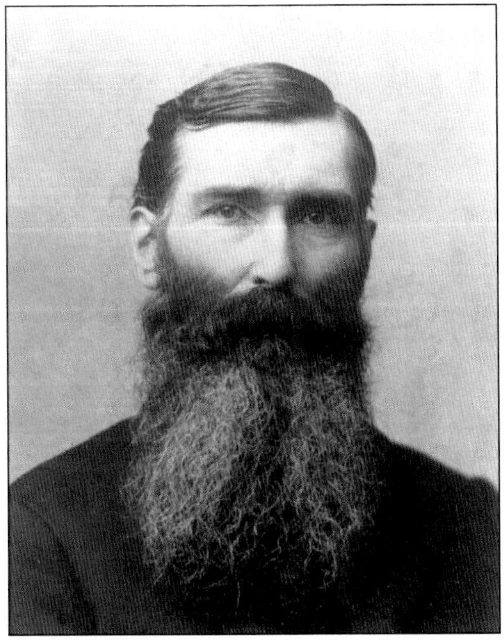

An enterprising merchant, Julius Everson can be credited for his foresight into what the railroad would mean in the future. He recognized the potential of moving the town's business to the railroad tracks and station. The key to the future was through the middle of the property of the Kerr brothers. The present Main Street, Elk Grove Boulevard, was the dividing line between the ranches of Joseph Kerr (left) and George Harvey Kerr (right). Below is Joseph Kerr's house, which stood at the northeast corner of Elk Grove Boulevard and Elk Grove-Florin Road where the bank is now.

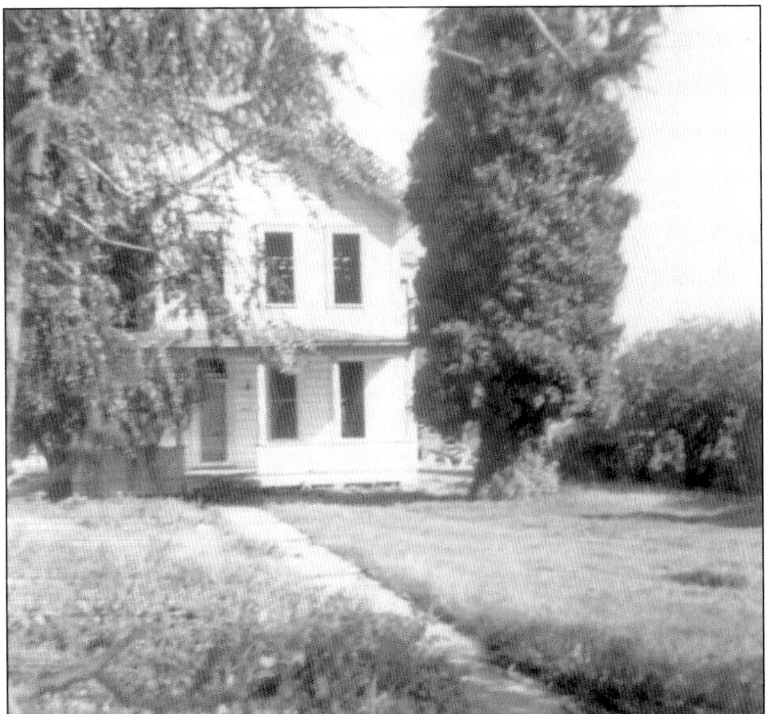

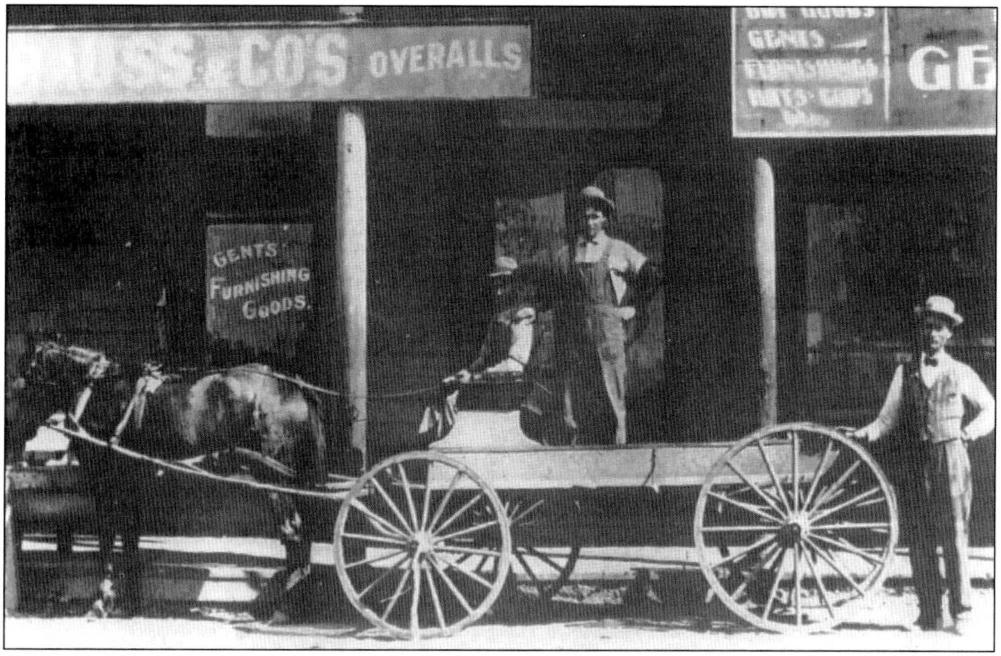

Julius Everson created the Elk Grove Building Association in 1876, and with his partner, Mr. Chittenden, was ready for business with a 30- by 60-foot building filled with merchandise. Only 16 months later, the partners claimed to have had $52,000 worth of business. The town grew by the railroad, and by 1880, there were 500 people living there. The former site was called Old Elk Grove, and the original stage stop was a residence by that time.

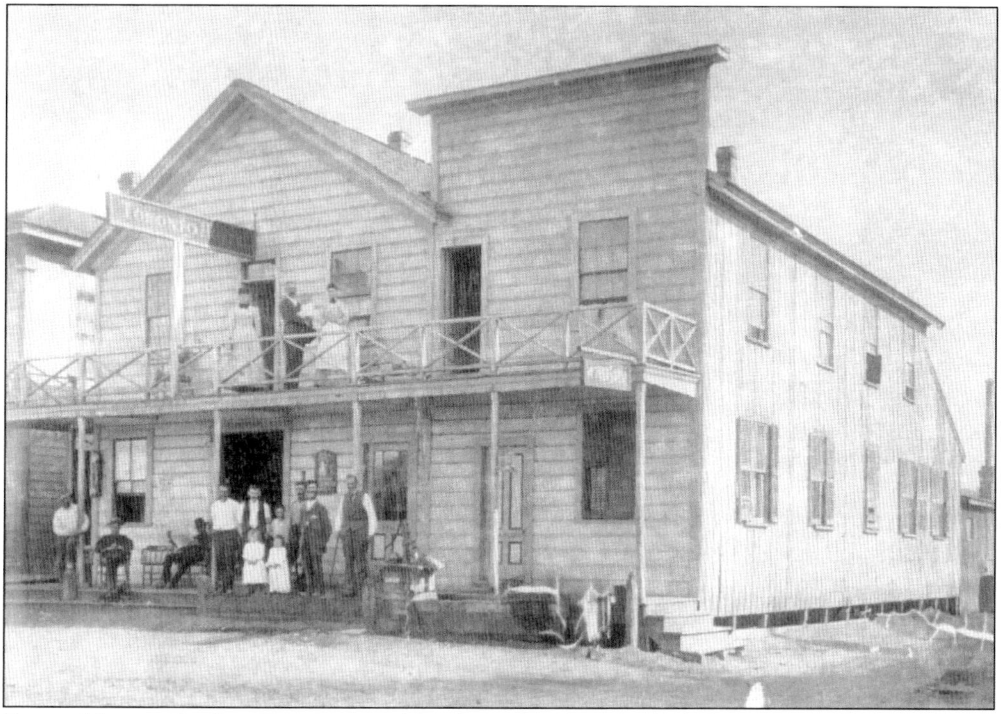

Pictured here is the first Toronto Hotel by the railroad tracks, built by Frank Graham in 1888.

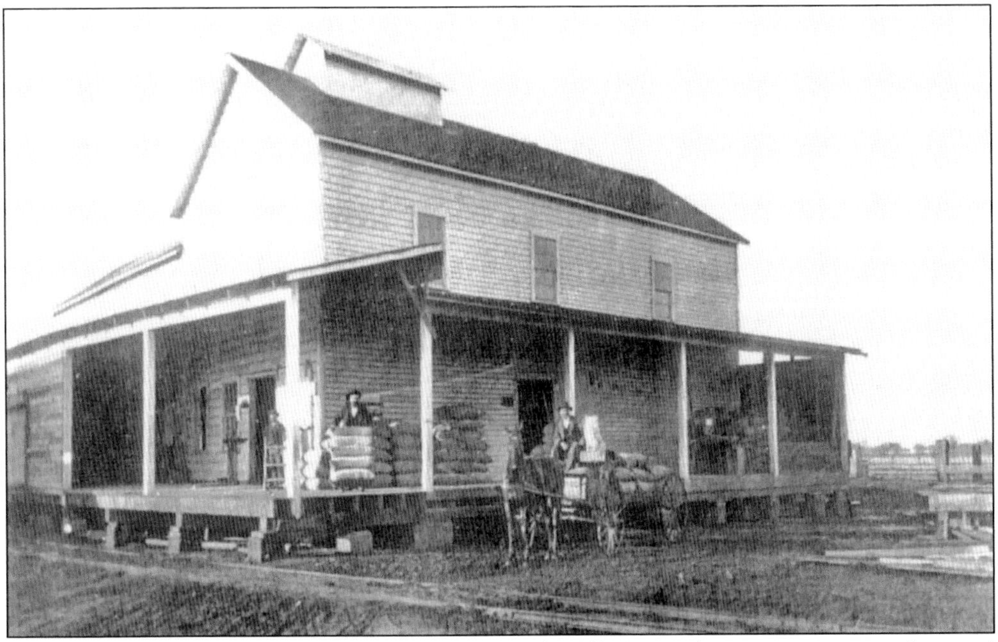

The hay and grain store, like all other buildings in the Elk Grove that were constructed around the railroad tracks, was made of wood. Disaster struck on a hot July afternoon in 1892 when sparks from a train ignited dry grass along the tracks. Despite the valiant efforts of the townspeople, most of the buildings in the entire town burned down. (Courtesy of Elk Grove Historical Society.)

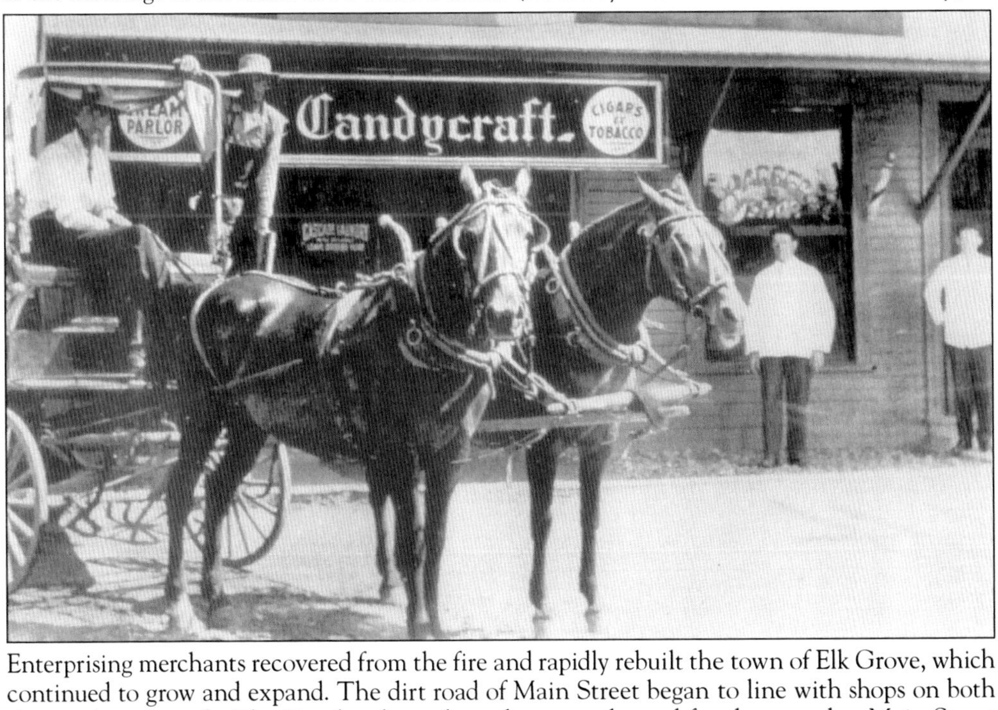

Enterprising merchants recovered from the fire and rapidly rebuilt the town of Elk Grove, which continued to grow and expand. The dirt road of Main Street began to line with shops on both the north and south. The Kerr brothers planted trees and cared for them so that Main Street would be attractive and prosperous. The Candycraft was a popular place in the 1900s. (Courtesy of Elk Grove Historical Society.)

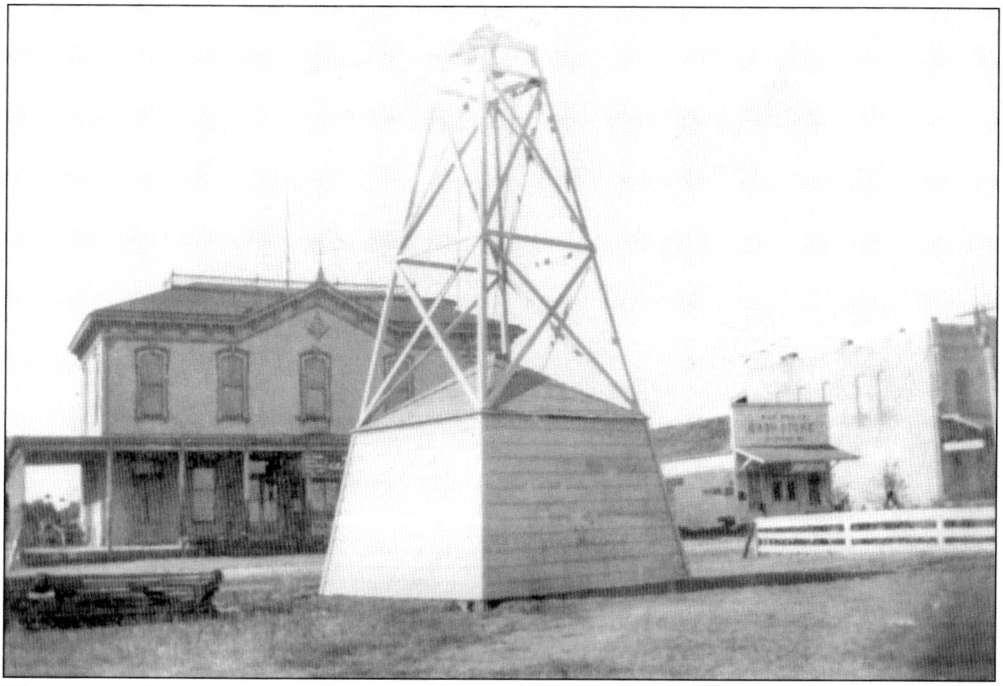

The terrible fire of 1892 that destroyed most of Elk Grove was the catalyst for two important activities of the local citizens. One was the establishment of an adequate water supply, and the other was the creation of a volunteer fire department. This 1900 photograph shows the 80-foot tower and hose cart shed. In the background is the Masonic Hall. (Courtesy of Gerald Derr.)

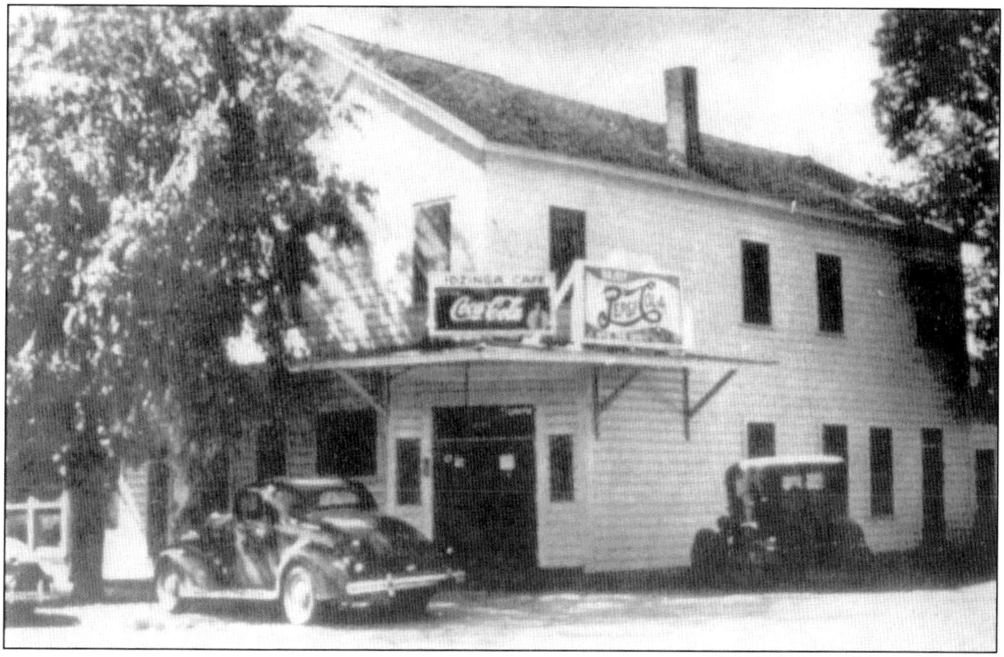

This is a much later image of the only building that survived the terrible Elk Grove fire. It was the Railroad Hotel in 1892, and today it is known as Bob's Club. (Courtesy of Elk Grove Historical Society.)

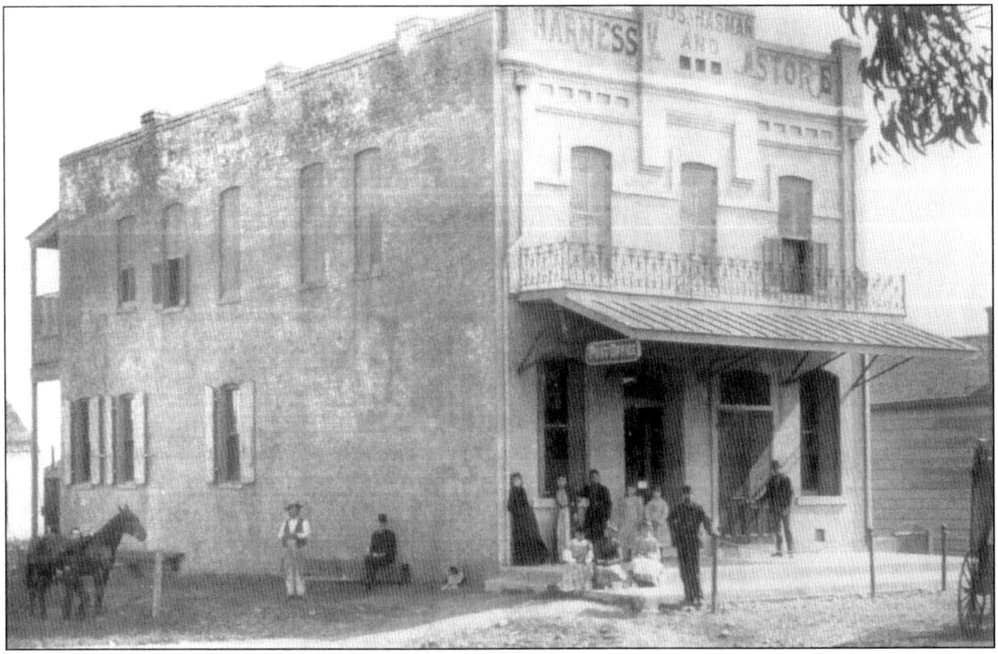

The two magnificent buildings on this page still stand in Old Town Elk Grove. Both were rebuilt after the fire, and they have had many different uses over the years. The Harness Store (above), created by Joseph Hasman, and the International Order of Odd Fellows Building (below), with its IOOF emblem still clearly visible, have been home to a variety of businesses in their prominent places on Elk Grove's Main Street. (Courtesy of Elk Grove Historical Society.)

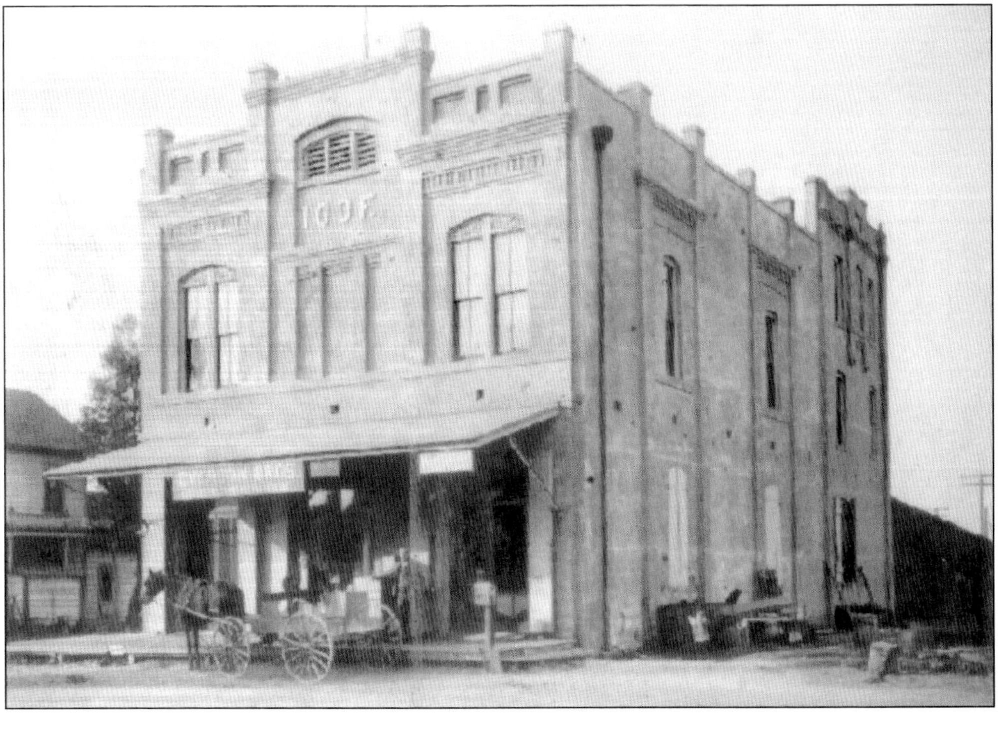

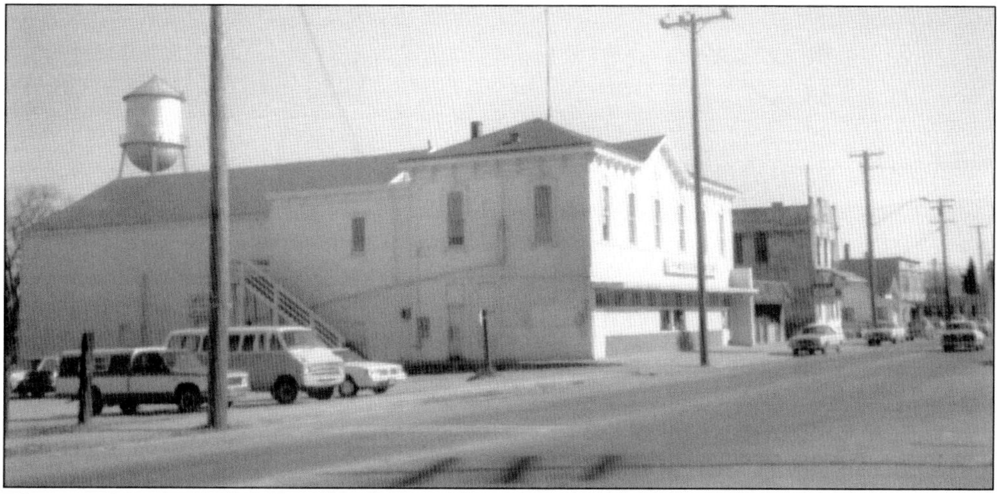

This was the Masonic Hall for more than 100 years, from 1880 to 1986. The building is unique in how it has changed its face over time. In 1926, more room was needed, so the building was cut in half and moved to create more space, with the six windows pictured here. The original structure had only five windows. The present building was rebuilt after a fire, and the original design of five windows is what is now seen. Many different shops filled the first floor over the years, as they still do today. The lodge hall was on the second floor.

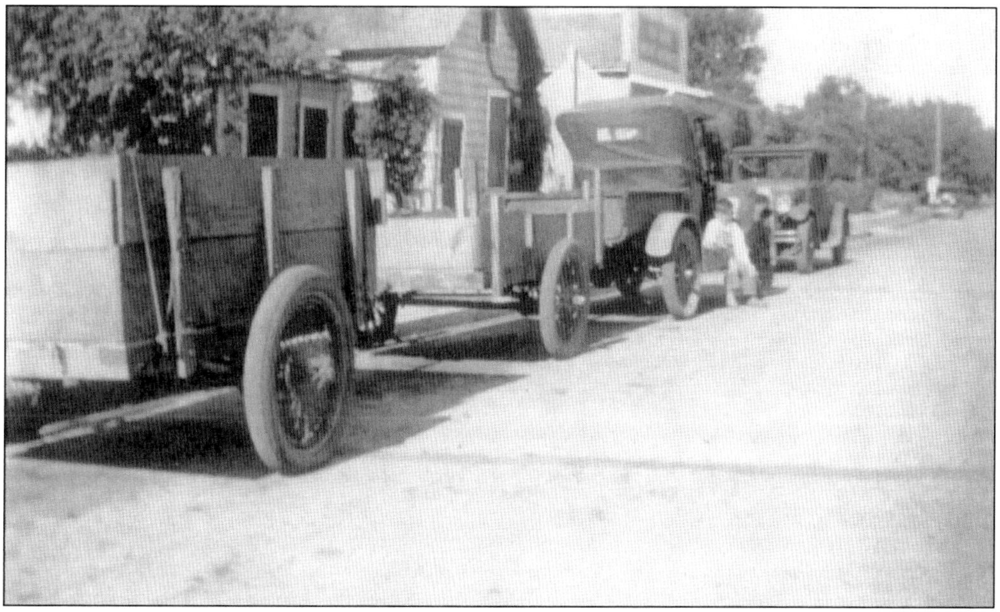

Cars changed the lives of everyone in Elk Grove just as they did across the nation. The local livery stable got rid of its horses and used the new gasoline-powered vehicles to pull the wagons.

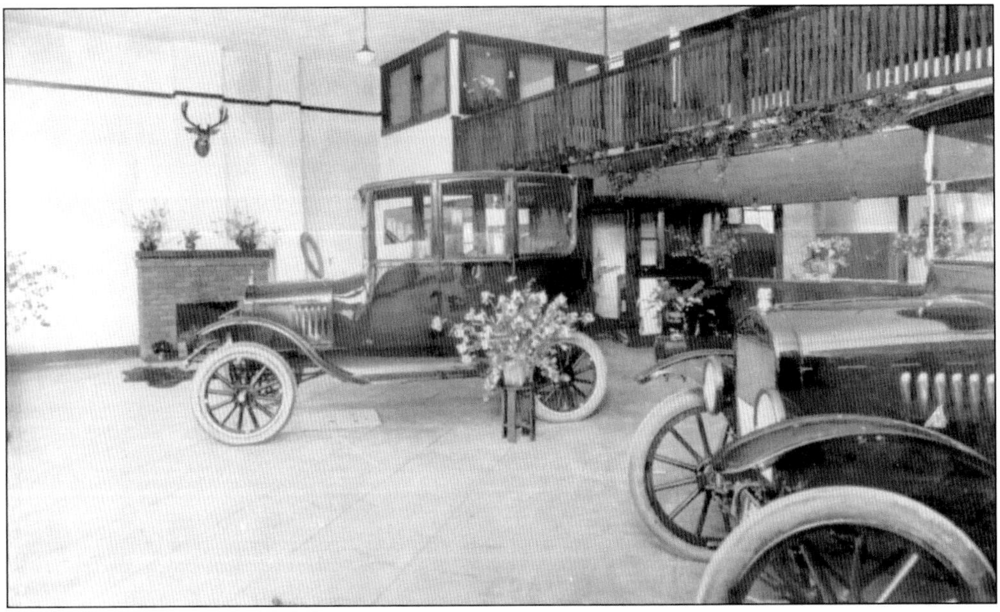

Big changes began to occur in Elk Grove in the 1900s when automobiles became available. A trip to Sacramento by horse-and-buggy took all day, but the partnership of Henry L. Ehrhardt and George Rhoades changed it all. They created the first automobile dealership in Elk Grove in 1919, the Ford Model T Agency. (Courtesy of Elk Grove Historical Society.)

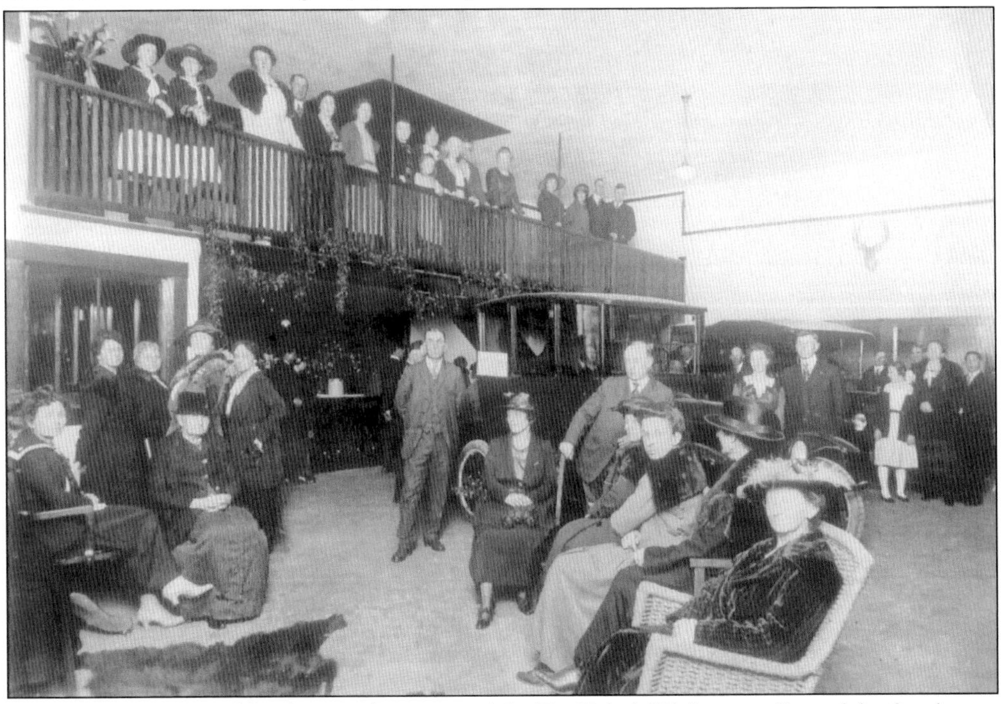

A huge crowd gathered for the grand opening of the Ford Model T Agency. One of the first buyers was the town doctor, who quickly recognized how he could improve his services for farm families. Those long-ago families would be surprised to see the variety available at Elk Grove's Auto Mall of 2006. (Courtesy of Elk Grove Historical Society.)

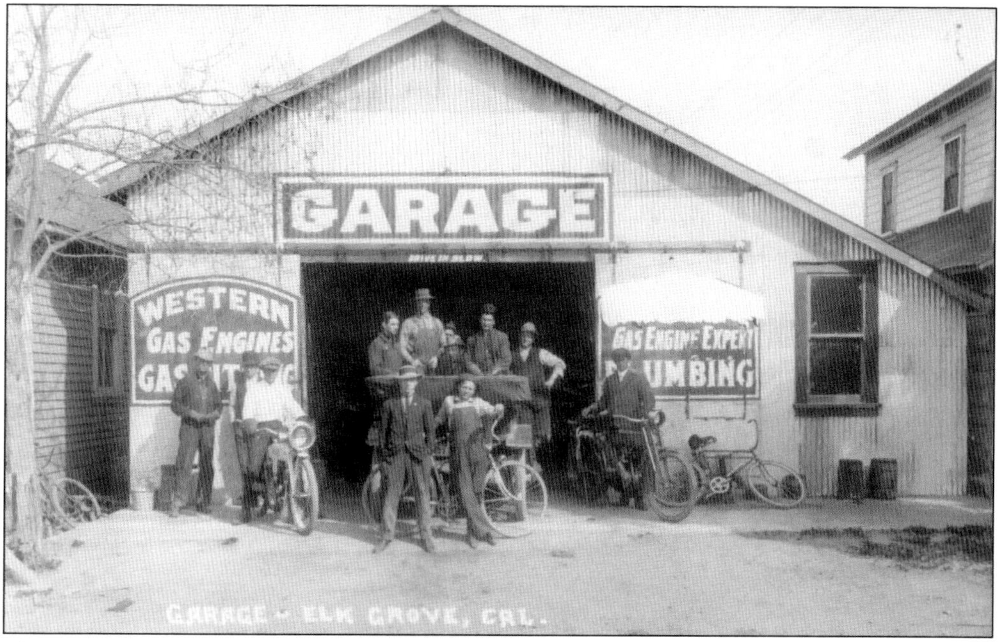

These are blacksmith shops and machine shops turned into garages. Men learned new skills to keep the cars running.

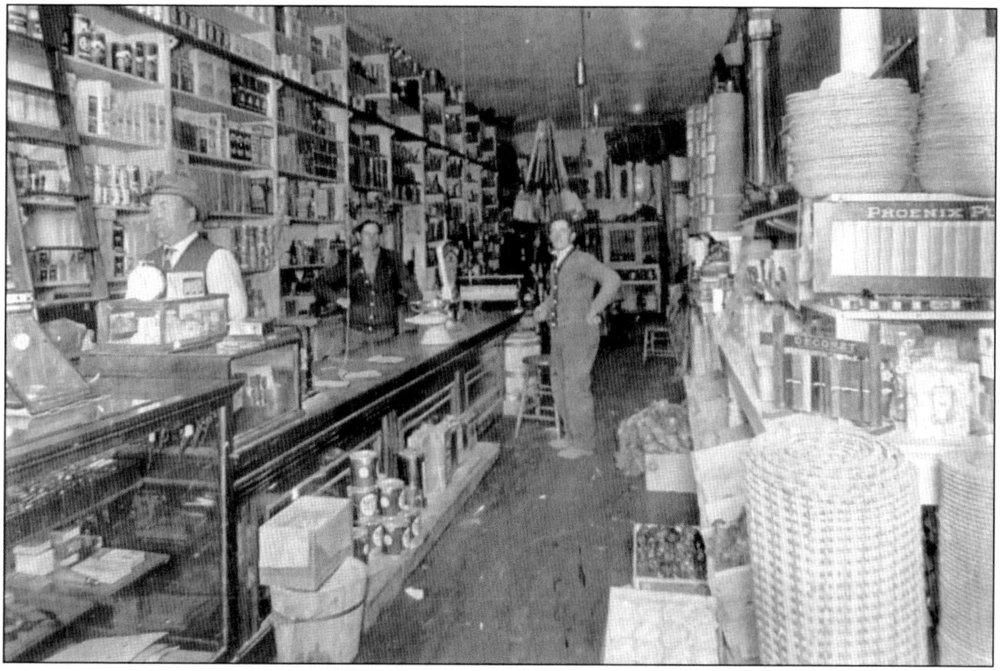

The combination of railroad and automobiles greatly improved transportation for families. General stores with groceries and other items began to spring up at crossroads and other locations near the railroad tracks. The 1920 Foster's General Store in the Hasman Building on Main Street is pictured here. Later it was the Smith and Welch Store, and still later the Red and White Store. The Elk Grove area is served by a variety of grocery stores, and some of them are managed by the next generations of families such as Steve Fischlin at the Waterman Bel Air Store.

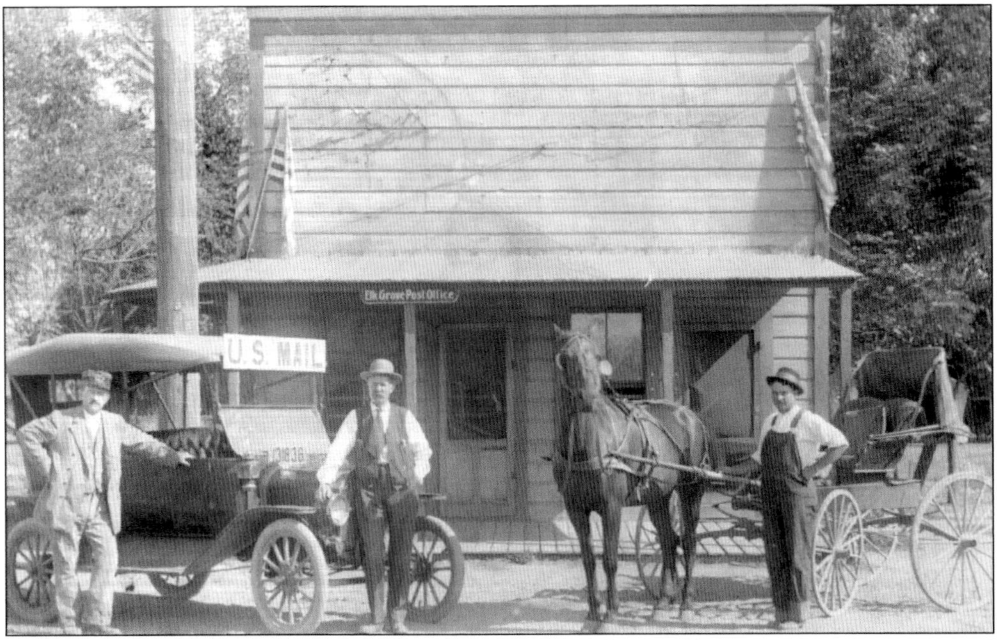

This photograph celebrates a new age of mail delivery with its publication on a penny postcard from 1915. This comment was provided by Mr. Coons: "We are not allowed to have anyone ride with us." Ed Garrish, center, is by the car, and Lloyd Coons is the rural route mailman.

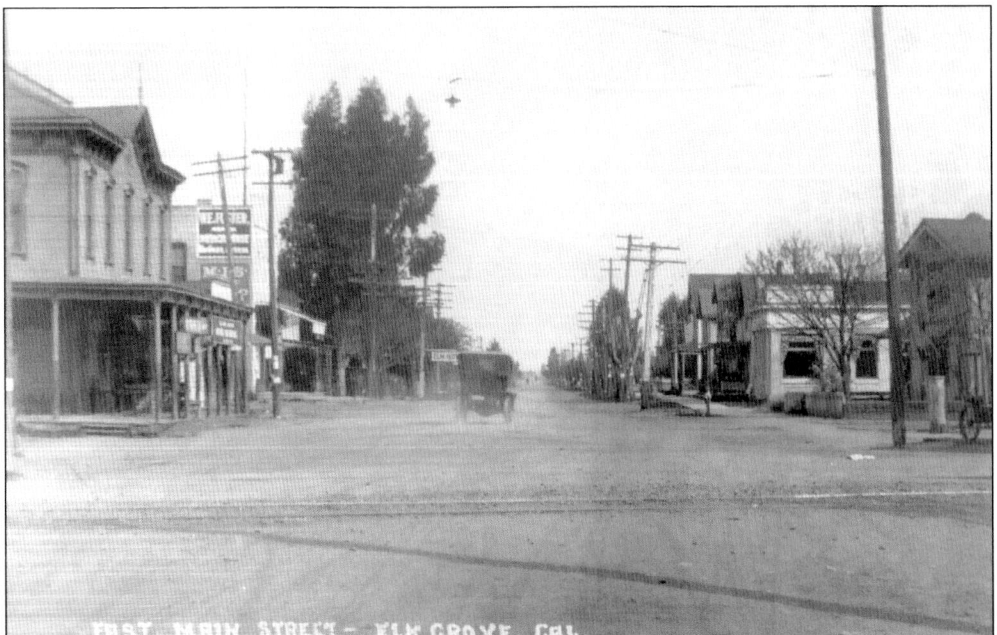

In this photograph, Main Street changes from horses to cars.

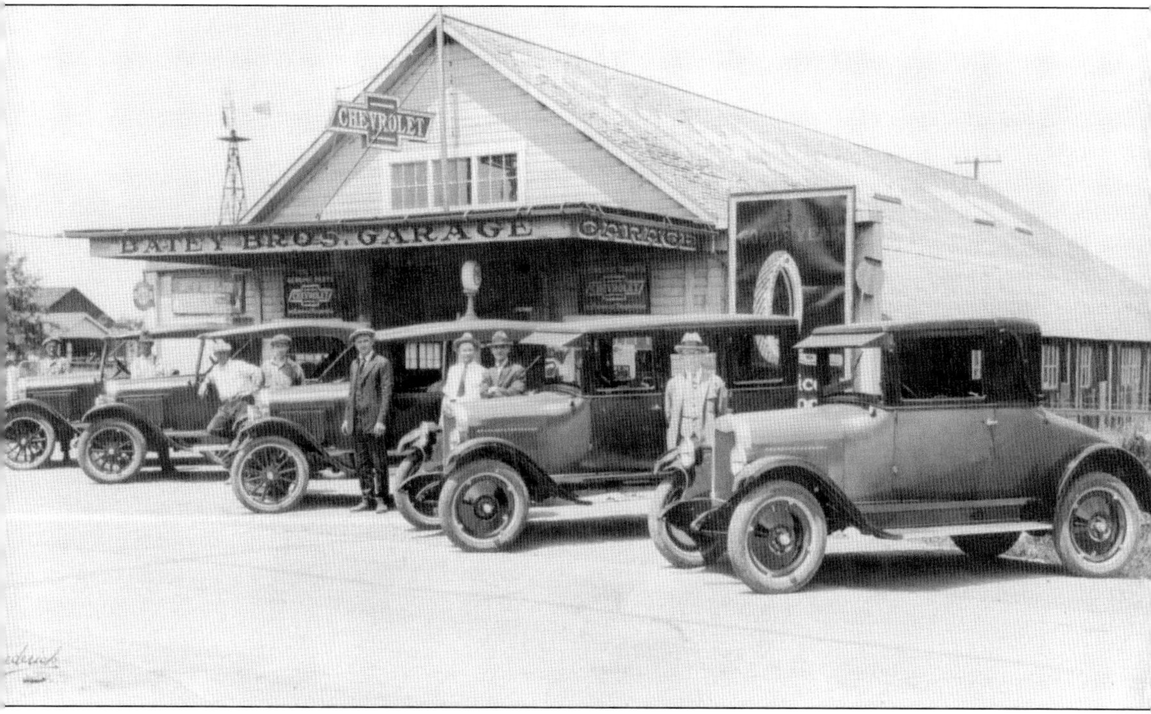

Matt and Bill Batey came to Elk Grove from England in 1919 and set up a pump and machine repair shop on Main Street. Other family members joined them, and their brother Bob entered the business. The Bateys recognized the machine of the future and joined the growing automobile market. Batey Chevrolet, continued by Matt's son Robert (known as Bob) was a premier family owned business until almost the end of the 20th century. This photograph (also on the cover of this book), is of the Batey Brothers and their new 1926 Chevies. According to Mr. Batey, his father and uncles went to Oakland to see the new cars and were greatly impressed with the new models. The car had four-wheel brakes, and Matt Batey claimed that "there would never be more perfect cars." The automobiles were shipped to Elk Grove by train, and everyone lined up for a photograph. Pictured here from left to right are Bill Batey, owner; Elton Ronk, mechanic; Matt Batey, owner and Robert's father; Bill Dixon, salesman; Bob Batey, owner; and Roy Hand, insurance salesman. (Courtesy of Robert [Bob] Batey.)

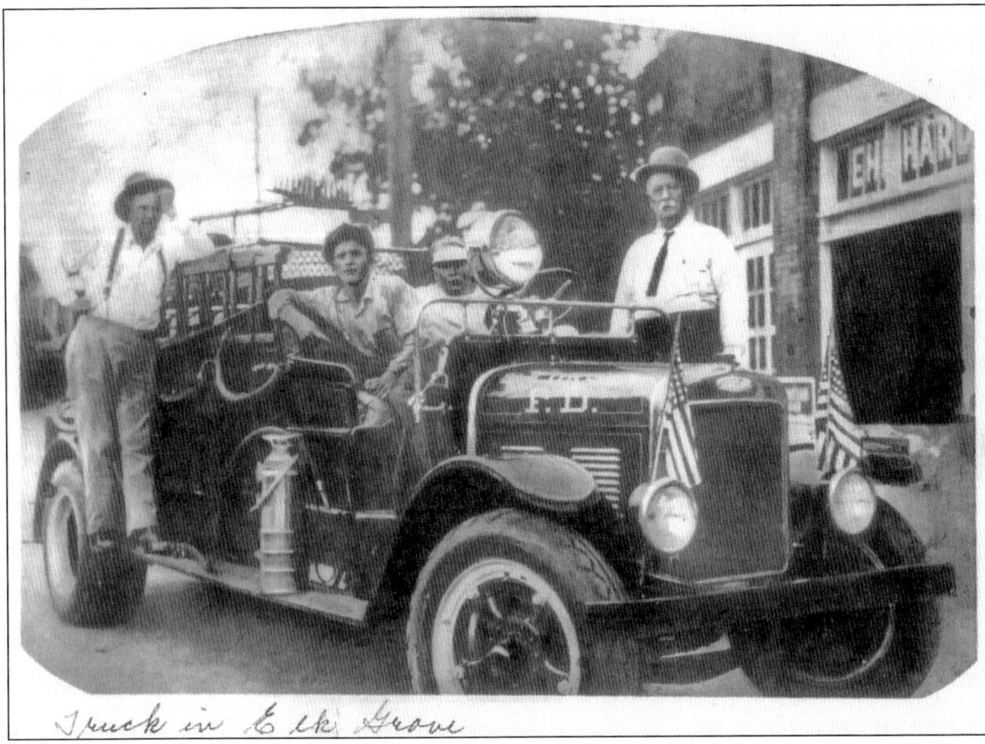

The volunteer fire department raised funds through community events to improve firefighting. A Paige Roadster to transport the water tanks was donated in 1920 by Del Cann, the first fire chief. Pictured here are Del Cann, Frank Everson, Bud Jones, and W. E. Everson.

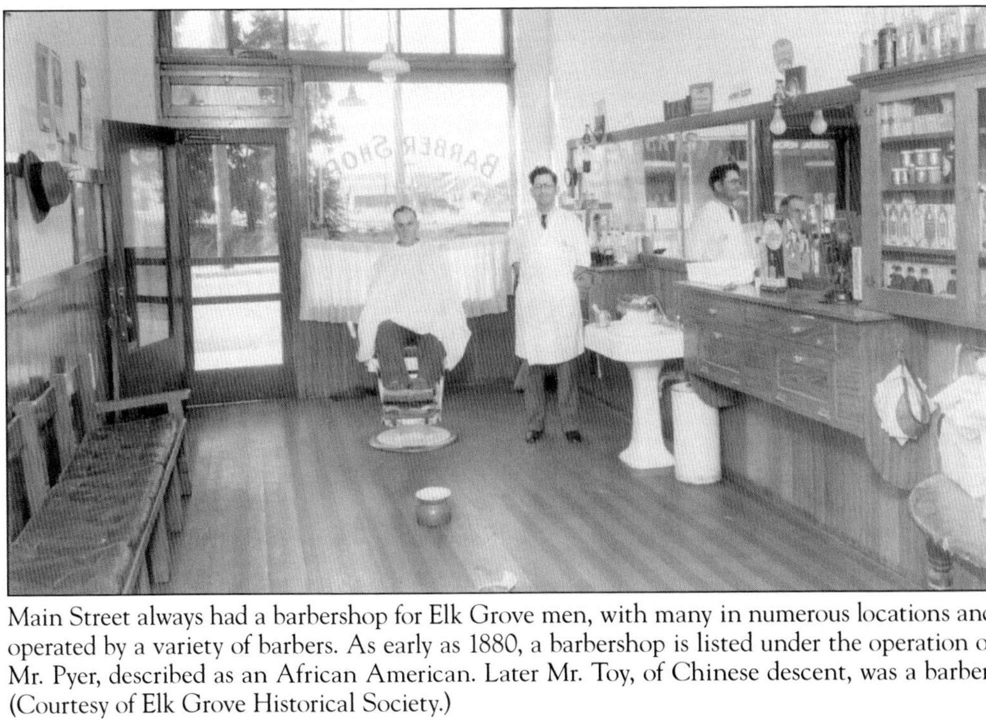

Main Street always had a barbershop for Elk Grove men, with many in numerous locations and operated by a variety of barbers. As early as 1880, a barbershop is listed under the operation of Mr. Pyer, described as an African American. Later Mr. Toy, of Chinese descent, was a barber. (Courtesy of Elk Grove Historical Society.)

James Hall was Elk Grove's first justice of the peace in 1850. The justice court, a small building near the railroad tracks, was in place by the late 1800s. Local citizens acquired a jail cell from Sacramento's floating jail ship, the *LaGrange*, which had sunk in the Sacramento River during the 1862 flood. The original justice court building was moved to Elk Grove Park by the Sacramento County Sheriff's Delta Patrol in the 1980s, and it has been restored by the Elk Grove Historical Society. (Courtesy of Jane Morse.)

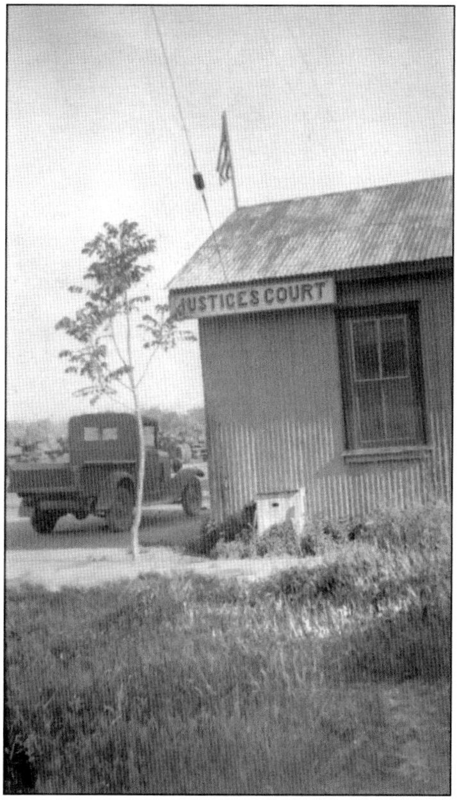

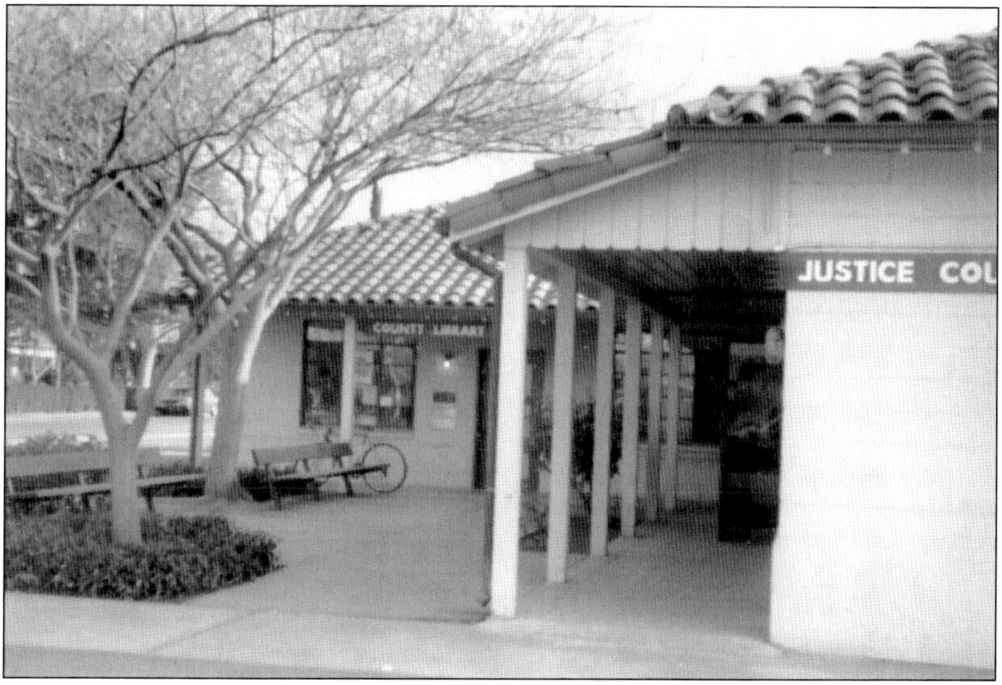

This 1950s building on Main Street served as the justice court until 2004. The library was originally in the building, but it was moved down the street where more space was available.

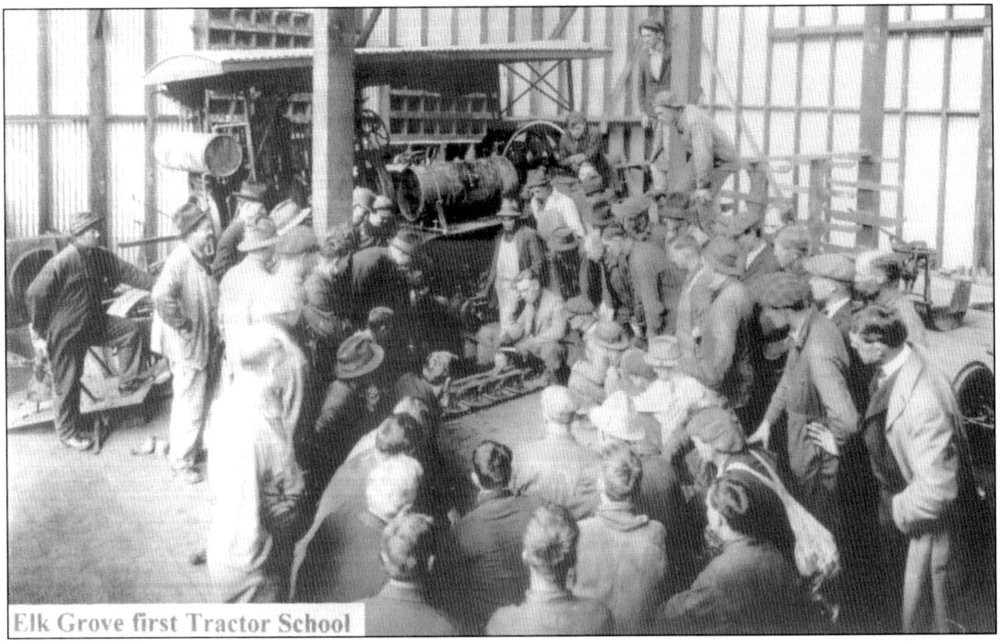

The needs of the local farmers were quickly addressed by the automobile dealerships in the 1920s, as they added tractors to their lines of merchandise. The next step was to offer tractor schools so that farmers could learn how to operate the new machines. Classes were held in the sales room, and the students practiced out in the fields. (Courtesy of Elk Grove Historical Society.)

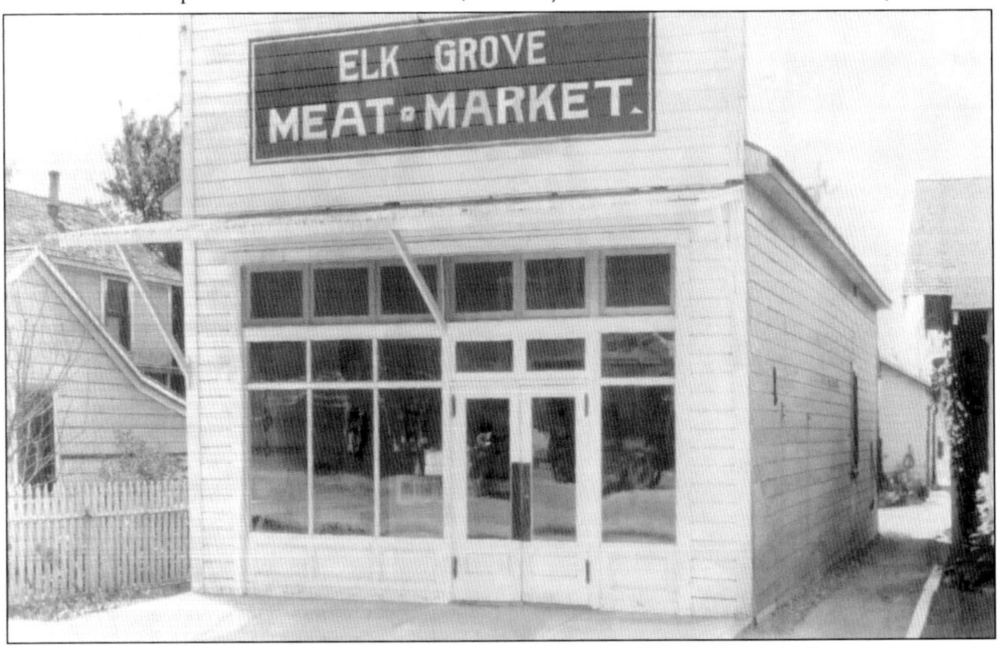

As transportation improved more and more, businesses developed on Main Street to meet the needs of local families. James Hayes operated the Meat Market from 1901 to 1929. From 1944 to the 2000s, the building and adjoining residence have housed an auto repair shop, pump shop, bike sales, grocery store, dress shop, children's wear shop, real estate office, pet shop, and nail shop. (Courtesy of Elk Grove Historical Society.)

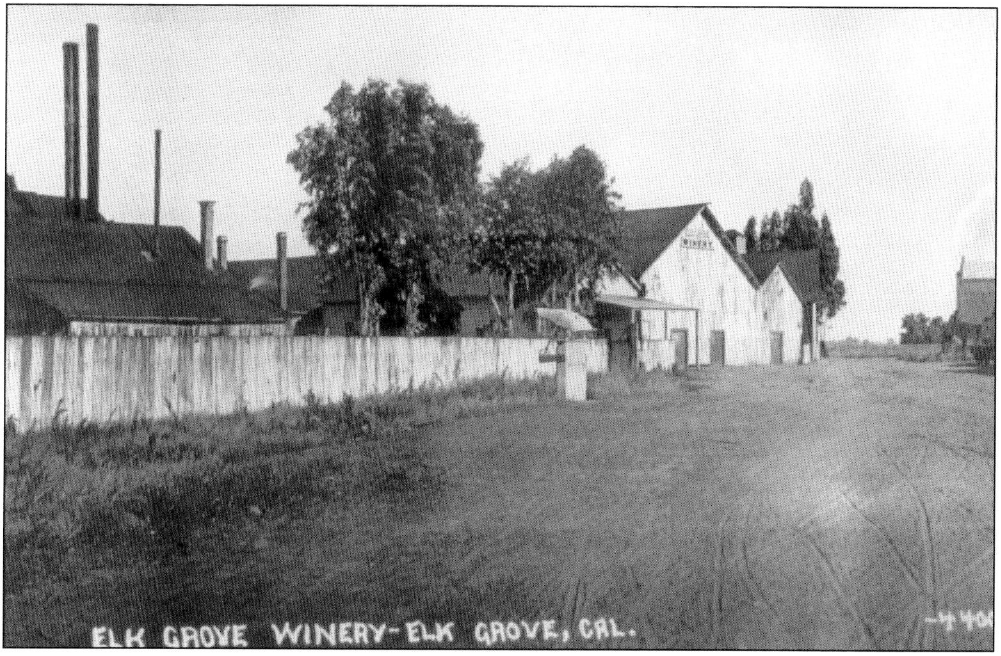

The first Elk Grove winery was established by George Harvey Kerr in the 1860s. By the early 1900s, there were at least five wineries in Elk Grove, Franklin, and Florin. Kerr's winery was taken over by the granddaughter of a third Kerr brother and was called the DaRosa Winery. Later it was the DaRosa-Neves Winery. Many Elk Grove residents are familiar with the Gibson Wine Company that was in operation from 1940 until the 1980s. Some of the Gibson specialties were fruit, berry, and honey wines. The photograph below shows grapes being prepared for shipment by Colonial Grape Products. (Courtesy of Elk Grove Historical Society.)

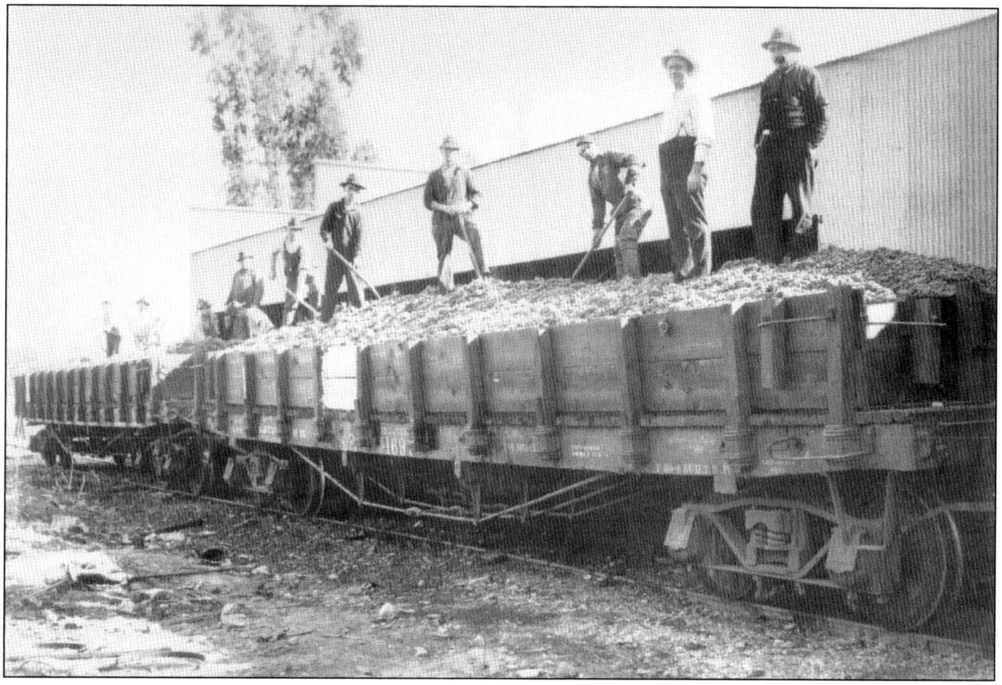

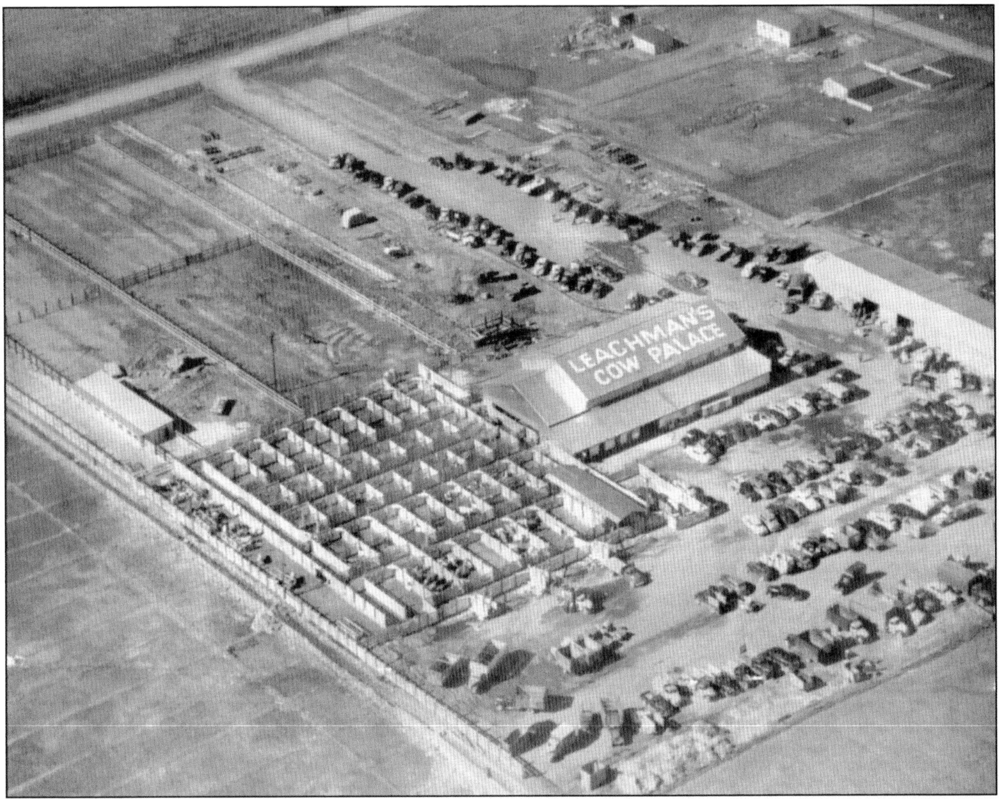

It is not too surprising that Elk Grove had its own cattle yard and auction place. Known as the Cow Palace, and sometimes as the Cattle Palace, many transactions took place at this site in southeast Elk Grove. The railroad was only a few blocks away, and the slaughterhouse, used to dispose of animals when necessary, was to the east. No one thought anything of cows walking down Main Street from one site to another. The aerial view (above) shows the placement of the corrals as well as the empty fields that surrounded the operation. (Courtesy of Elk Grove Historical Society.)

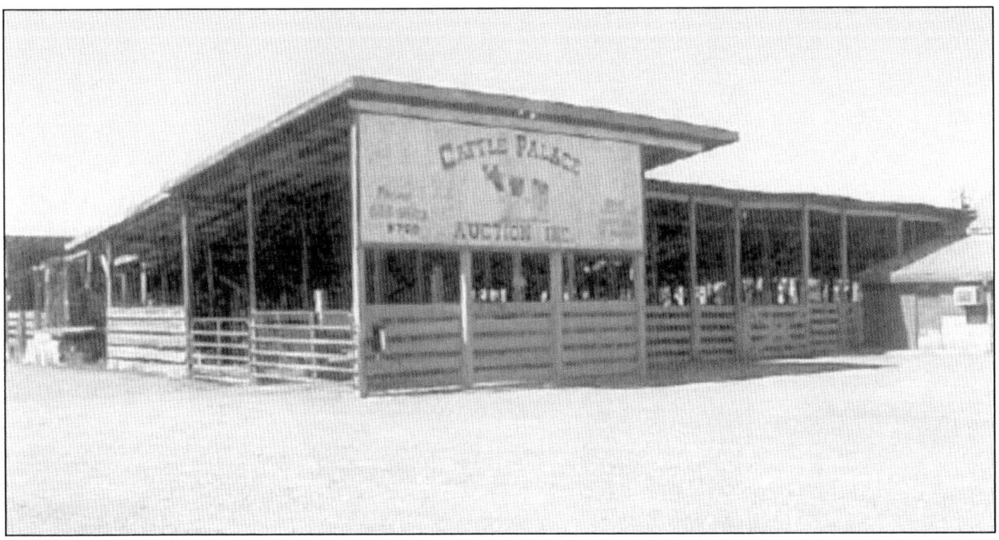

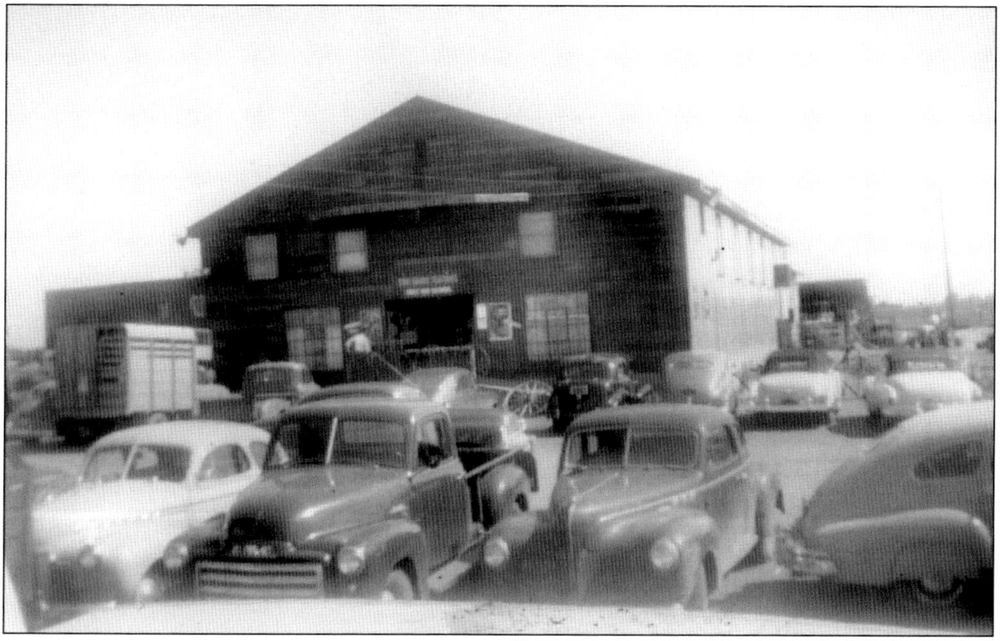

Many Elk Grove families cherish their memories of "movie days," for when Carl Amundson opened the town's first theater there was much to celebrate. Families no longer had to go to Sacramento to see a movie when the Cow Palace Theater debuted in 1949. Carl later opened the Boulevard Theater on Main Street because it was in a more desirable location. The theater days were short lived, however, as the building burned down in 1957 and was not replaced. (Courtesy of Elk Grove Historical Society.)

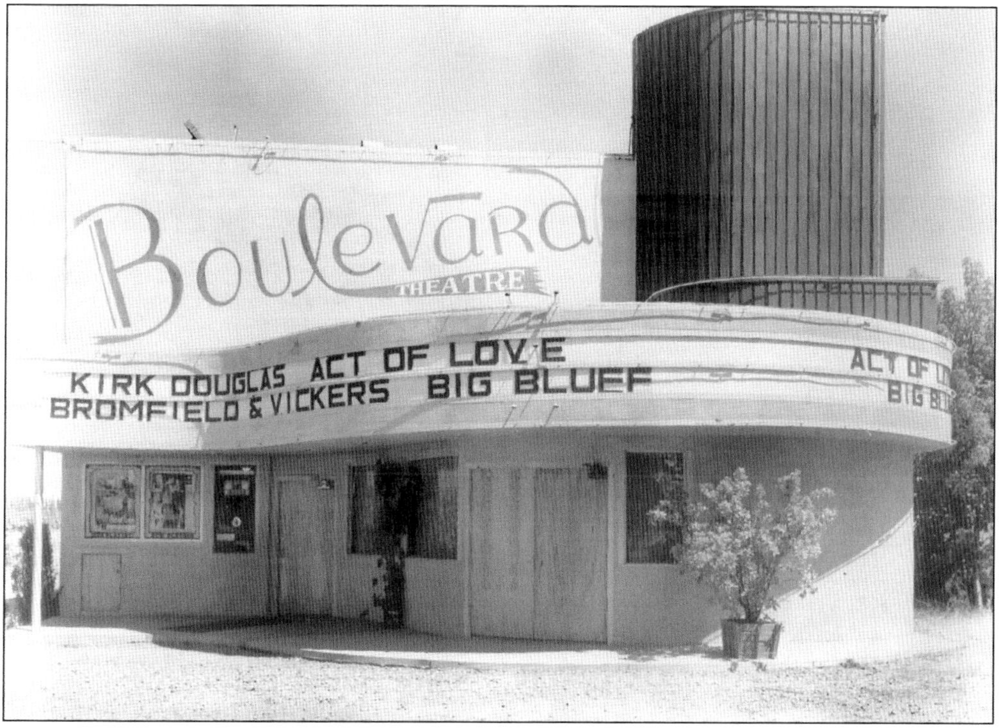

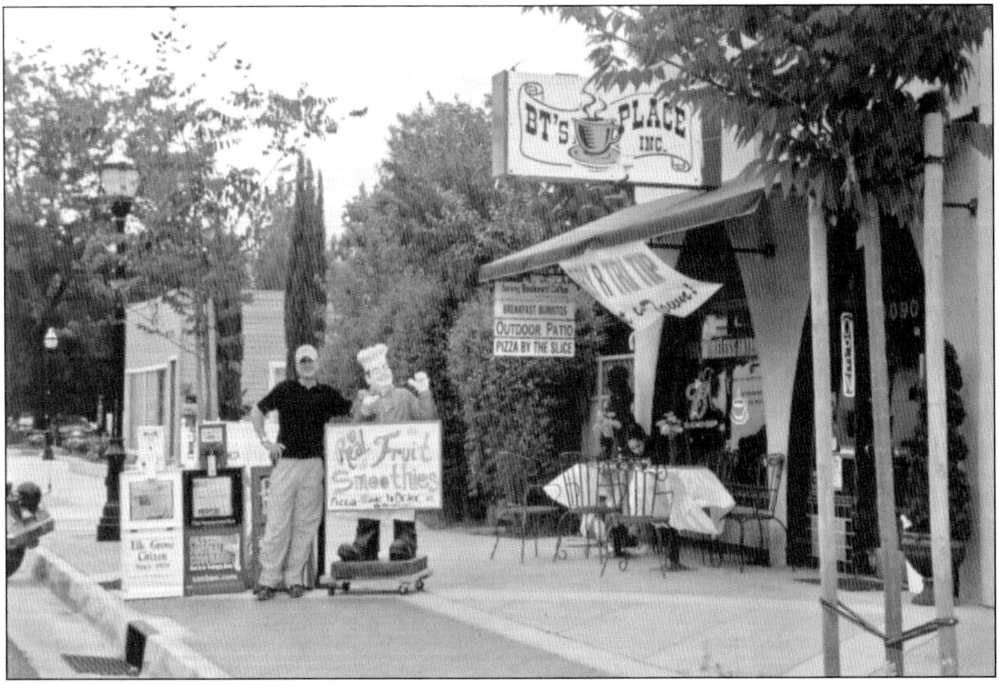

The distinctive arches on the building that houses BT's Place bring memories of Warren's Shoe Store to old-timers. Braulio Torres (BT) continues to change his coffee shop to meet the needs of today's residents who frequent Old Town.

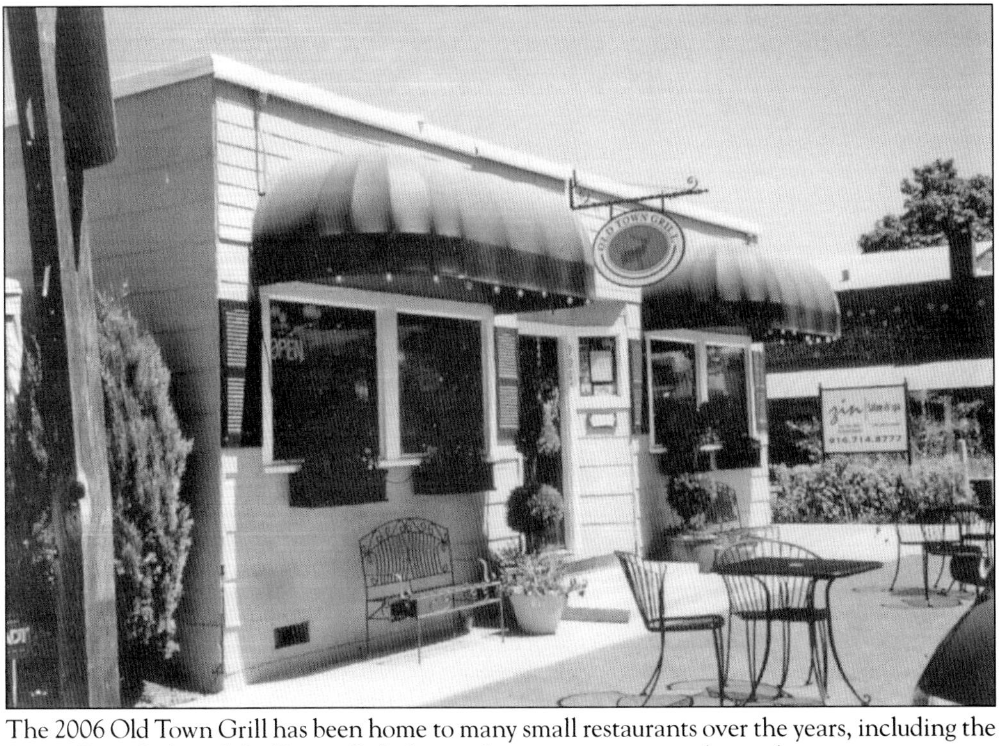

The 2006 Old Town Grill has been home to many small restaurants over the years, including the Sunny Rose Café and the Depot Café. It too changes to meet new demands.

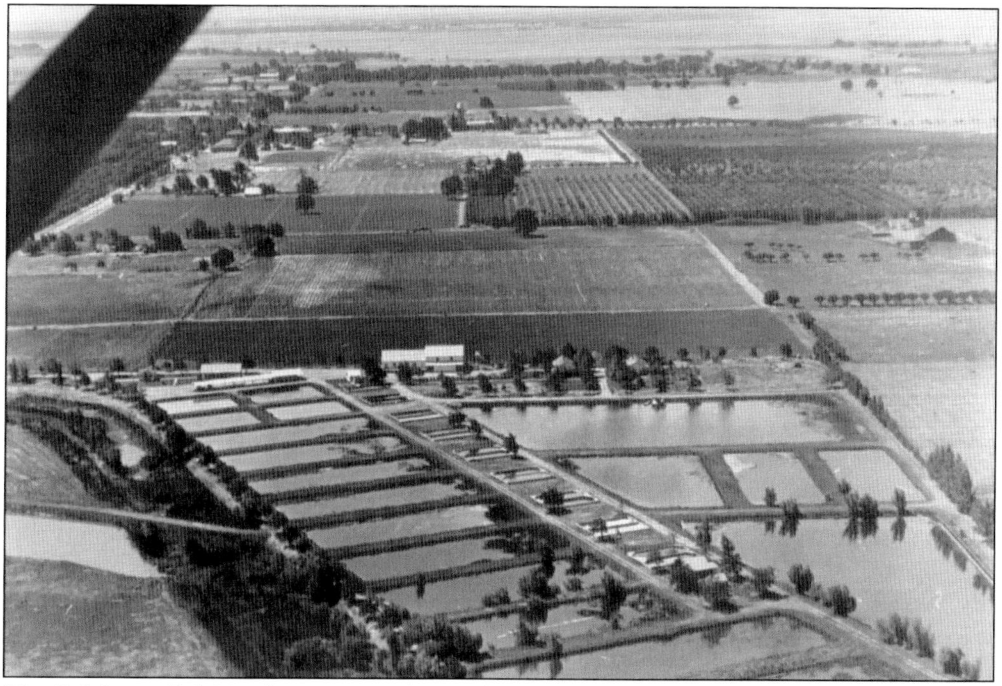

The California Fish Hatchery was on the southwest corner of Elk Grove-Florin Road and Bond Road on what is now called Laguna Creek. The hatchery was a prominent feature of Elk Grove and a great place to take children to fish. Today the ponds have all been covered, and instead of the hatchery, there are houses and a shopping center. There's even a Starbucks at the corner, but Laguna Creek is still there as an important part of the Elk Grove Trail that meanders through the city. The State of California Fish and Game agency maintains an aquatic toxicology laboratory at a portion of the former hatchery site.

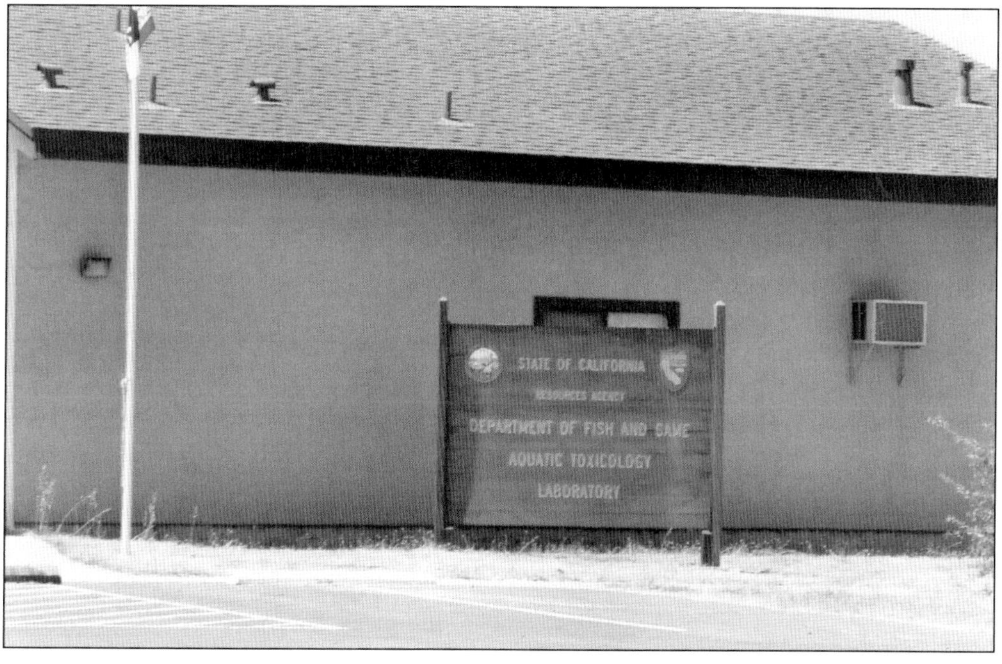

The original Central Pacific Railroad that ran through the middle of Elk Grove became the Southern Pacific and then the Union Pacific. But by the 1970s, it was apparent that passenger service would no longer be a part of the offerings available for those who wished to travel to and from Elk Grove. The railroad depot on the southeast side of the tracks was closed and available to the highest bidder who would move it from the site. A community effort was just getting started to save the building when it was loaded onto a truck and hauled away. Some said it was to be used in an amusement park in southern California. Others said it would be restored somewhere as part of a history project. As of 2006, the whereabouts of the building are unknown, but stories persist that the dismantled building is stored somewhere in a barn in the San Joaquin Valley. The trains, though, are still there—dozens of them every day and some with more than a 100 cars. They continue their routes through the middle of town, much to the dismay of many, but to the delight of those who love the sound of trains.

Seven

THE PEOPLE

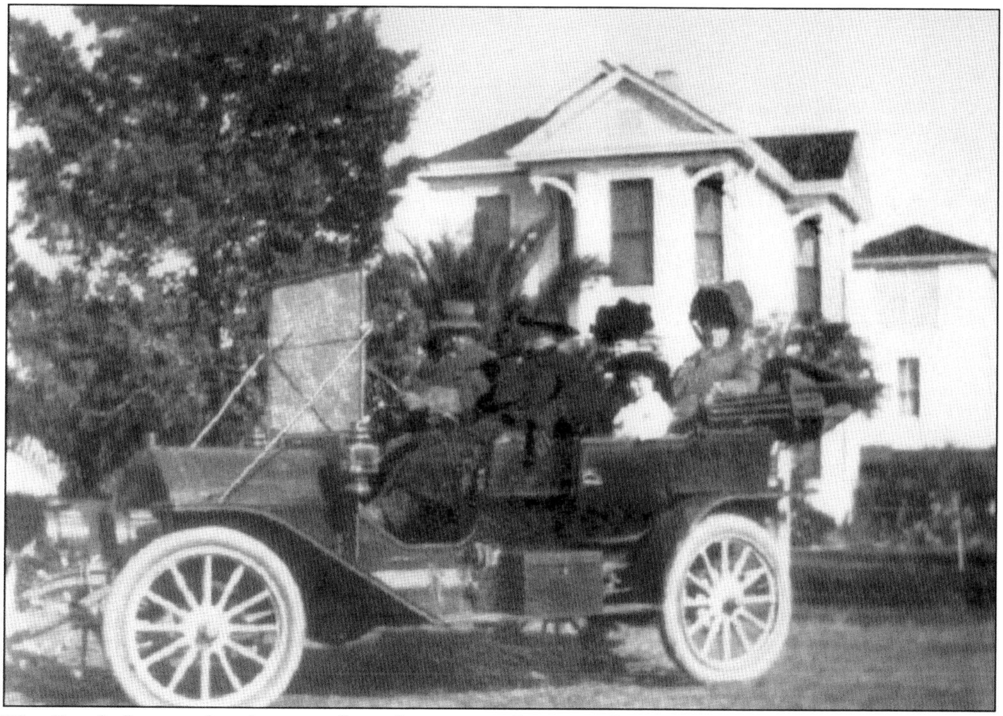

The Bartholomew family is out for a drive on a pleasant afternoon in Elk Grove. Although the roads of the 1920s left a lot to be desired, the owners of the new cars did not hesitate to try out their motoring skills. Even trips to Lake Tahoe were done on mountain roads that were far from ready for their later freeway status. The Bartholomew family was prominent in the development of Elk Grove throughout the 20th century and continues that involvement into the 21st century. Alvin Bartholomew was one of the main supporters of cityhood for Elk Grove. (Courtesy of Bartholomew family.)

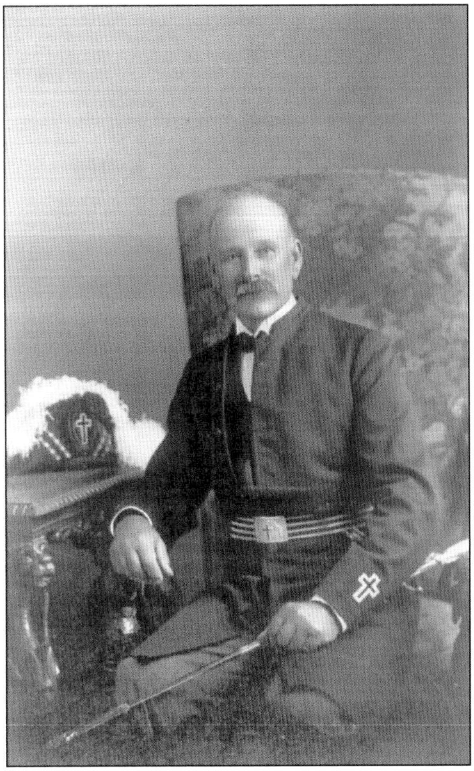

William Chauncey Sheldon was the son of Jared Dixon and Catherine Rhoads Sheldon. Born in 1848, he was only three years old when his father was killed in a dispute with miners. He is pictured here in his Masonic regalia. (Courtesy of Ellen Rosa.)

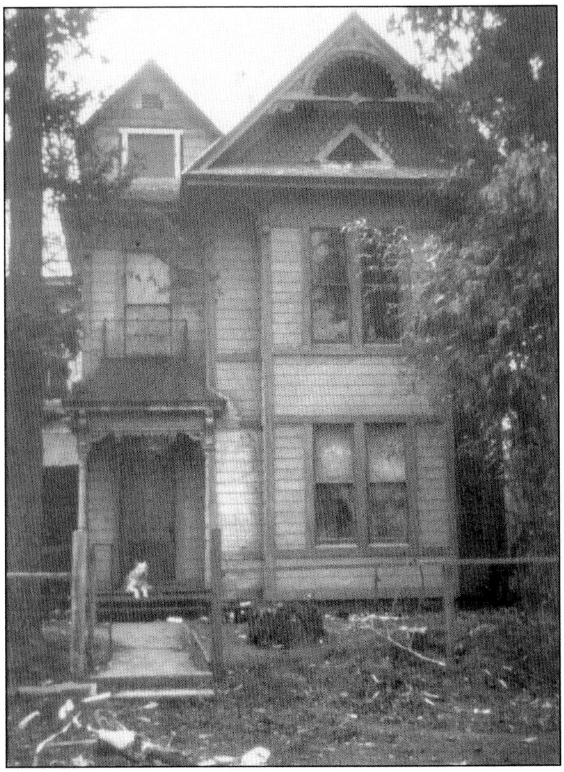

The Sheldon home on Sloughhouse Road was a showpiece. The house was built in 1889 for $15,000, a huge sum at the time. In a natural setting on Deer Creek, not far from the Cosumnes River, the house was surrounded by cottonwoods, oaks, willows, grapes, elderberries, and blackberries. Sheldon imported a variety of plants and animals from other countries for his country estate. The photograph shows the grand old house shortly before it burned to the ground in the 1970s.

Alexander Hamilton Willard was the blacksmith for the Lewis and Clark Expedition of 1803. He and his wife came to California in 1851 following the urging of their son who had come for gold two years earlier. Willard settled in Franklin, known then as Georgetown, and lived there until he died in 1865. He is buried in the Franklin Cemetery, a true hero of the United States and its westward expansion. Willard is pictured here with his wife, Eleanor.

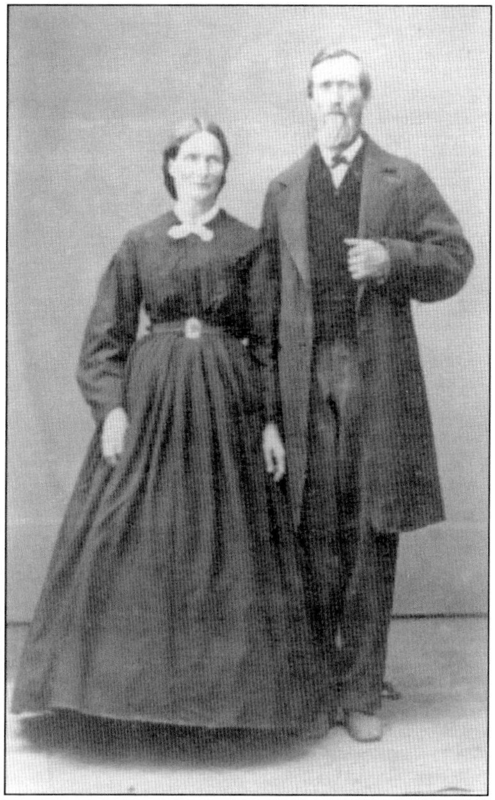

Willard's grave is marked with a historical plaque, placed there by the Daughters and Founders and Patriots of America.

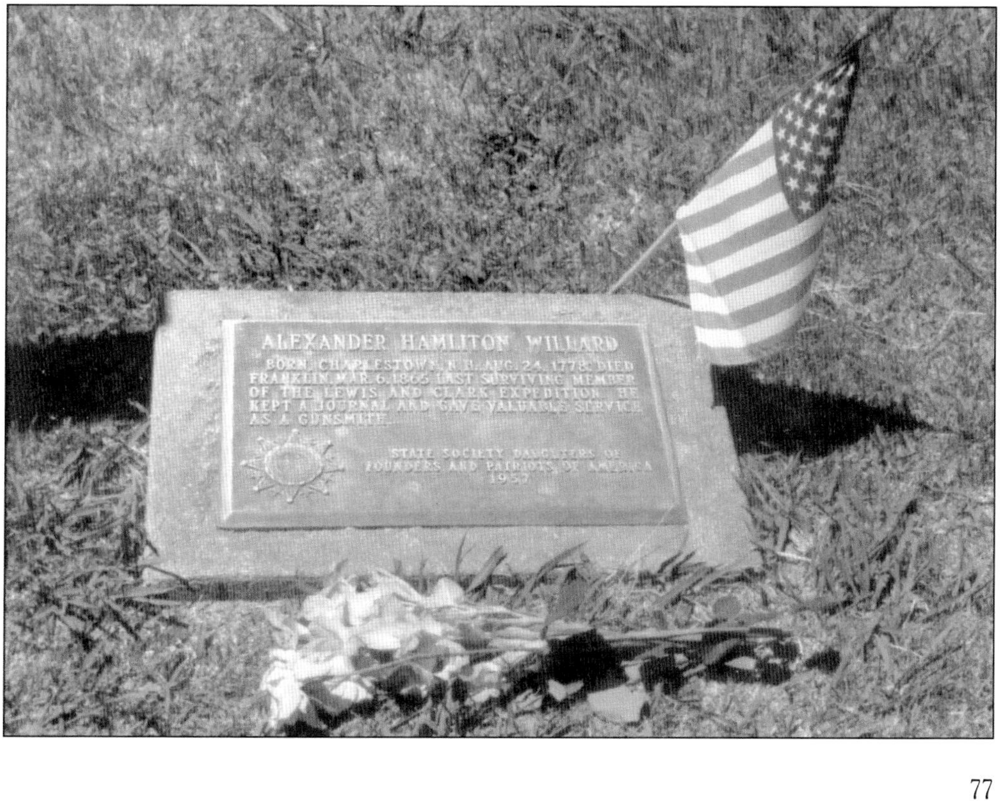

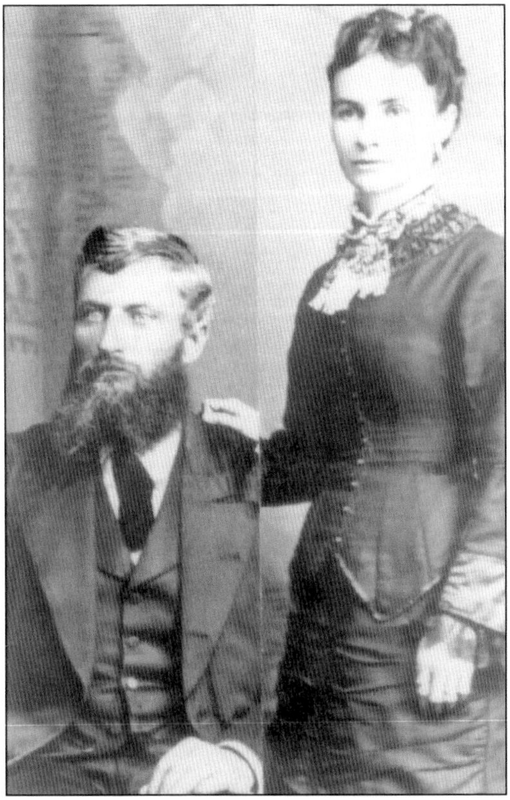

Samuel Kennedy was born on September 9, 1850, the day that California became a state. It may explain why he was destined to be a leader in Florin and Elk Grove. Kennedy was six years old when he traveled across the plains and mountains as part of the Kennedy-Jackson wagon train. The families settled east of Stockton Road in the Sheldon/Calvine/Gerber area. They founded the Ebenezer Baptist Church and the Jackson School. Uncle Sam, as Kennedy was known, helped to form Elk Grove Union High School. He is pictured here with his wife, Mary. (Courtesy of Ellen Rosa.)

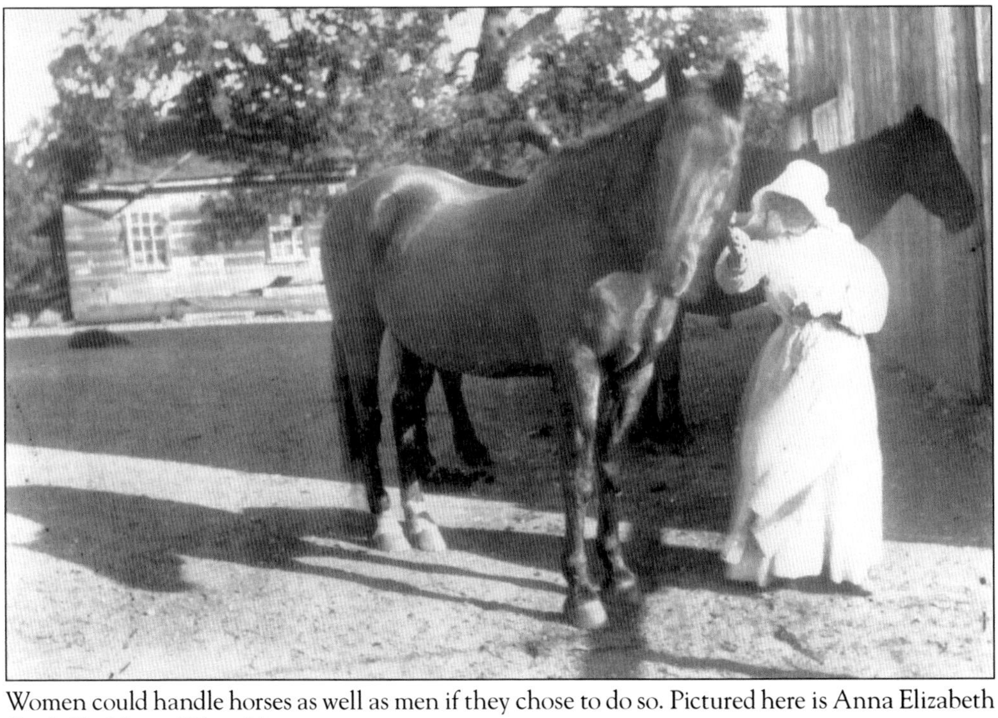

Women could handle horses as well as men if they chose to do so. Pictured here is Anna Elizabeth Cook Sheldon of Sloughhouse.

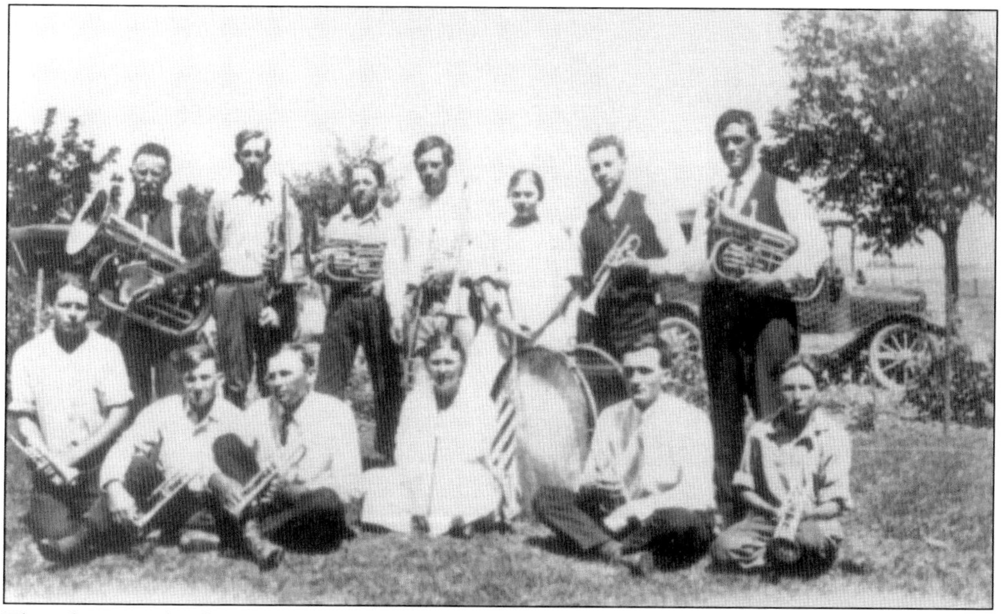

This photograph of Point Pleasant residents with their musical group was taken in 1923. They called themselves the Dutch Flat Band. (Courtesy of Dennis Buscher.)

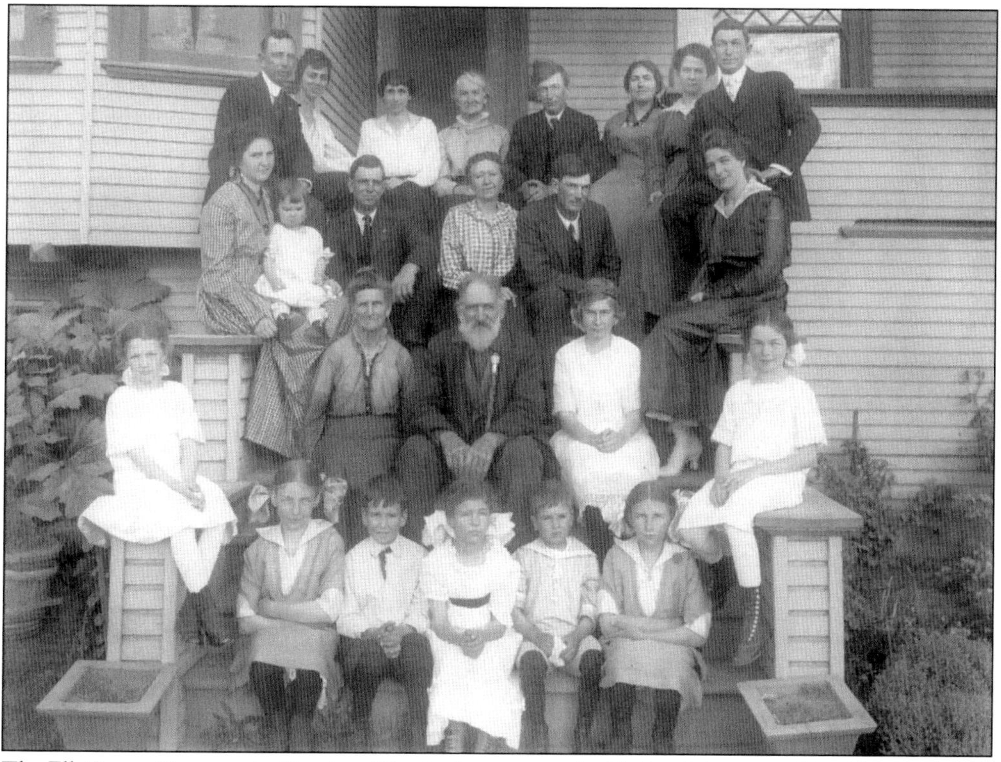

The Elk Grove Community Services District is restoring the Ehrhardt house on Franklin Boulevard to be a centerpiece of the park that is located there. Elk Grove also has a John Ehrhardt Elementary School. Members of the John Ehrhardt family are pictured here in 1915 celebrating a 50th anniversary. (Courtesy of the Ehrhardt family.)

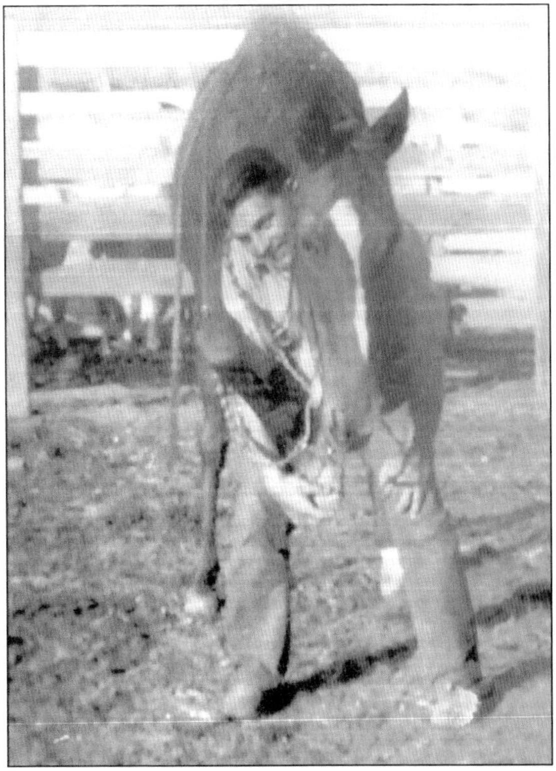

Elk Grove's rodeo star, Ernie Carli, is seen here in 1928. A farm boy of an immigrant family from Italy, young Ernie grew up in the Excelsior-Highland area near what is now Sunrise Boulevard. As a young man, he became fascinated with rodeos and earned quite a reputation for his daredevil antics. To keep his hobby a secret from his mother, he changed his "cowboy" name to William Carli and became known as Bill. In regard to the photograph, he said, "Today men ride horses, but when I was young, the horses rode the men."

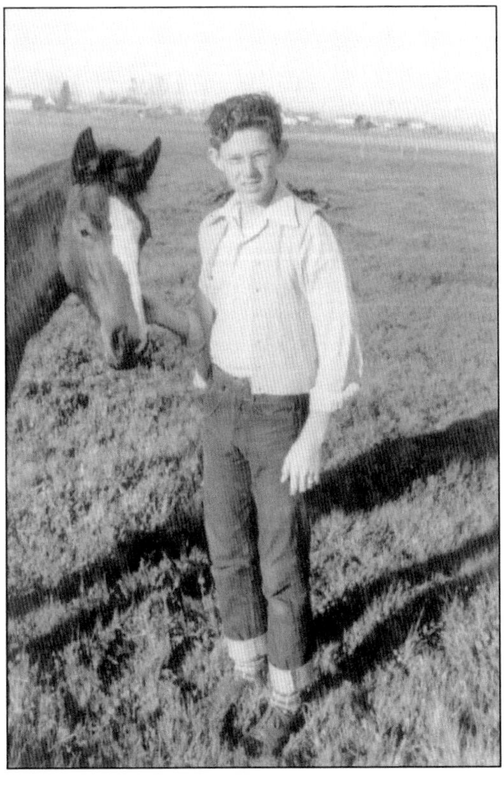

Teenager Jim Ring is pictured here with his horse, Blaze, in the late 1930s. Ring and his wife, Virginia, live in Wilton. Both are active community volunteers with the Rhoads School as well as other endeavors. (Courtesy of Jim and Virginia Ring.)

Ouida Hanks, pictured here with Jane and Dave Morse, was the granddaughter of Elk Grove's well-known constable, Del Cann. Hanks was one of the first women in the Sacramento area to volunteer in the beginning of World War II for the Women's Army Auxiliary Corp, the predecessor of the WACS. She worked in a hospital in Australia and frequently met Gen. Douglas MacArthur in the halls.

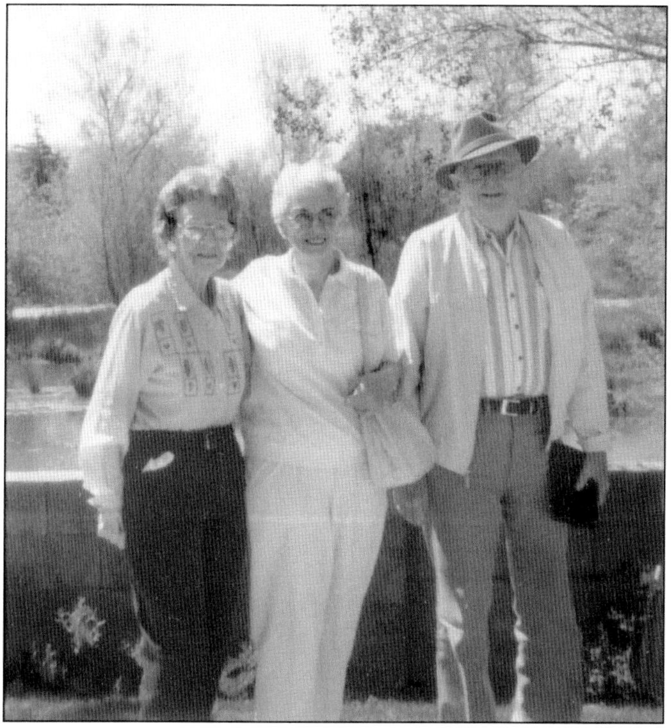

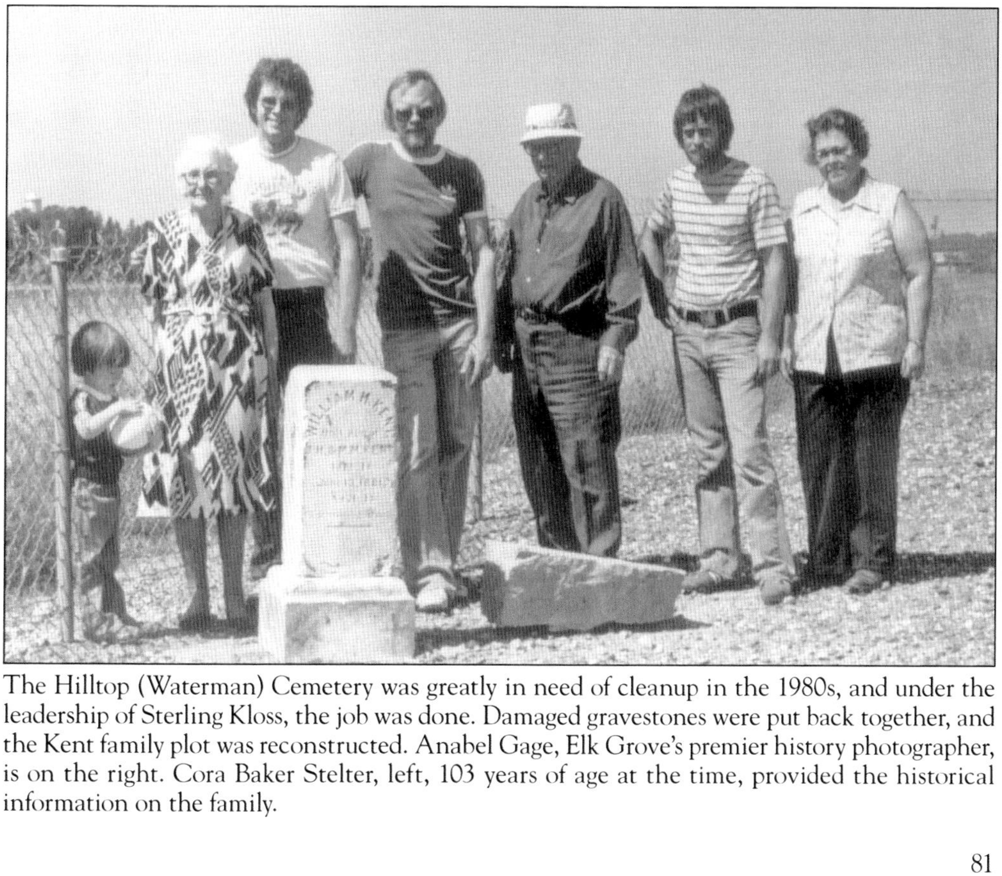

The Hilltop (Waterman) Cemetery was greatly in need of cleanup in the 1980s, and under the leadership of Sterling Kloss, the job was done. Damaged gravestones were put back together, and the Kent family plot was reconstructed. Anabel Gage, Elk Grove's premier history photographer, is on the right. Cora Baker Stelter, left, 103 years of age at the time, provided the historical information on the family.

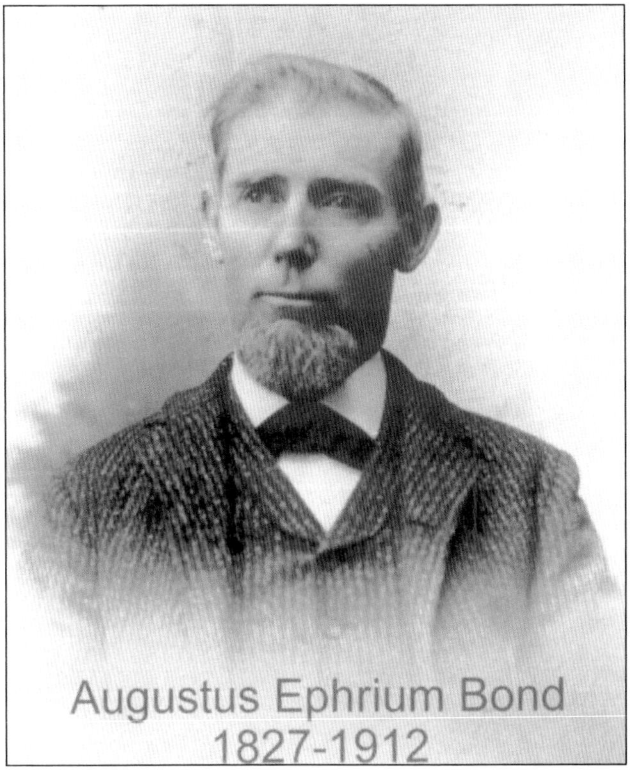

Augustus Bond, known as Gus, came to California for gold but ended up with 320 acres at what is now the northeast corner of Bond and Elk Grove-Florin Roads. He married Frances Eustis, the niece of George Donner. Frances sewed Donner's money belts for his California venture. The Donner girls, who survived the Sierra winter of 1846–1847, were frequent visitors of the Bonds at their Elk Grove home.

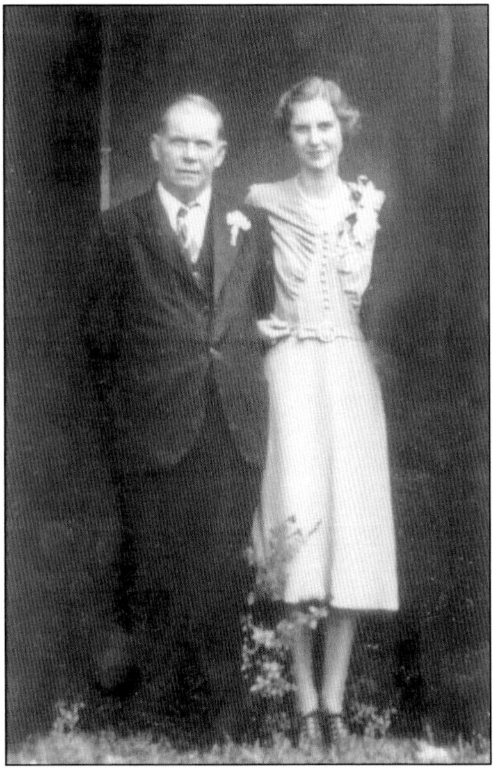

Pictured here in the 1930s are John M. Brown and his daughter Grace, who married Mark Wightman, a frequent contributor to local history and a supporter of the Elk Grove Historical Society. The Browns owned the property of the original Elk Grove Hotel and Stage Stop. (Courtesy of Mark Wightman.)

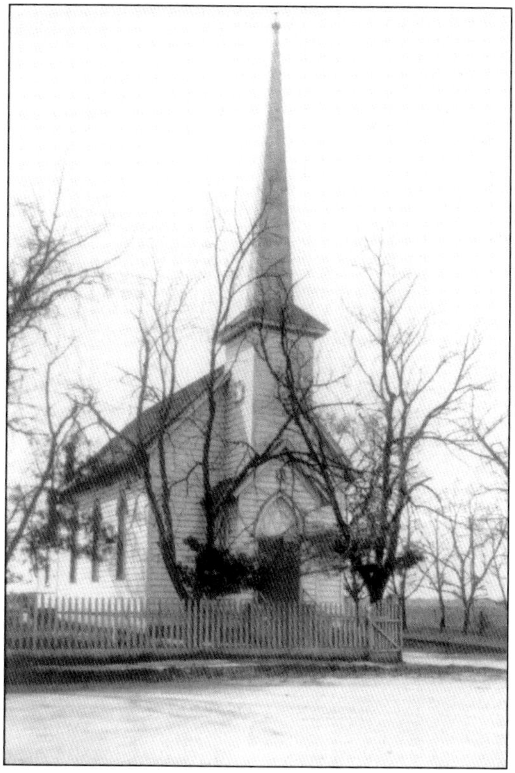

Churches have been important in the Elk Grove community and in the lives of families. In 1880, two churches anchored the businesses on Main Street. The Presbyterian church (right) was where the Methodist church is today. The Methodist church (below) was at the other end of town. Both were on the south side of the street on property that had been the ranch of George Harvey Kerr. The Methodist church joined the Presbyterian church in 1919. The former parsonage building, however, is still there on the east side of town. (Courtesy of Elk Grove Historical Society.)

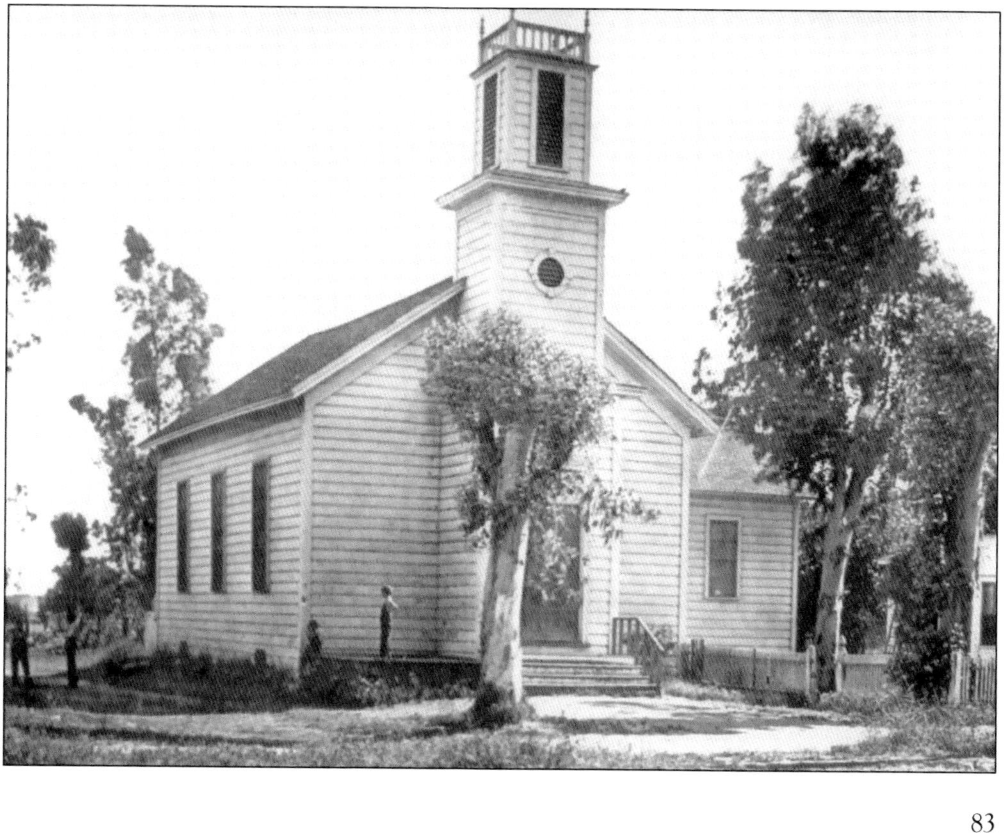

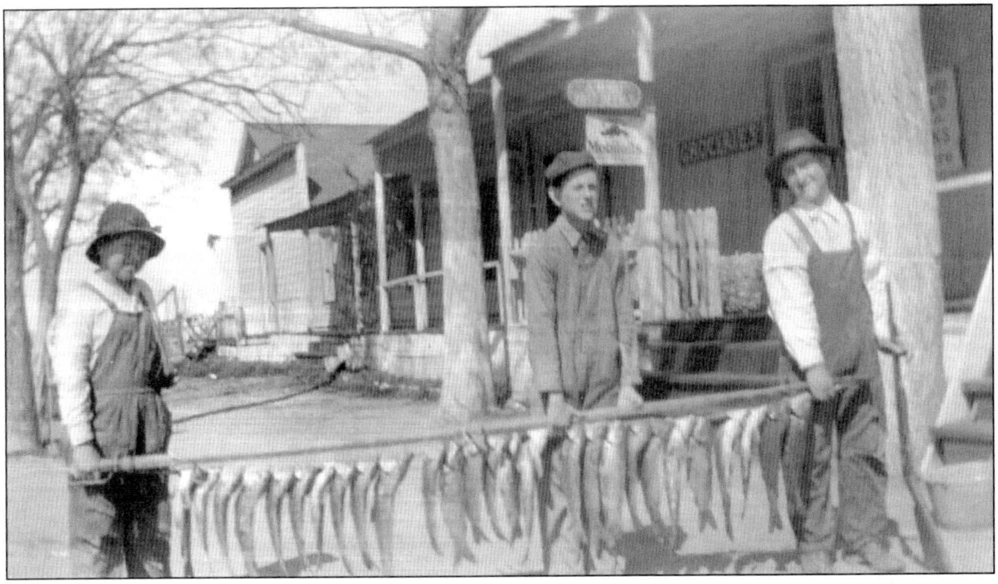

The community of Arno replaced long-ago Hicksville, but Arno is gone now too. This image, taken in 1921, shows the dance hall, post office, general store, and saloon. The Arno school was combined with Herald and Colony schools to form the Arcohe School District, using the first two letters of each name. (Courtesy of Jacquelyn Hanson.)

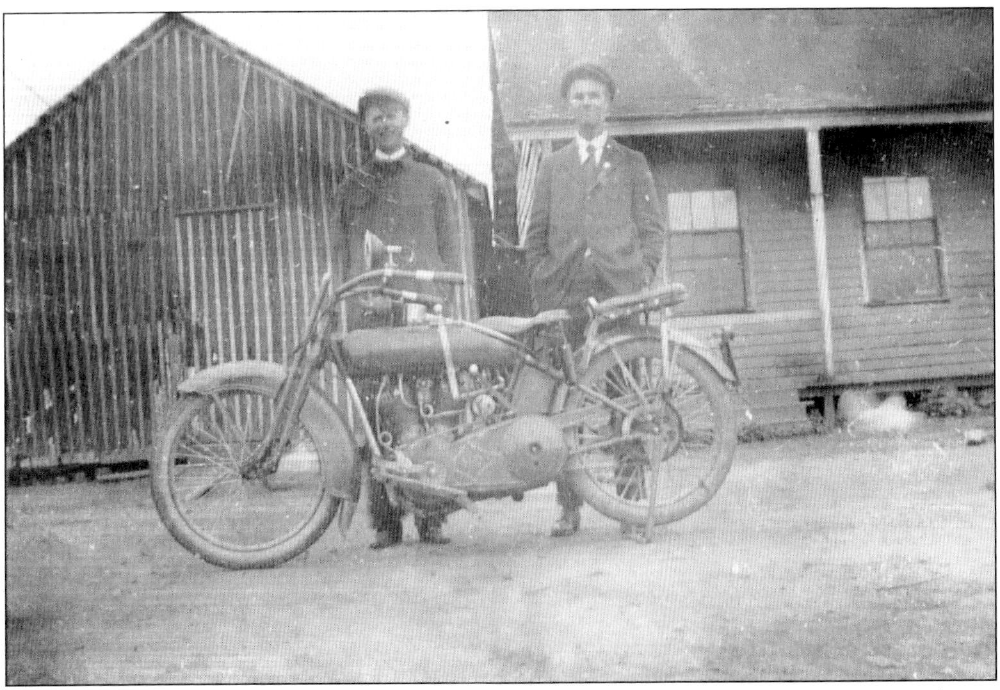

The Buscher brothers, Frank and Hurbert, of Point Pleasant show off their new motor cycle.

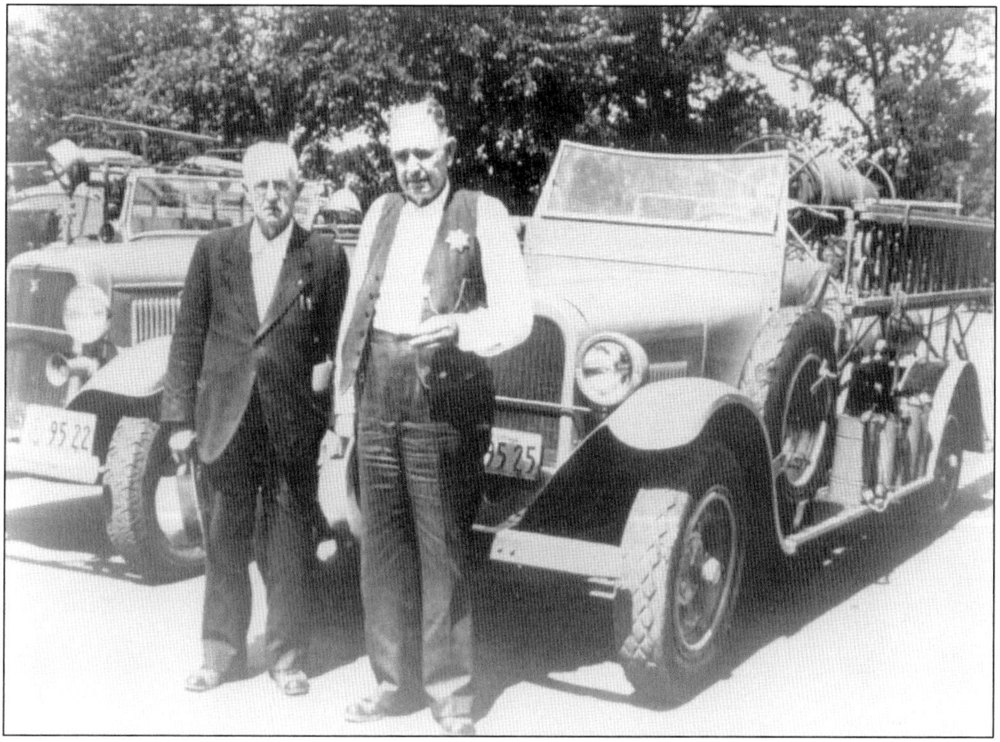

Judge W. E. Everson and constable Del Cann pose in front of an early fire department truck. (Courtesy of Gerald Derr.)

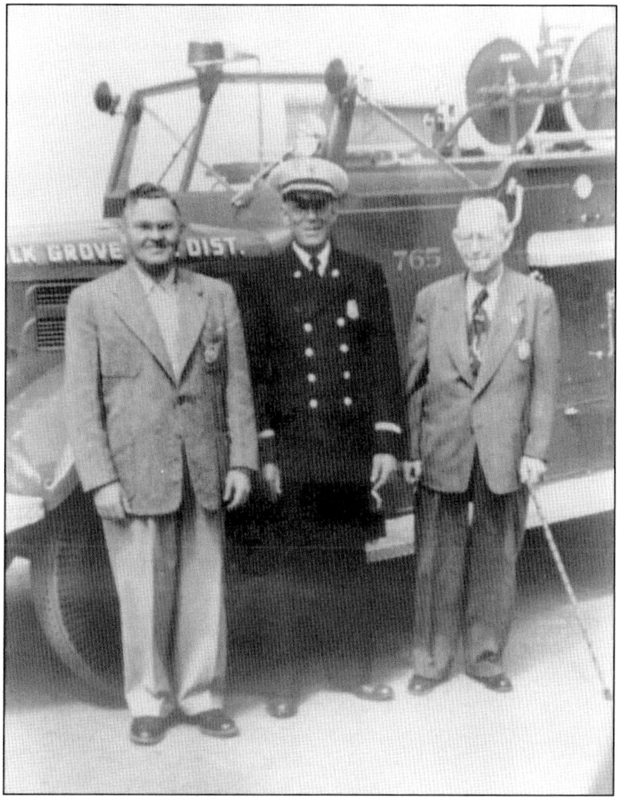

The Elk Grove Fire Department was the first fire district in Sacramento County to hire a full-time chief in 1940. Pictured here are director Bud Jones, Chief Perry Schulze, and director Creed Wackman. (Courtesy of Gerald Derr.)

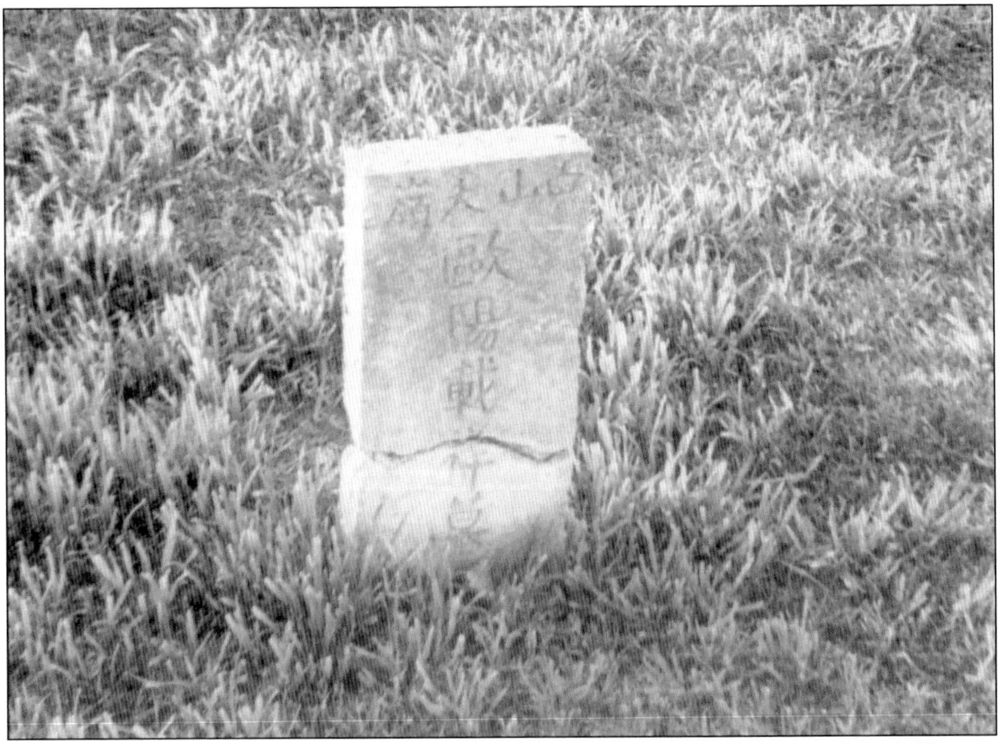

This Chinese grave marker is in Franklin Cemetery. At one time, a large number of Chinese people lived in the settlements along the Sacramento River, west of Franklin. Because of flooding, burials often took place on higher ground.

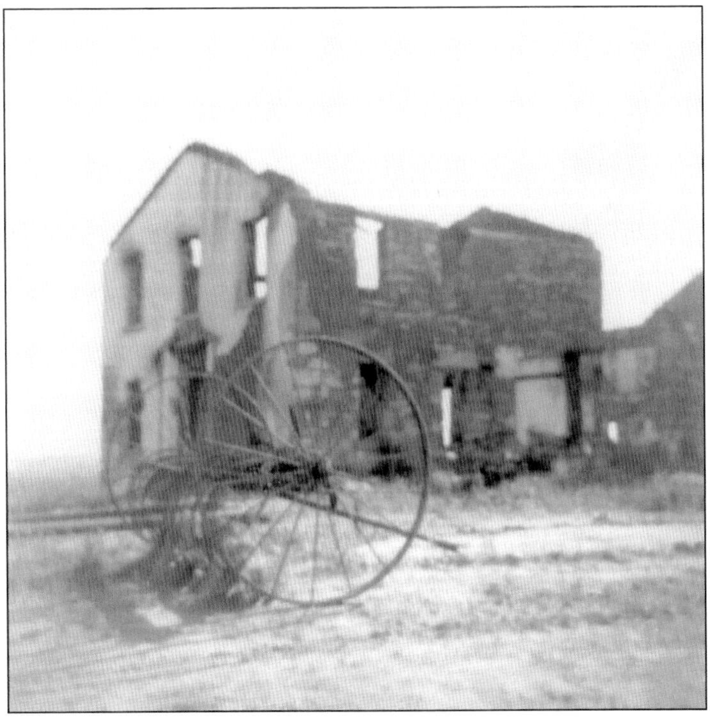

Pictured here in the 1970s are the remains of a sandstone house on the Pollock Ranch between Sloughhouse and Rancho Murieta. This house and a stone house with only one story were said to have been built in the 1870s by Chinese laborers who settled on the Cosumnes River after finishing their work on building the railroad. The long-gone Stone House School and the present Stone House Road get their names from these buildings. (Courtesy of Dolleen Augustine.)

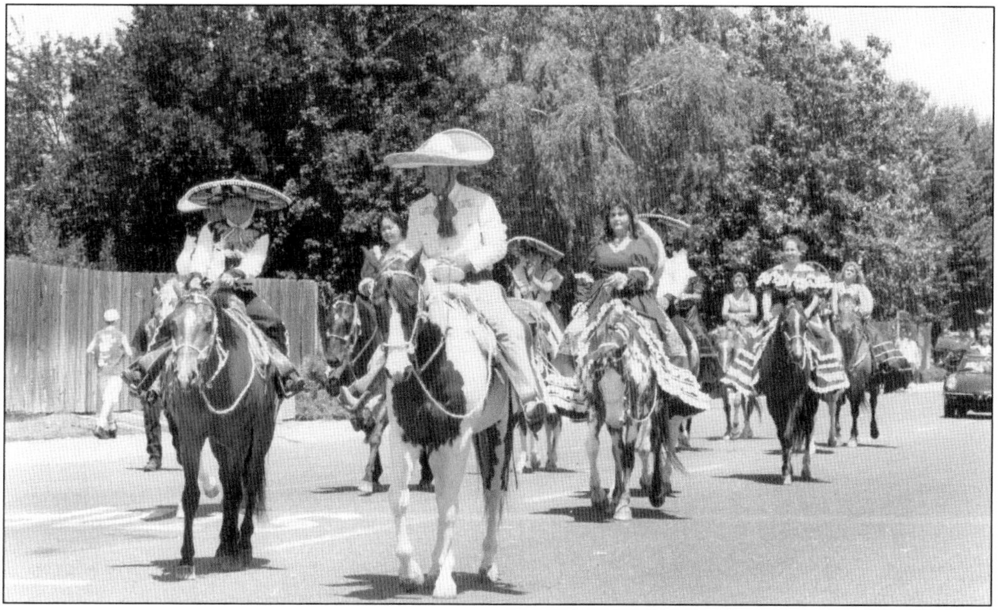

Many ethnicities and cultures are represented among the families of the Elk Grove area, including Russian Germans, Swiss, Dutch, Italian, Japanese, Hispanic-Latino, African American, and Chinese. In the past two decades, families have come from Southeast Asia, the former Russian provinces, India, Middle East countries, and the Pacific Islands. Students who attend the district schools in 2006 list more than 90 countries of origin, and they speak 70 different languages. Pictured here in a Western Festival activity is a Latino riding group.

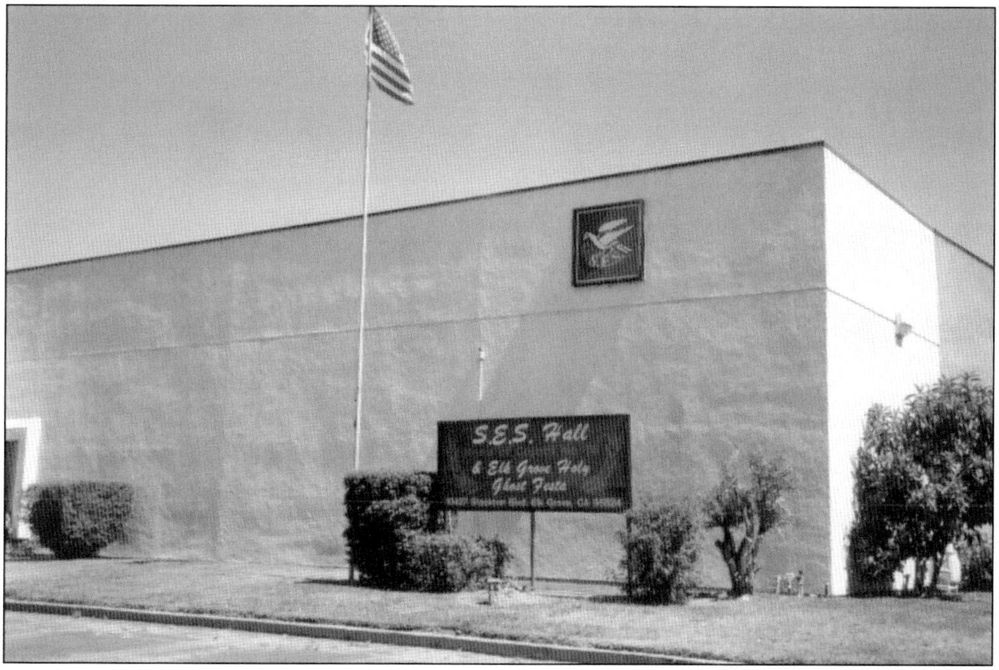

This is the Portuguese Hall, home of the Elk Grove Sociadade Do Espiorito Santo (SES). Portuguese families, originally from the Azores, have been active in community and farm groups for many years. The hall is a popular meeting place for many groups of people.

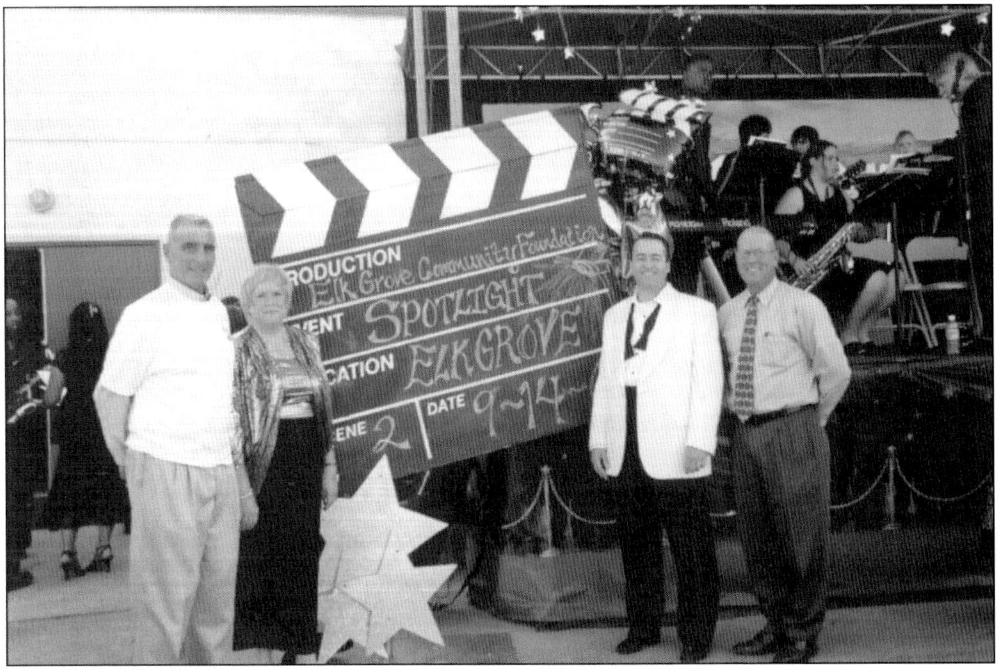

The Elk Grove Community Foundation traces its origins to 1987 when it began as a grassroots effort to support Elk Grove's youth. The foundation has grown significantly in its vision, with scholarships for 154 students totaling $134,000 in 2006. It expects to continue its growth and help more students to succeed each year. Pictured here from left to right at the yearly fund-raiser, Spotlight Elk Grove, are the 2006 organizers of the Hollywood-type event: Arnold Adreani, Marsha Holmes (2006 Citizen of the Year), Patrick Hume, and Dan Lawrence.

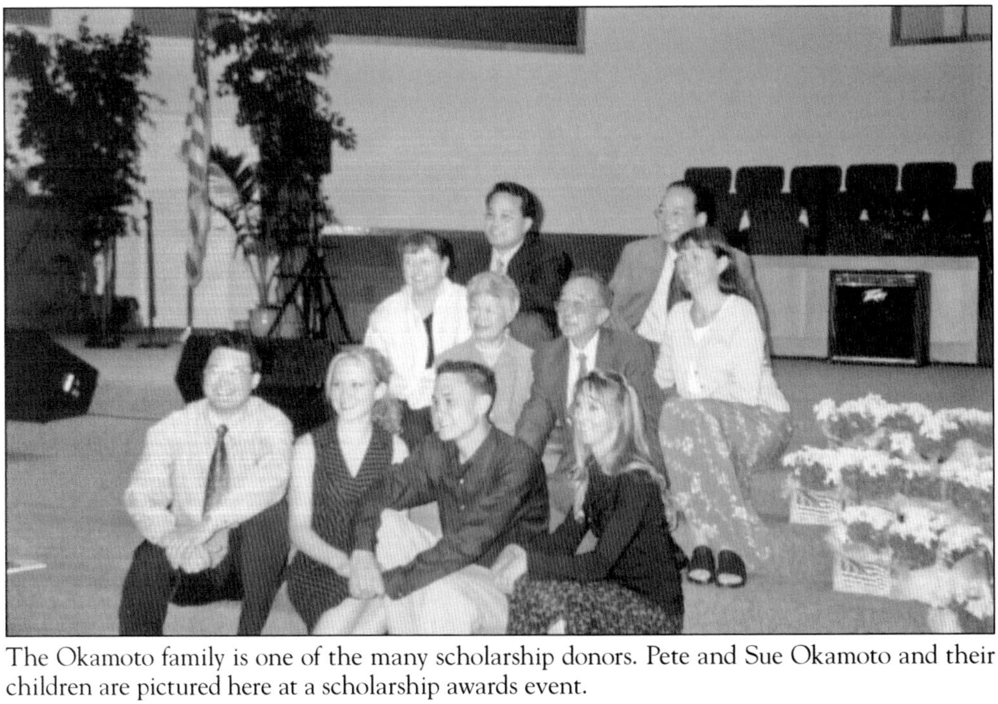

The Okamoto family is one of the many scholarship donors. Pete and Sue Okamoto and their children are pictured here at a scholarship awards event.

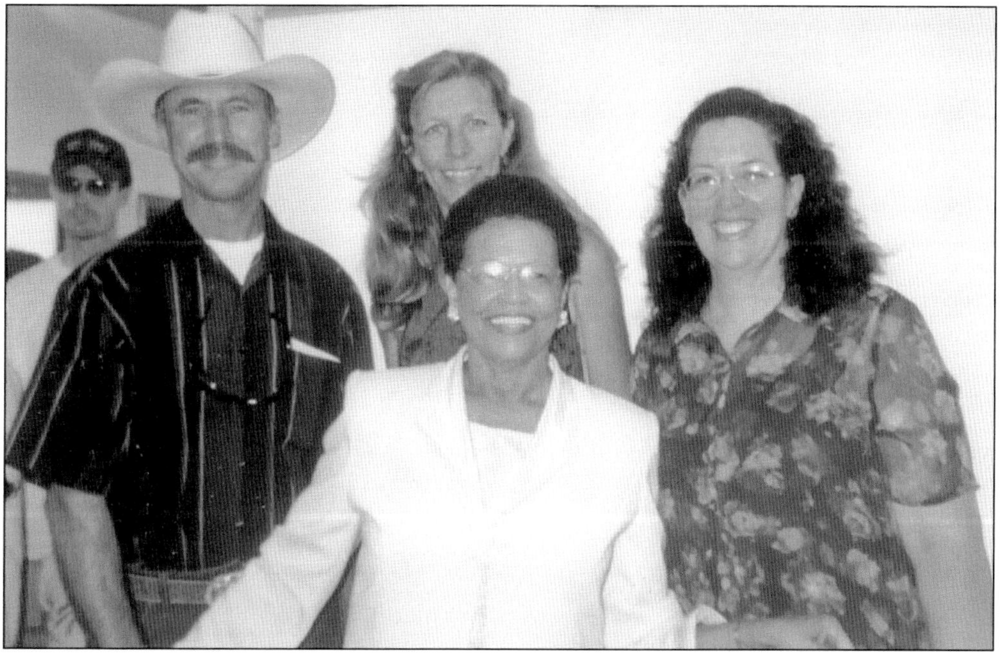

Irene West (center) came to Elk Grove to teach in 1962 shortly after the school district unified. She was a teacher and principal in a number of schools, including Elk Grove Elementary, James McKee, Florin, Prairie, Cosumnes River, and Franklin. She is pictured here with some of her former students at the dedication of Irene West Elementary School in 2002.

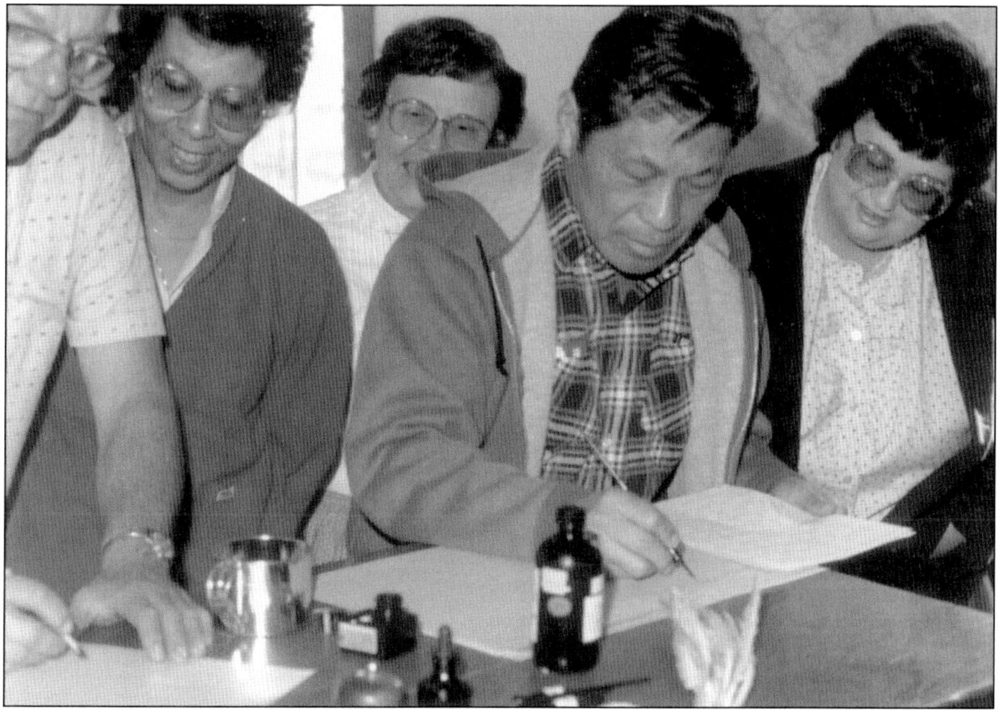

A group of Elk Grove educators participate in a calligraphy lesson at a workshop at the Rhoads School in the 1980s. Sam Yamamura is in the center.

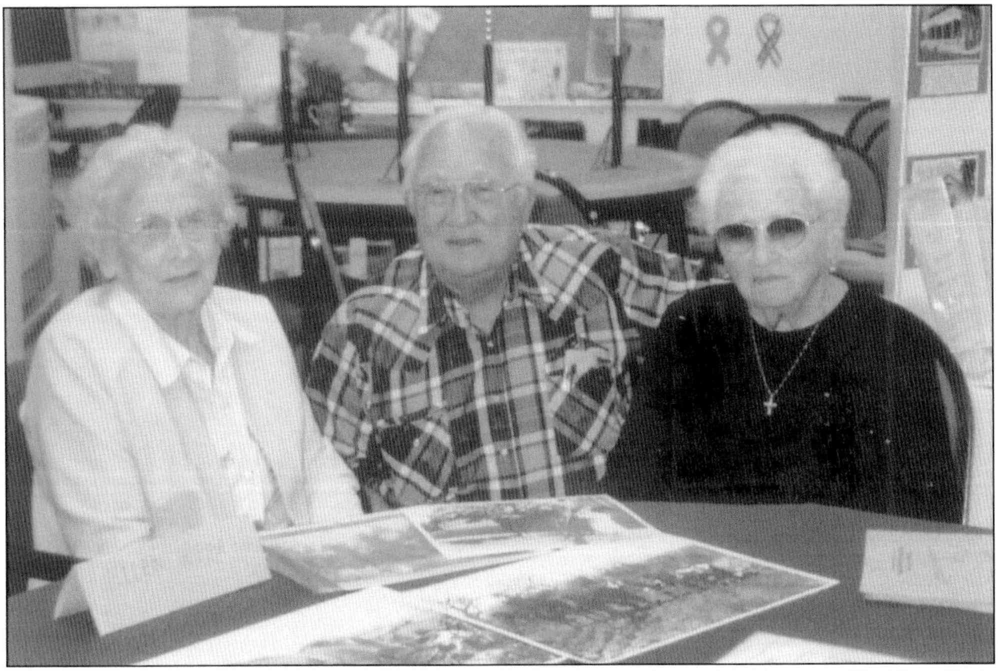

Ellen Rosa (left) is the great-granddaughter of Catherine Rhoads and Jared Dixon Sheldon. Each year, she organizes the Rhoads Cousins luncheon. Descendants of the Rhoads family come from all over to attend these events. Ellen's mother was Kittie Sheldon Cothrin whose father was William Chauncey Sheldon. Pictured with Ellen at the Sheldon Fair are Douglas Keith, a newcomer to the Sheldon area, and Janice Thomas, a native of Pleasant Grove.

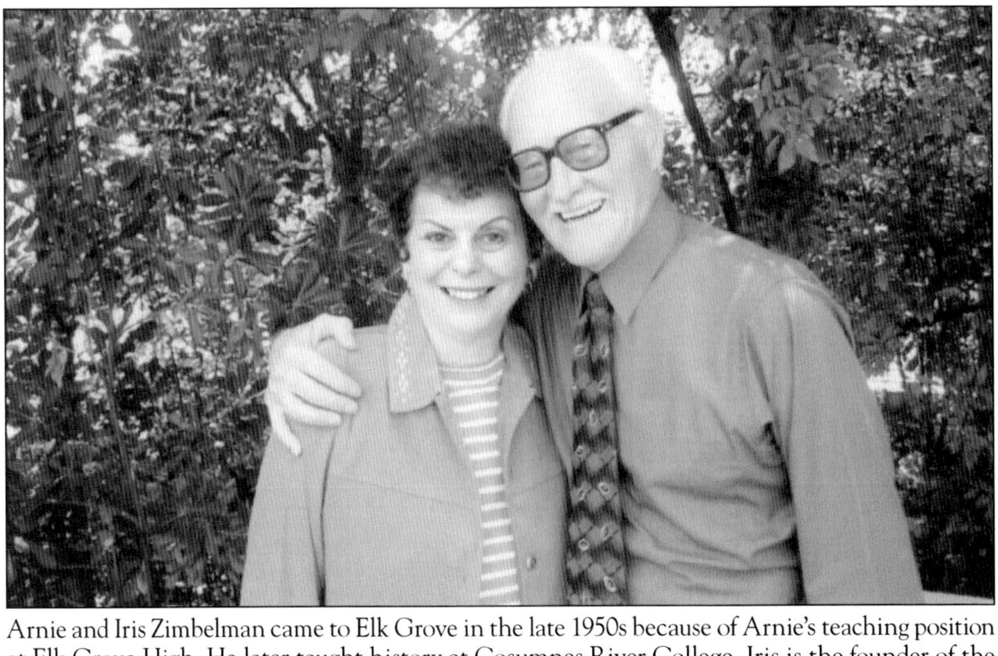

Arnie and Iris Zimbelman came to Elk Grove in the late 1950s because of Arnie's teaching position at Elk Grove High. He later taught history at Cosumnes River College. Iris is the founder of the Strauss Festival, a yearly musical and dance activity for the past two decades. Both are active volunteers at the Rhoads School and in many other community projects.

Joyce and Carl Amundson spent many weeks getting the reconstructed Elk Grove Hotel and Stage Stop ready for its debut as a museum and community meeting place. They donated countless hours to the planning, construction, and decorating of the 1850 building. In earlier years, the Amundsons were involved with the Cow Palace and Boulevard Theaters along with dozens of community activities. Joyce is pictured here welcoming visitors to the hotel/museum.

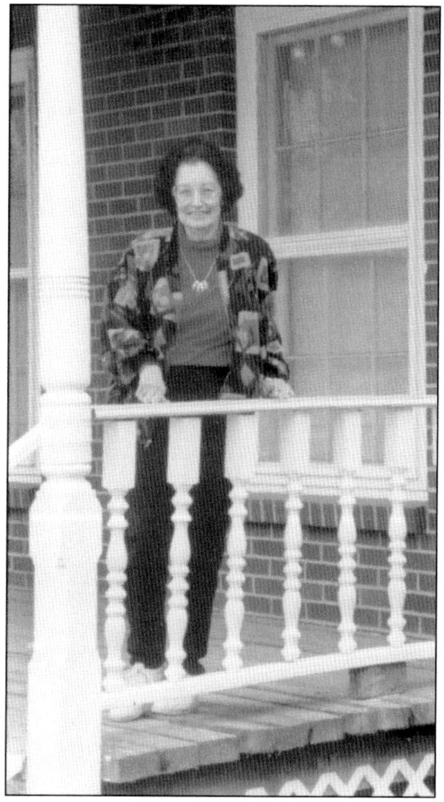

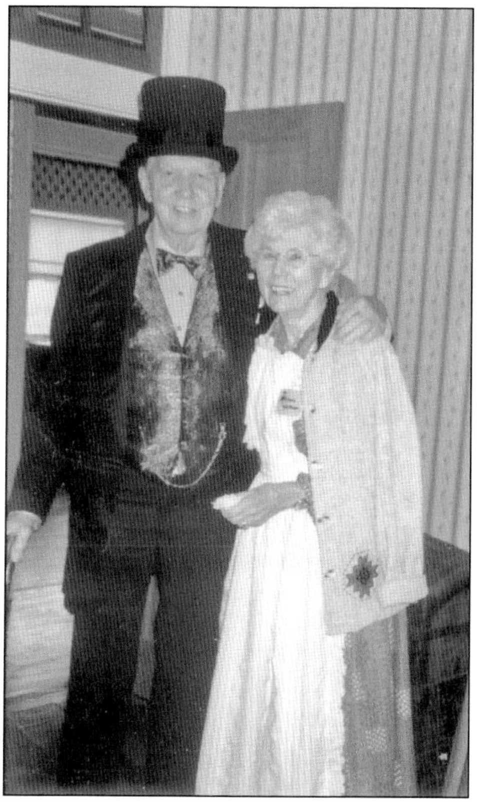

Carl Amundson and Mary Foulks Mauger are pictured here serving as docents in the hotel. Mary's mother, Bess Graham Foulks, was born in the old hotel building when it was the Graham home.

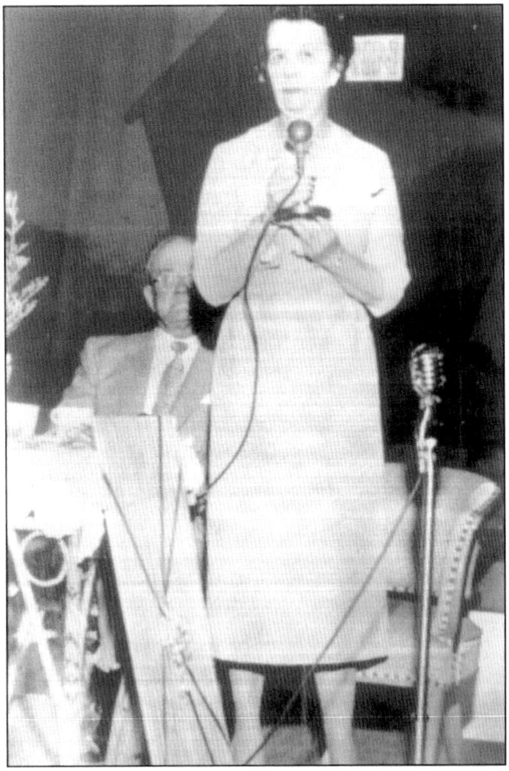

Isabelle Jackson, first a teacher and then a principal, was the influential superintendent of the Florin School District in the 1950s. She guided the post–World War II growth around Florin as housing developments began to replace vineyards and strawberry fields. The school became so overcrowded that by 1957 the trustees had to build a second school. The new school on Orange Avenue was named the Isabelle Jackson School. It is now the William Daylor School, and a new Elk Grove school is named for Isabelle Jackson.

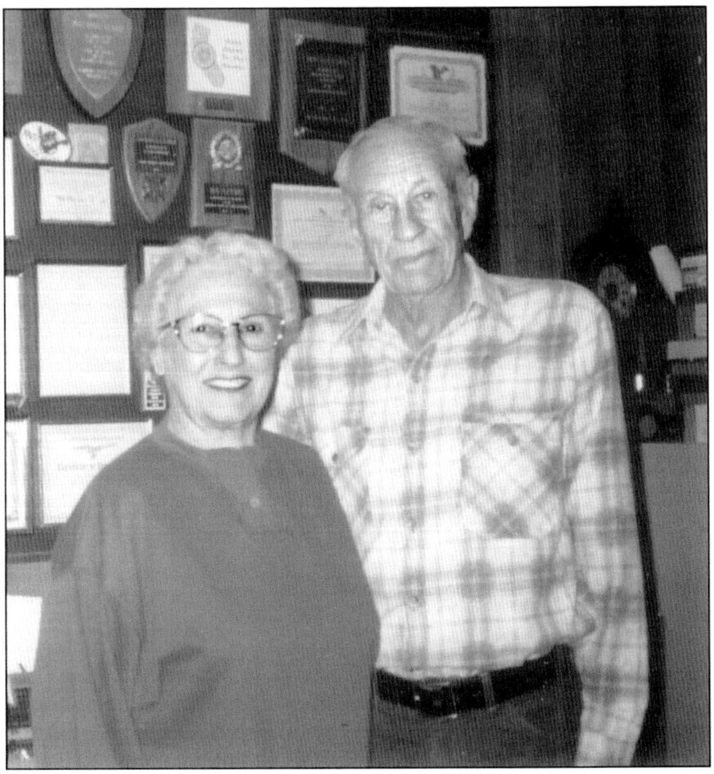

Bob and Theresa Fletcher are active Florin community members and volunteers. Their connections to Florin go back many years.

Eight

NEIGHBORING COMMUNITIES

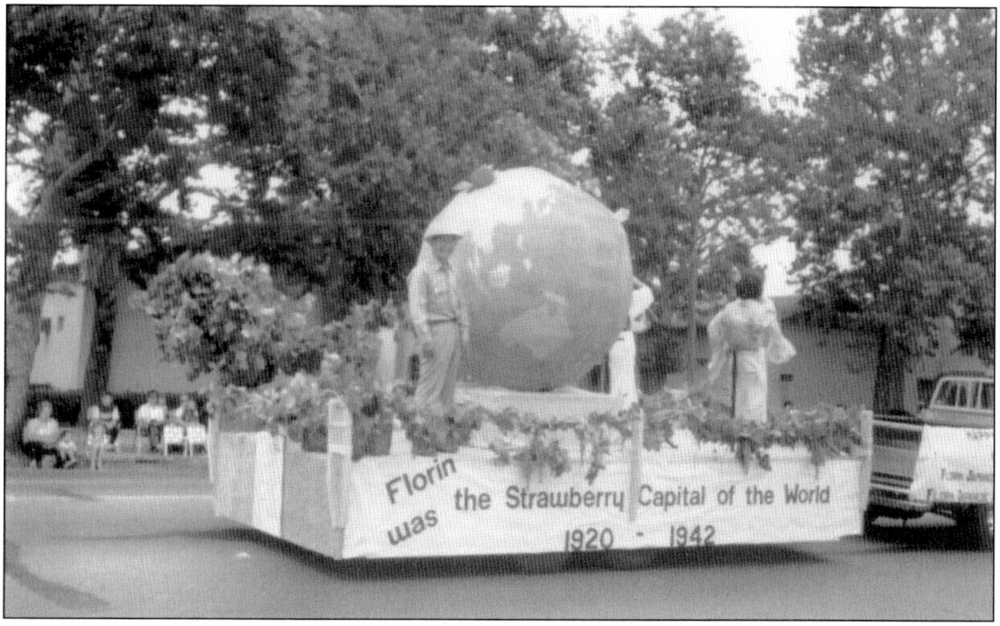

James Rutter and E. B. Crocker purchased 240 acres in Florin in 1852. Rutter planted fruit trees, experimented with grapes and seedlings, and started a winery. The town was established in 1875 when the railroad came through, and Judge Edwin Crocker is the one who gave Florin its name. The fields were covered with wildflowers, making it appropriate for the place to be named after the Latin word for flower, flora. The founders could not have known that Florin would become the strawberry capital of the world, as indicated on the "Once in a Life Time Reunion" float pictured here. The first trainload of strawberries from California was shipped from Florin in 1893. The city's peak record season of 1941 showed 133 carloads of very perishable strawberries shipped by rail and hundreds of truckloads driven nightly to the Bay Area in Northern California and also Nevada. That same year, the grape growers shipped 130 carloads of Flame Tokay grapes to eastern markets. One of Florin's claims to fame is that Hiram Johnson, elected California governor in 1918, went to school in Florin.

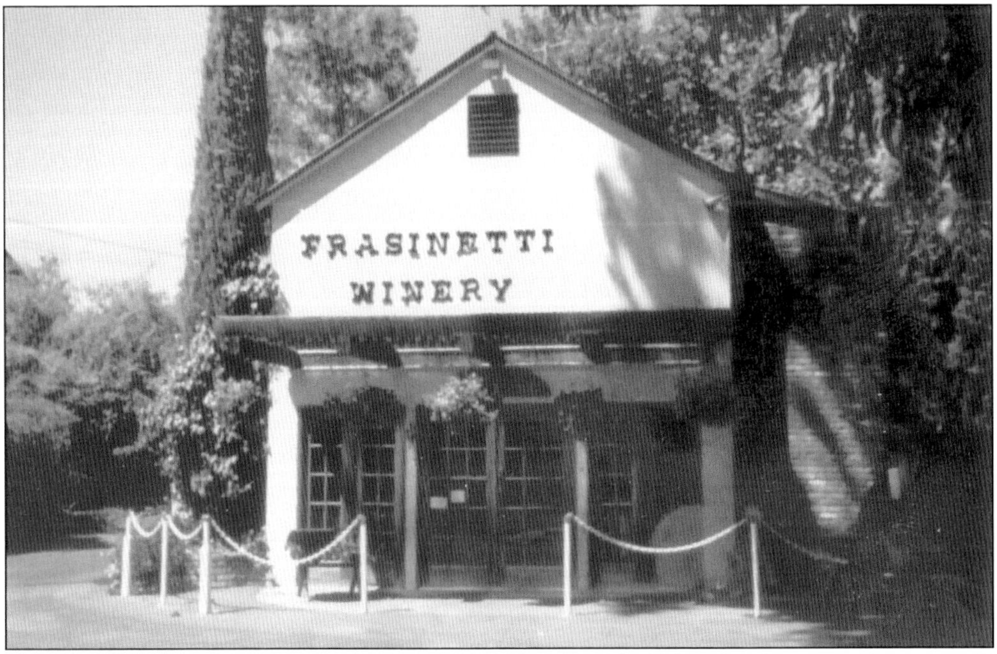

In 1897, James Frasinetti established the Frasinetti Winery, the oldest family operated winery still in continuous use in Northern California. An immigrant from Italy, Frasinetti had a great desire to create fine wines, and the winery prospered. Prohibition, however, brought a halt to winemaking, but the Frasinettis made "altar wine" for the church and began to raise and sell table grapes.

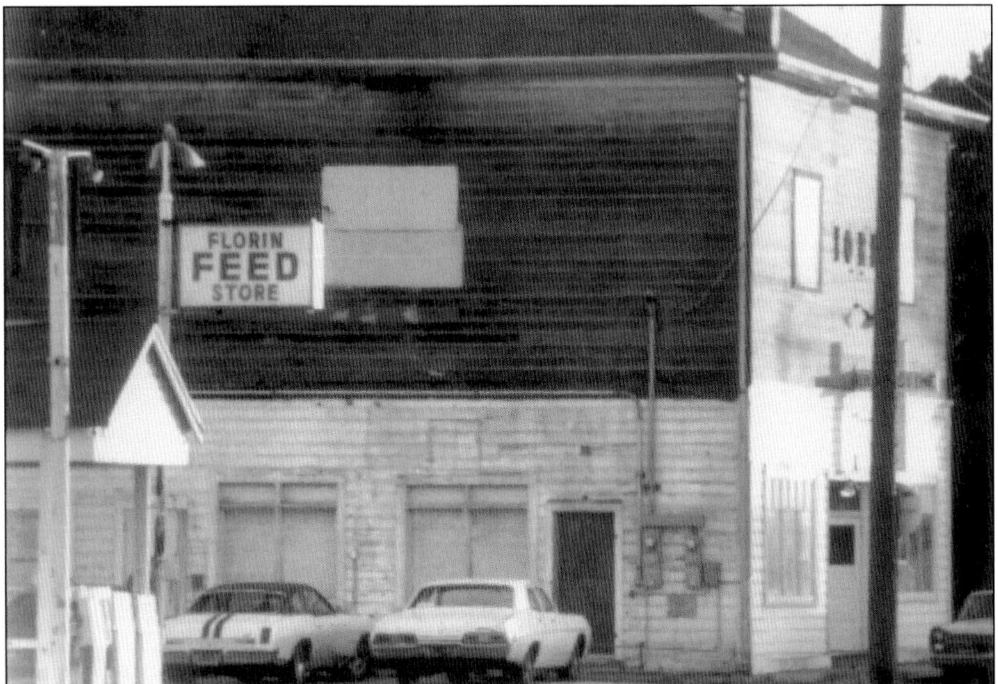

The Florin Feed Store was in the building of the lodge known as the Improved Order of Red Men, originally an organization for immigrants from Germany.

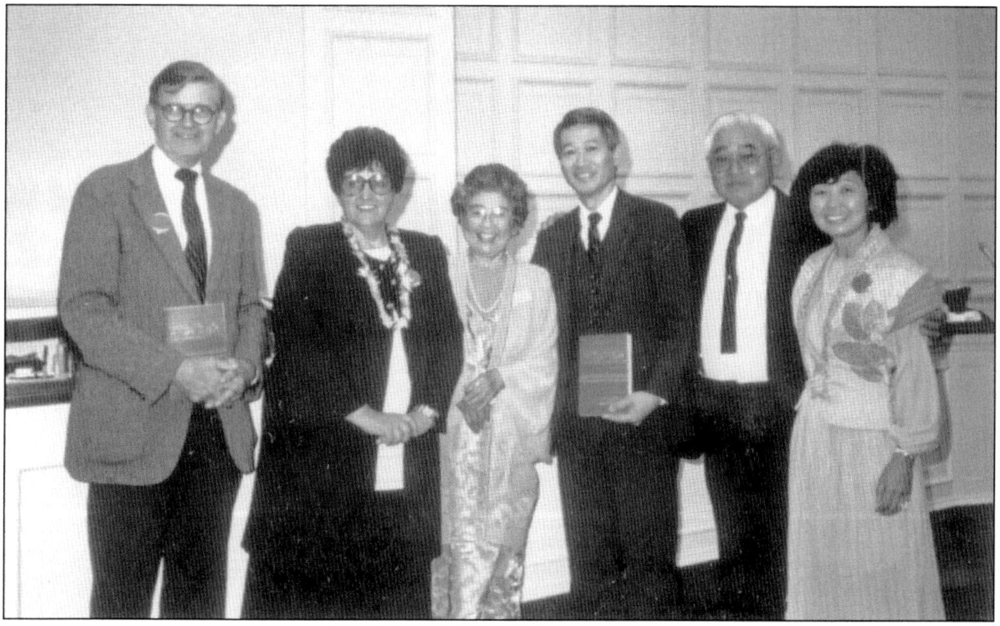

In 1987, many Florin residents of Japanese ancestry assisted with a special exhibit at the Smithsonian Institution in Washington, D.C. Created for the 200th anniversary of the United States Constitution, the exhibit focused on the failure of the government to protect the rights of its citizens in 1942 when Japanese Americans were interned. Pictured from left to right with Smithsonian curator Harold Langley are Elizabeth Pinkerton, Mary Tsukamoto, Congressman Robert Matsui, Al Tsukamoto, and Marielle Tsukamoto.

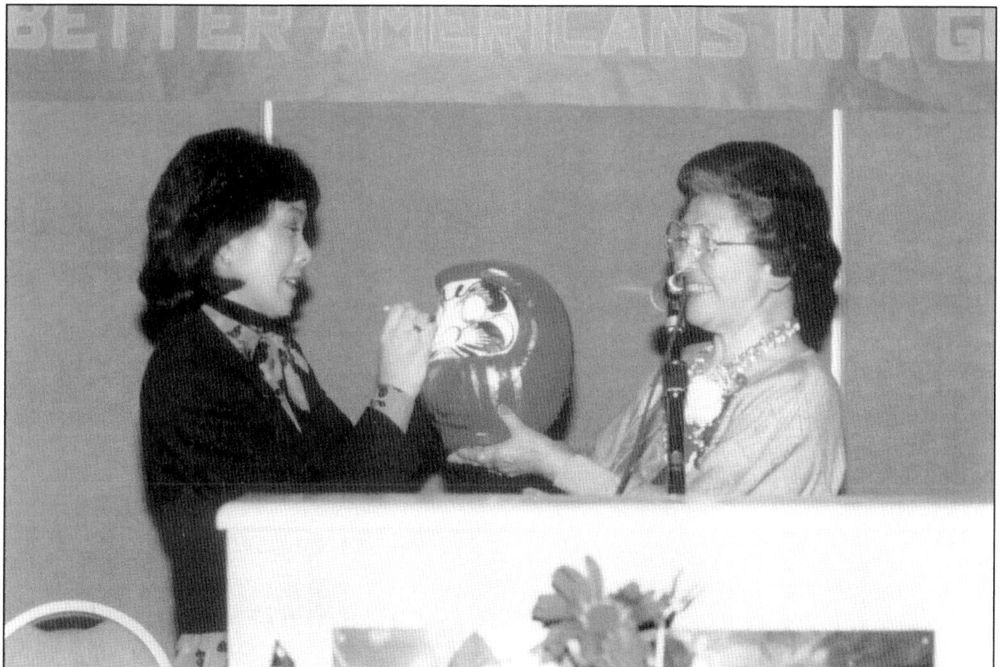

Doris Matsui, now the Congressional representative from Sacramento, symbolically paints the Daruma Doll to recognize the perseverance, patience, and dedication of Mary Tsukamoto.

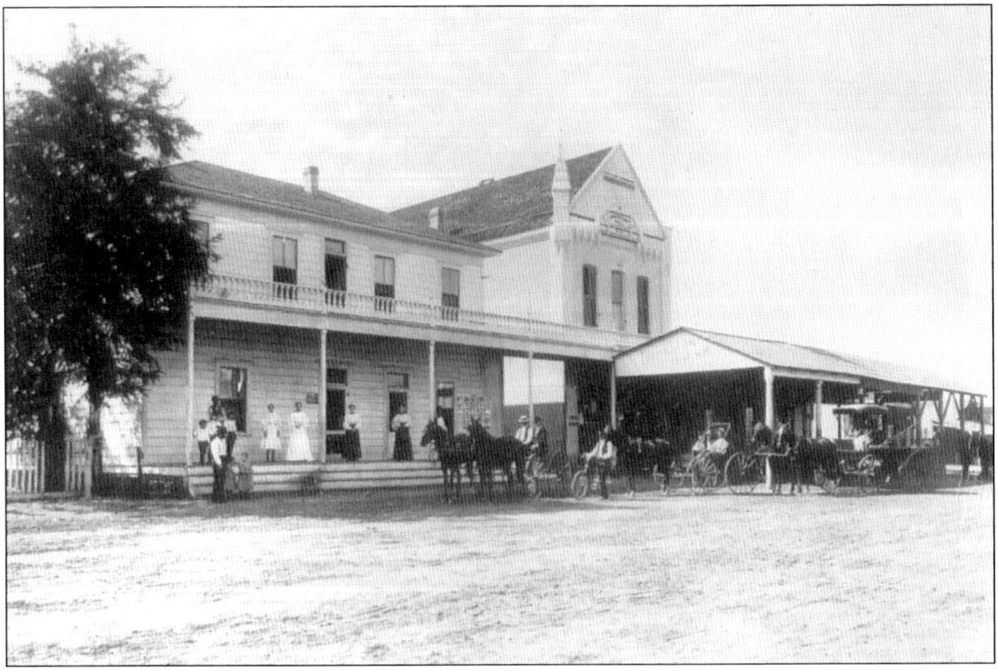

The town of Franklin was not always known as Franklin, for its original name was Georgetown. Andrew George built a stage stop on Lower Stockton Road, the road that took miners and travelers south from early day Sacramento. He called his place the Franklin House after his mother. When it was time for a post office, however, there was already one named Georgetown in the Sierra Nevada, so Franklin it became and Franklin it has been ever since. The historian of Franklin is Dennis Buscher, a Kunsting descendant. (Courtesy of Dennis Buscher.)

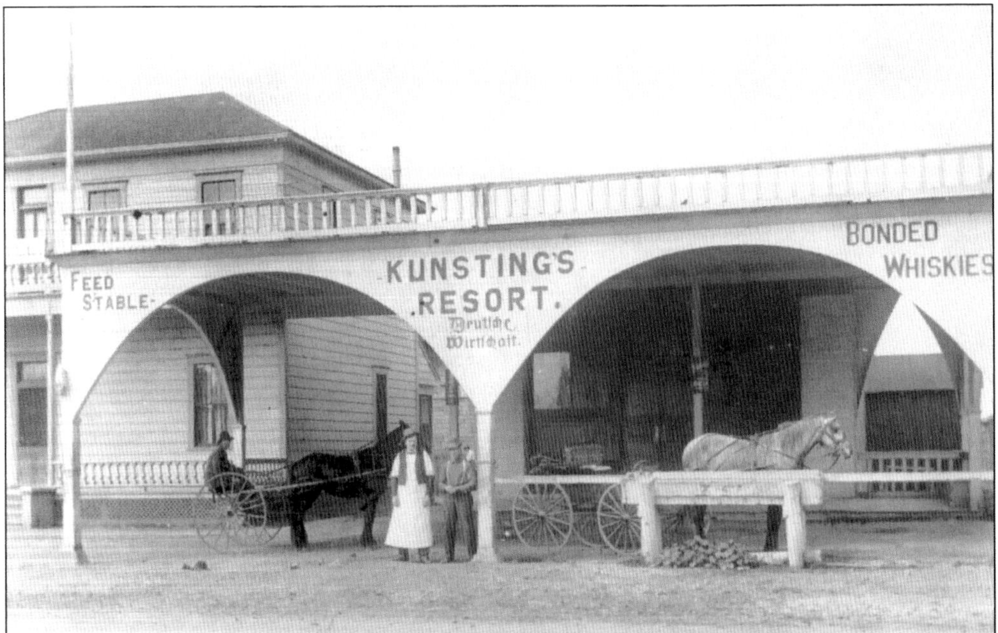

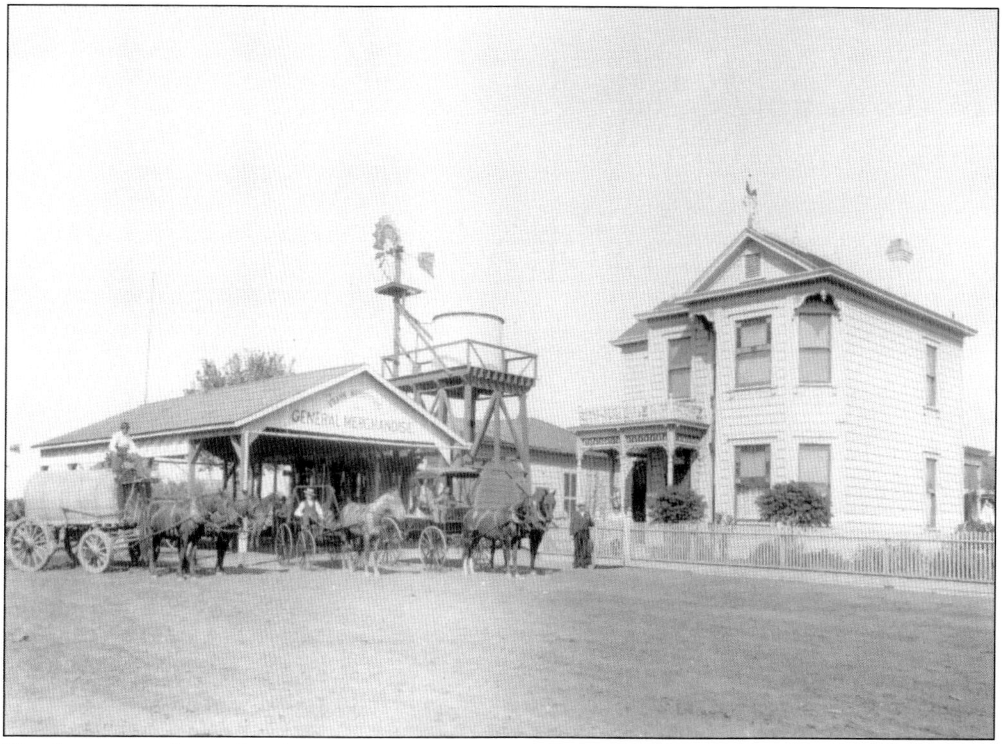

The house at right in the above photograph of downtown Franklin is no longer there, but its resemblance to the house in the image at right is not by chance. The house was moved by Dennis Buscher to Bilby Road, where he has painstakingly restored and refurbished it to its Queen Anne elegance. (Above courtesy of Dennis Buscher; right courtesy Tom Russell.)

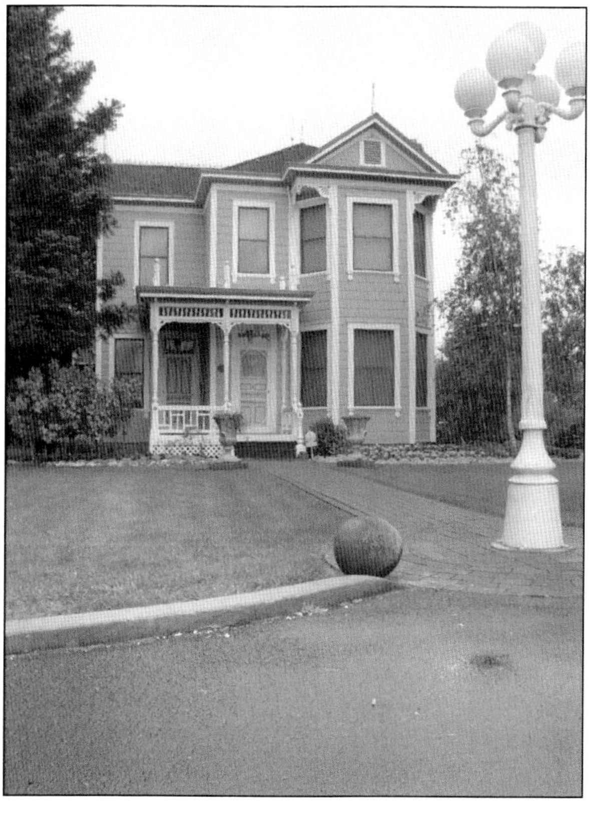

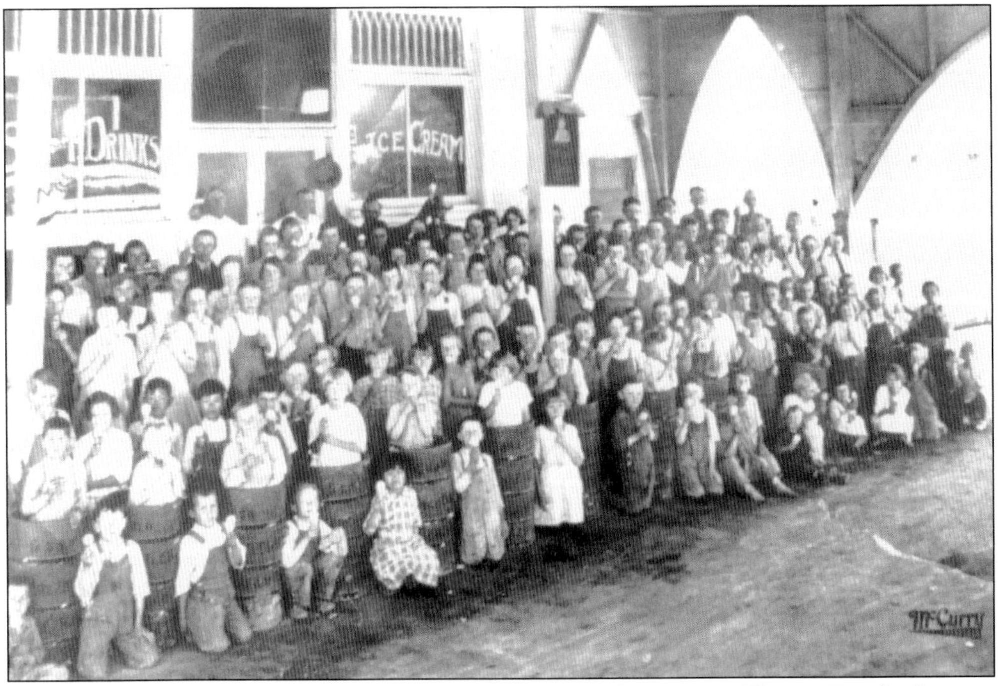

Children at the Franklin School enjoy an ice cream treat. (Courtesy of Dennis Buscher.)

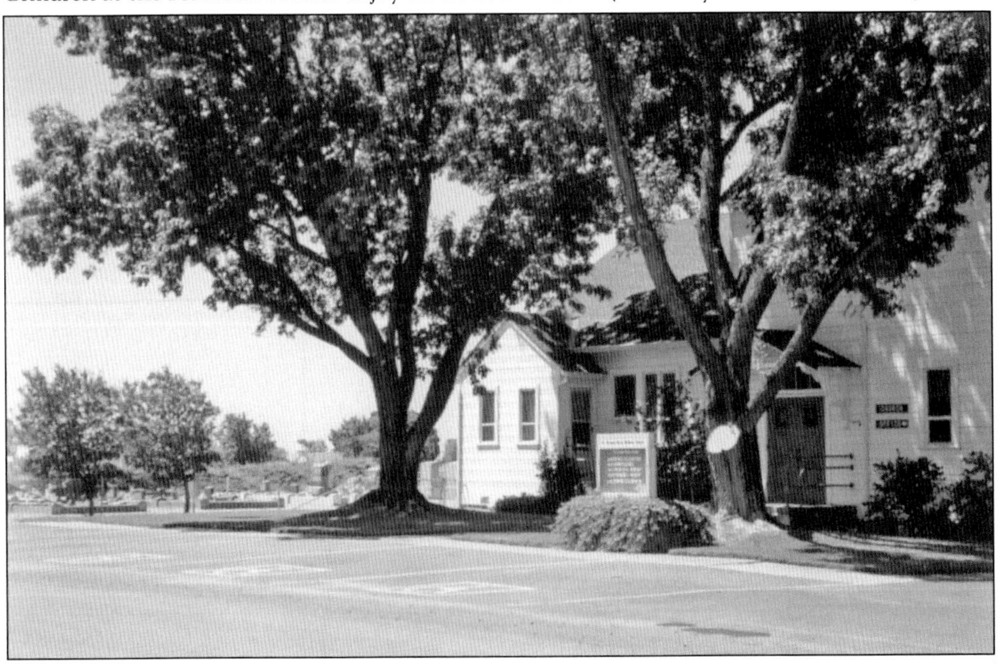

This photograph is of the Point Pleasant Methodist Church in the little farming community of the same name that is nestled against Interstate 5 south of Franklin. The farming community is still home to families of German descent, many who came from South Dakota in the early 1900s. The church dates to 1885, when it was organized by a Lutheran minister. It was the Evangelical United Brethren Church in 1946 and now is the Point Pleasant Methodist Church. But it is still the center of the community.

Barns such as the one pictured here were once seen all around the Elk Grove area. Many have disappeared as housing developments and shopping centers have taken their places.

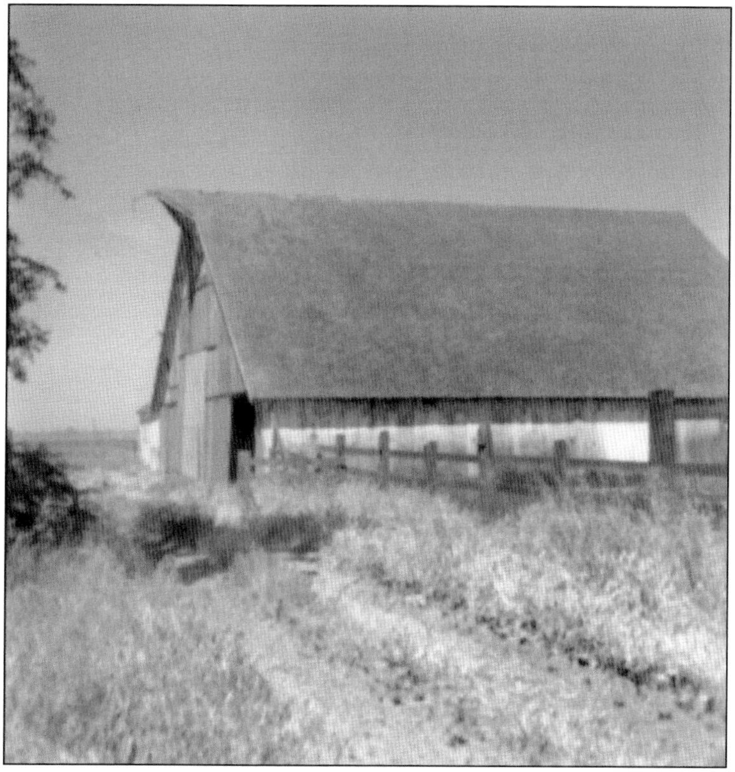

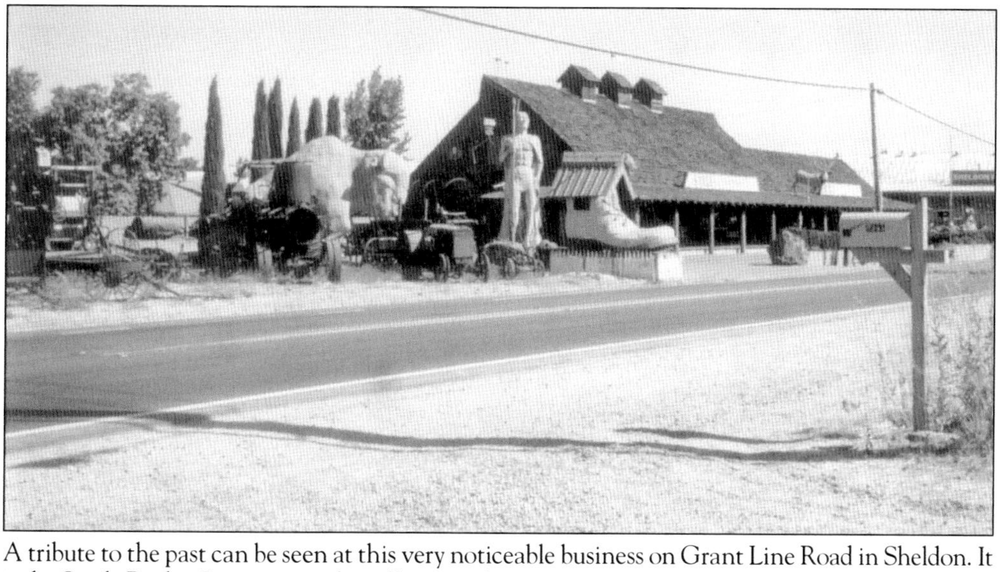

A tribute to the past can be seen at this very noticeable business on Grant Line Road in Sheldon. It is the Steele Realty Company, and a collection of items resides in this historical place that originated in the gold days. A concern of local citizens in 2006 is the planned widening of Grant Line Road, which has become a major thoroughfare of south Sacramento County and Elk Grove.

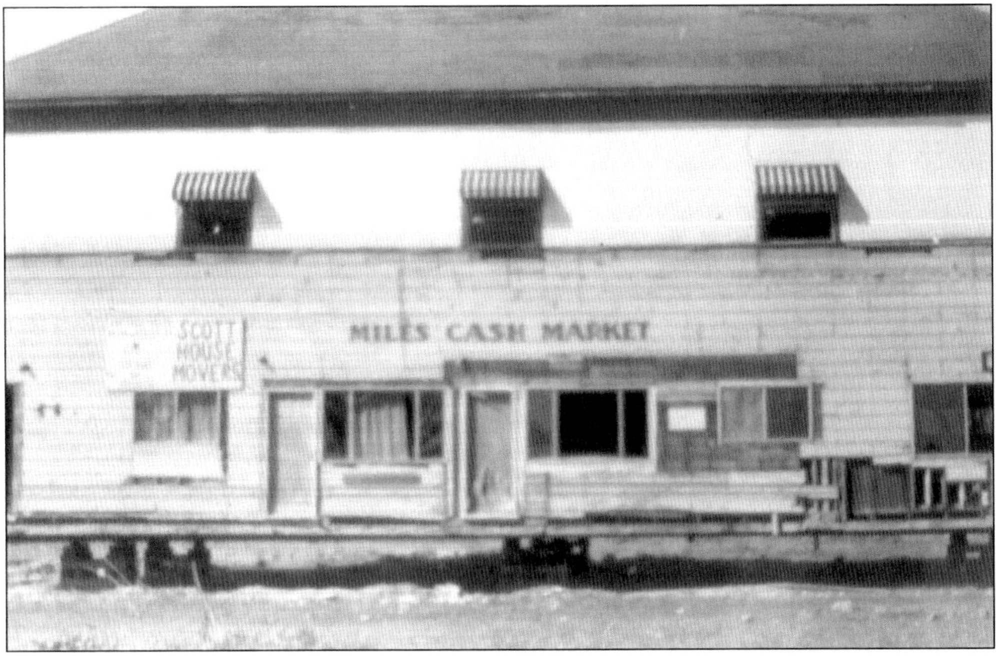

The community of Sheldon has a longer history than all other places along the Cosumnes River except Sloughhouse, as it was a wagon-making place during the gold days. In this photograph, the building that once housed Miles Cash Market was in the process of being moved farther back on Grant Line Road in the 1980s.

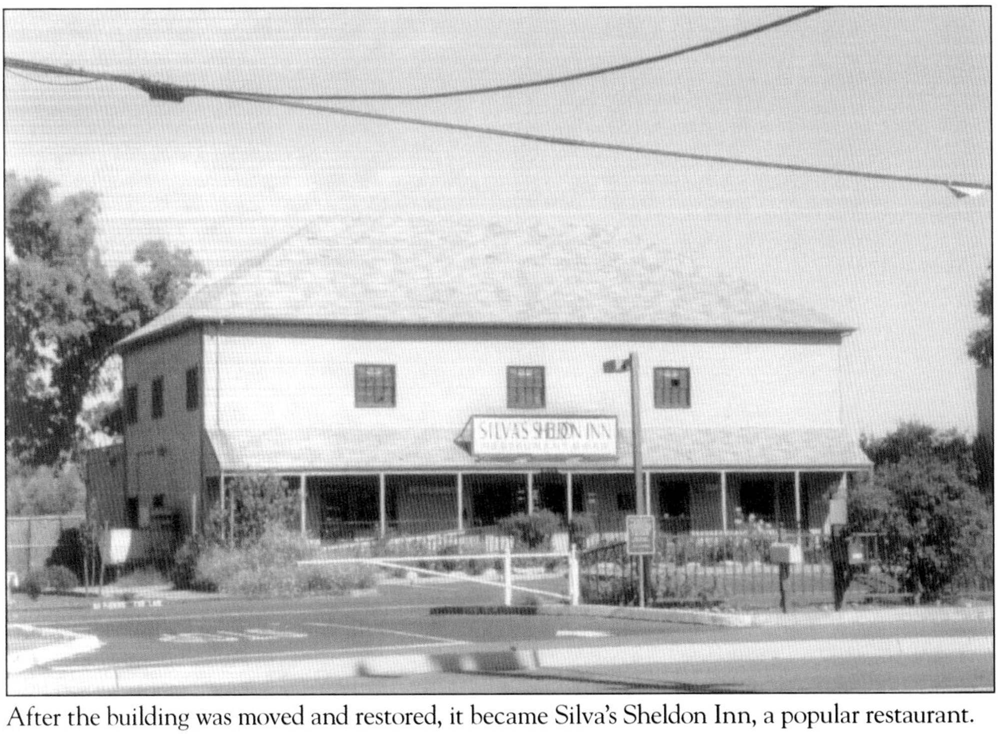

After the building was moved and restored, it became Silva's Sheldon Inn, a popular restaurant.

The community of Wilton has changed very little over the past several decades. Located on Wilton Road south of the Cosumnes River and north of Dillard Road, these structures have had many uses over the years. The building at right, a hardware store in the 1970s, was an antique store in the 1990s (below). Originally, however, it was a community clubhouse and dance hall. Survivors of the 1906 San Francisco earthquake were encouraged to settle in Wilton, and in 1910, the California Traction Line Railroad brought new life to Wilton and to its neighboring community of Dillard.

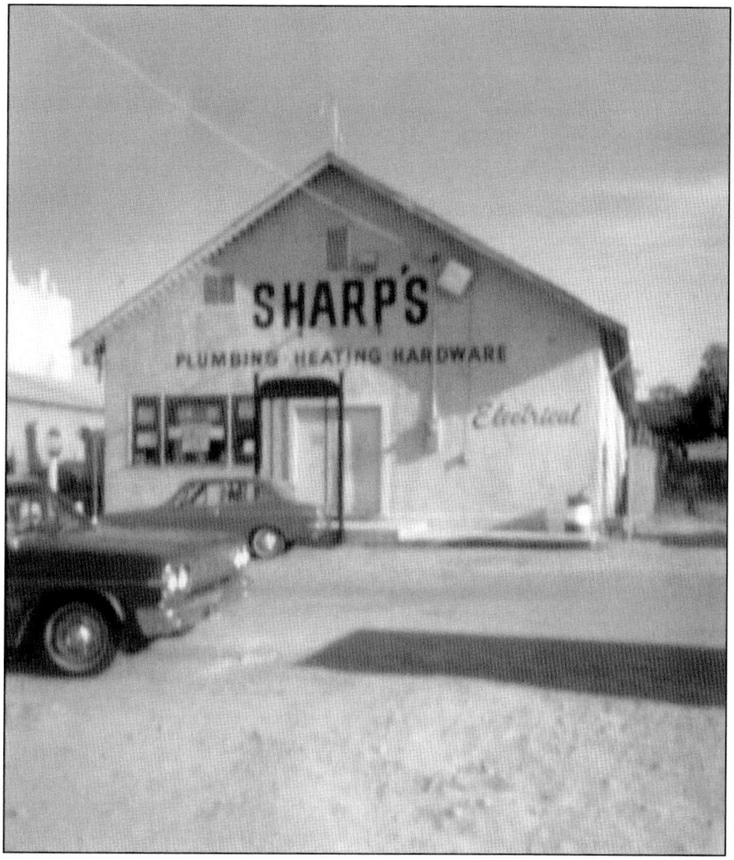

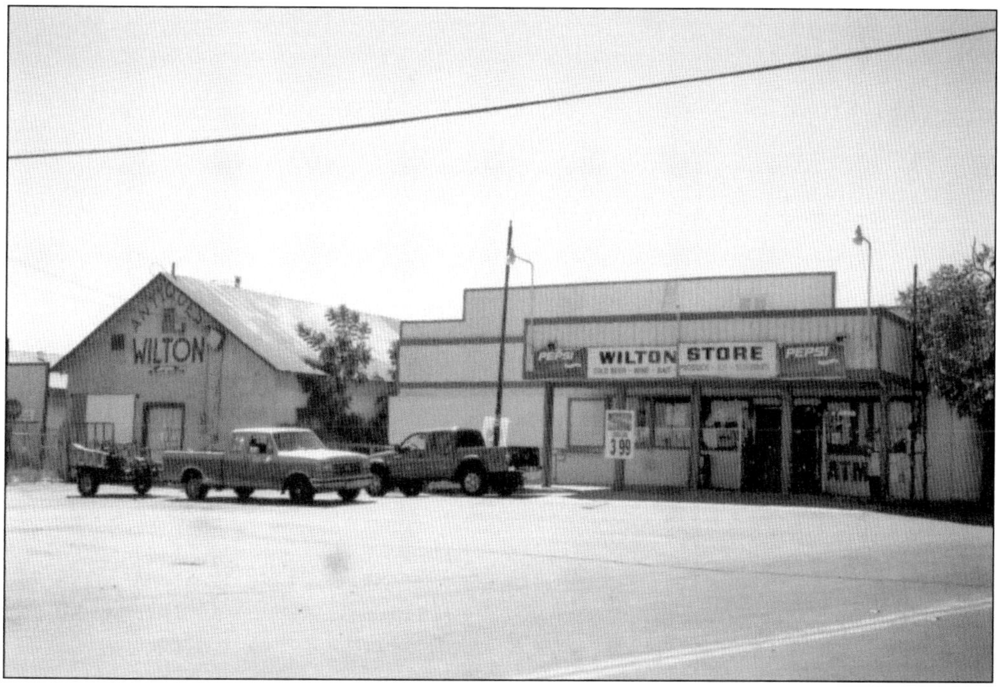

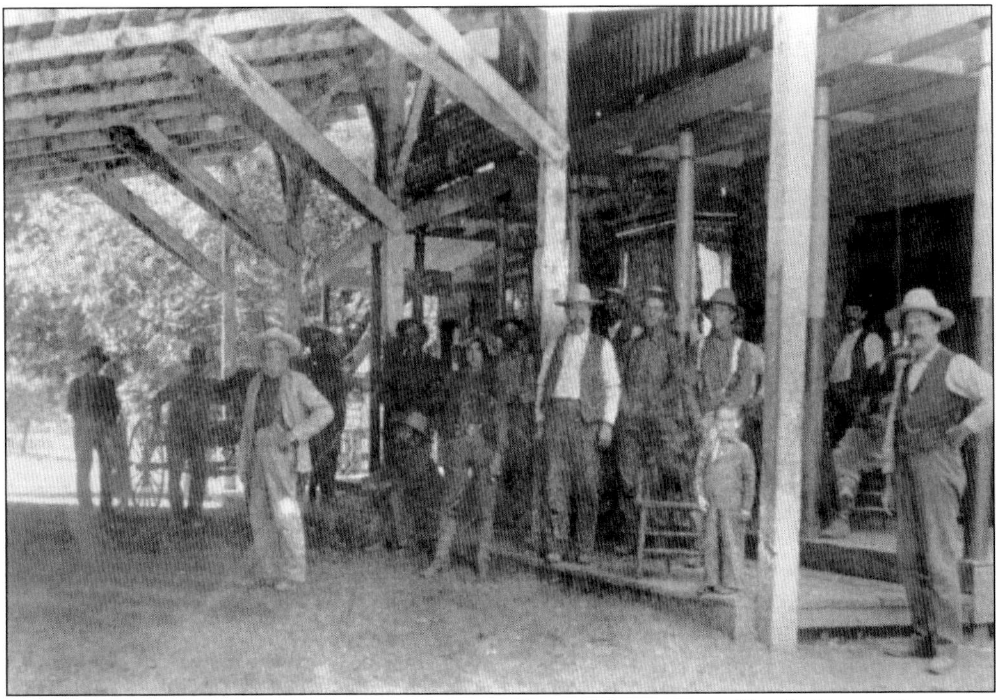

The main stage stops on the Jackson Highway in the gold days were at Slough House, Cosumne, and Bridge House. All three of these survived as places of business into the 20th century. The location originally known as Daylor's Place became Cosumne, and there was a post office there. After the death of William Daylor, his wife, Sarah, married William Robinson Grimshaw, who had been a bookkeeper for John Sutter. The General Merchandise store at Cosumne (below) was under the management of John E. Givens in the early 1900s. Both of the photographs on this page were taken at Cosumne.

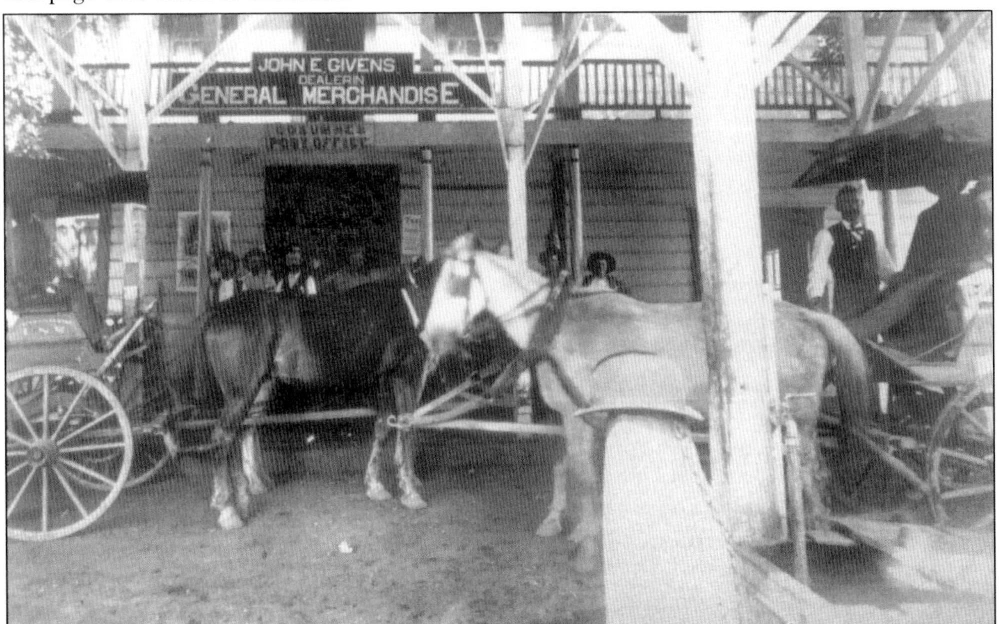

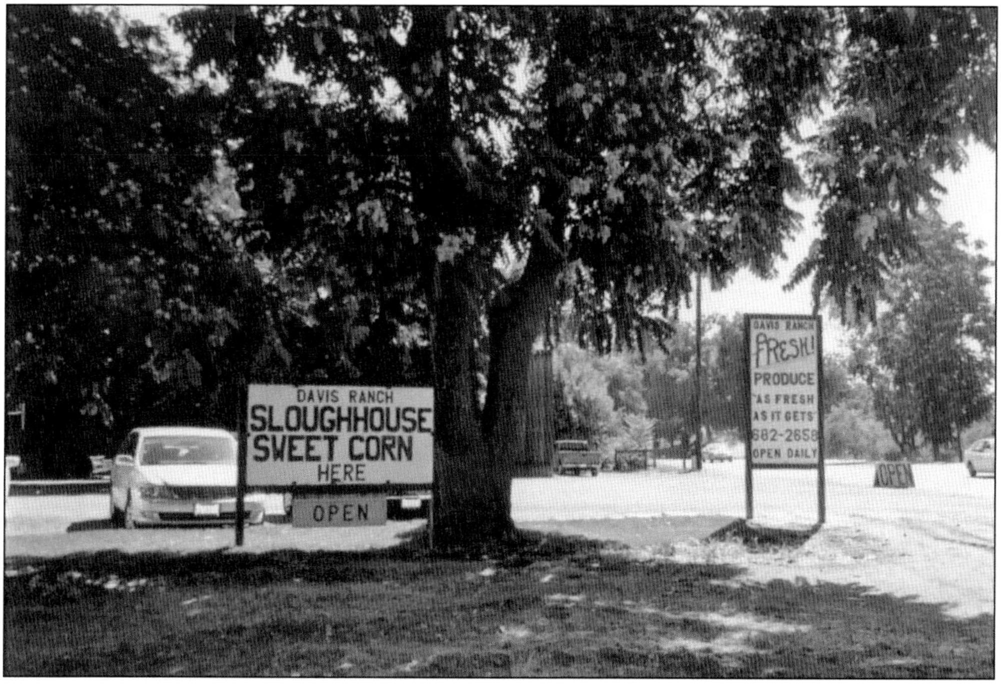

In 2006, the Cosumne site is no longer known by that name, but the location is a very popular place for purchasing fresh produce. The Davis Ranch features Sloughhouse corn all summer long.

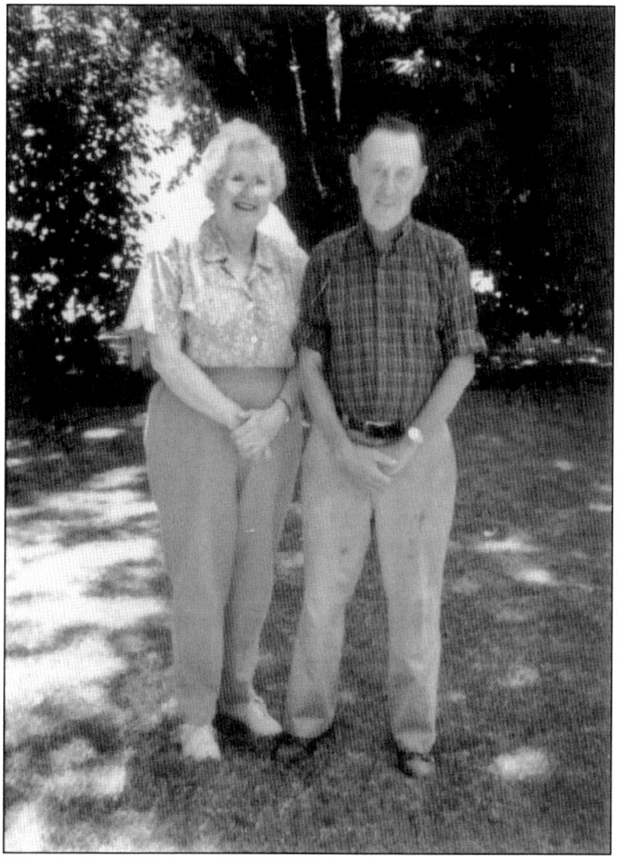

George and Virginia Signorotti lived on Jackson Road just past Sloughhouse and the long-gone Cosumne. They could not have imagined that when this photograph was taken in the early 1950s they would operate the last hop ranch in California. But that is their legacy. (Courtesy of Olivia Franzoia.)

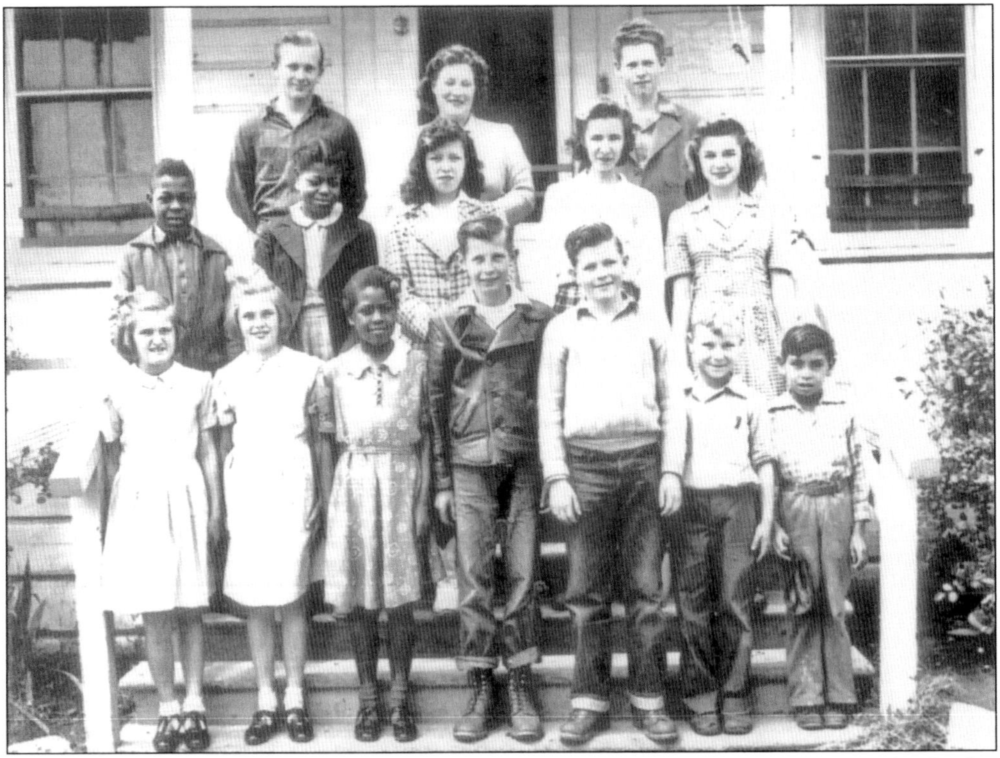

The Rhoads School closed in 1949, but in the above 1944 photograph are Leo Fassler, Lesley Ostman, and Betty Augustine. With the move of the school to Elk Grove Park and its subsequent restoration, many former students are able to talk about their long-ago memories there and at other one-room country schools. Below are George Waegell, Tony LaBrada, Delores Quintero, and Meg Waegell. (Above courtesy of Leo Fassler.)

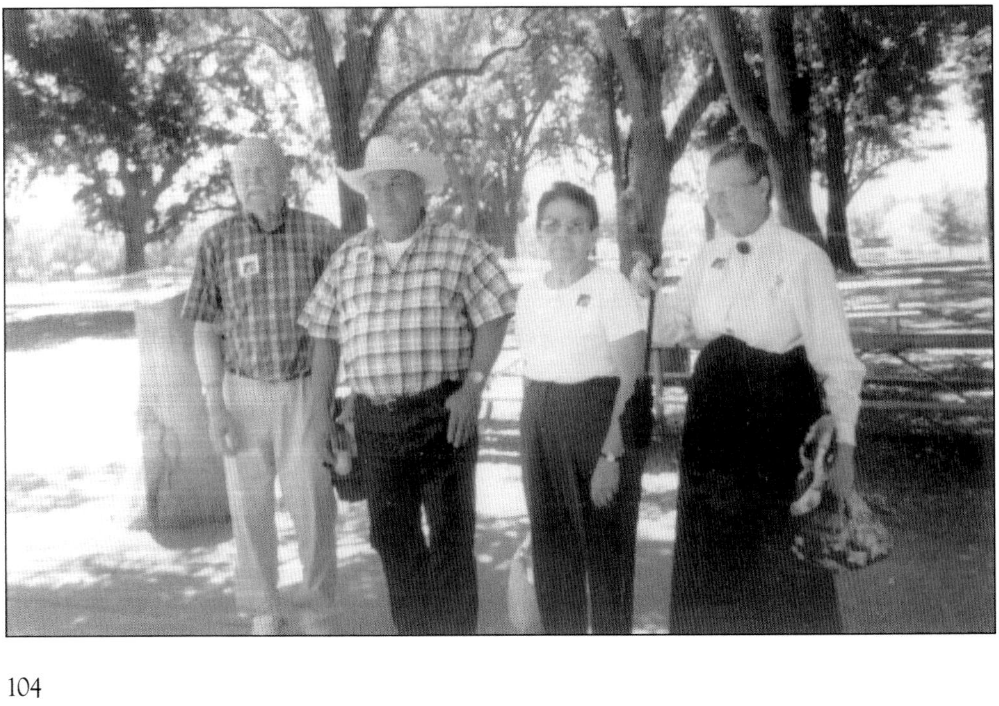

Nine

CHANGES 1900 TO 1950

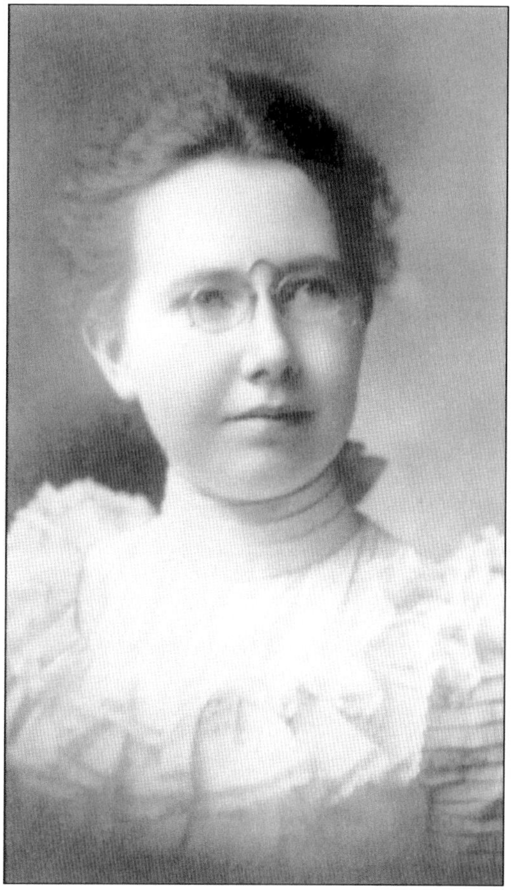

Harriet G. Eddy was the principal of Elk Grove High School in the early 1900s. This enterprising female educator was determined to get the high school on the accreditation list for the University of California. Without accreditation, Elk Grove's graduates had to attend a year of high school somewhere else before they could be admitted to a college or university. Eddy knew that a major obstacle was the lack of a school library to meet academic scholarship standards. What she did was take advantage of a new law that allowed the county library to establish branches in rural areas. Eddy set up a library in a corner of the Women's Christian Temperance Union (WCTU) building next door to the high school. High school students checked out books during the day, and Eddy worked there at night so that community members could avail themselves of the library's services. This was the first branch of a county free library in California. Harriet Eddy went on to establish libraries all over the state and in some European countries as well. She may also have been the first female principal of a high school in the state. (Courtesy of Harriet G. Eddy Middle School and librarian Paige Berry.)

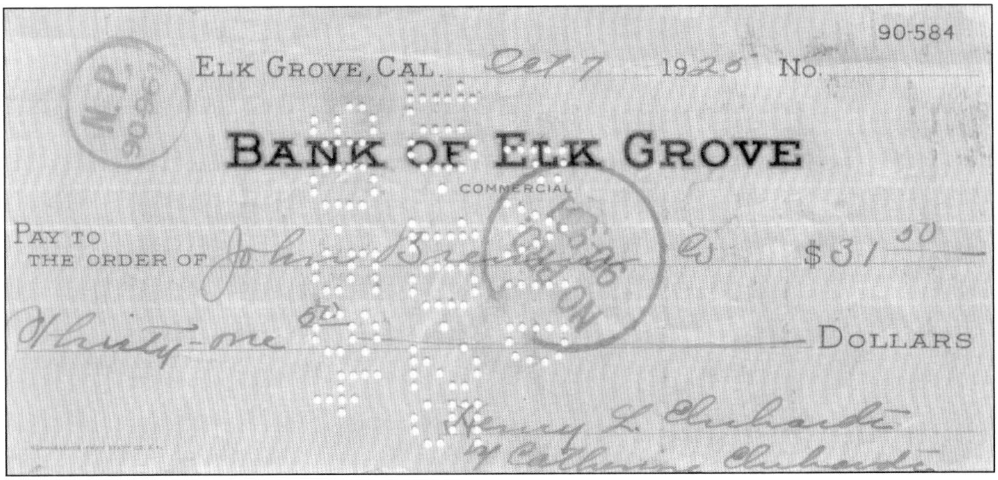

Elk Grove's first bank was the Bank of Elk Grove, created in 1910. The owner/directors were George Taverner, Tom Moroney, Charles Cooper, Dr. Hugh Beattie, G. Morris Colton, Zacheus Markofer, Hugh Bradford, Andrew Johnson, and L. J. Augustine. The bank was sold in 1928 and became the Bank of Italy, now known as the Bank of America.

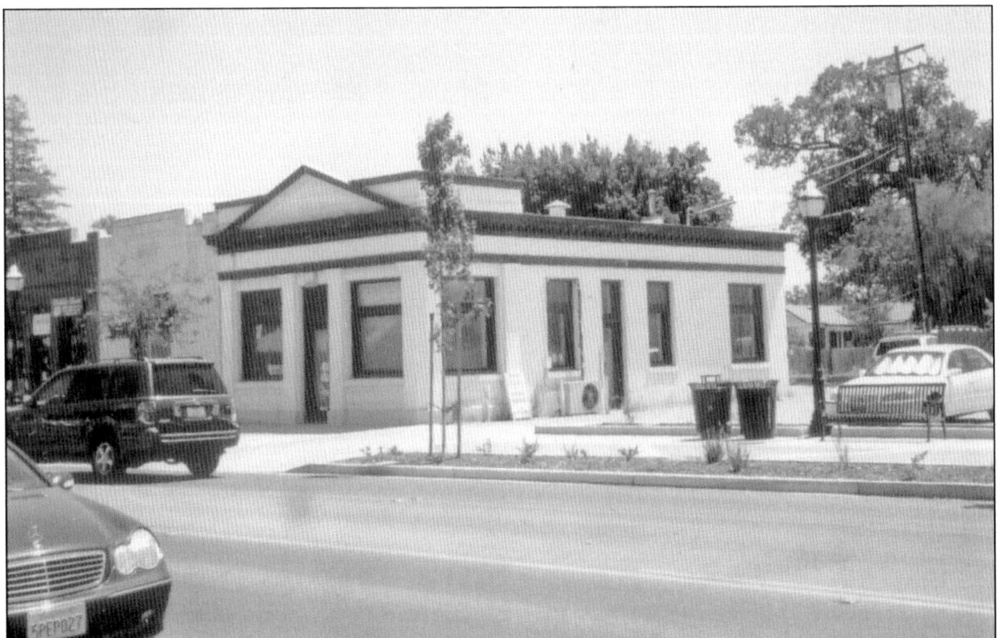

The original bank building has had many occupants over the years, but it stills stands proudly on the south side of Main Street in Old Town Elk Grove.

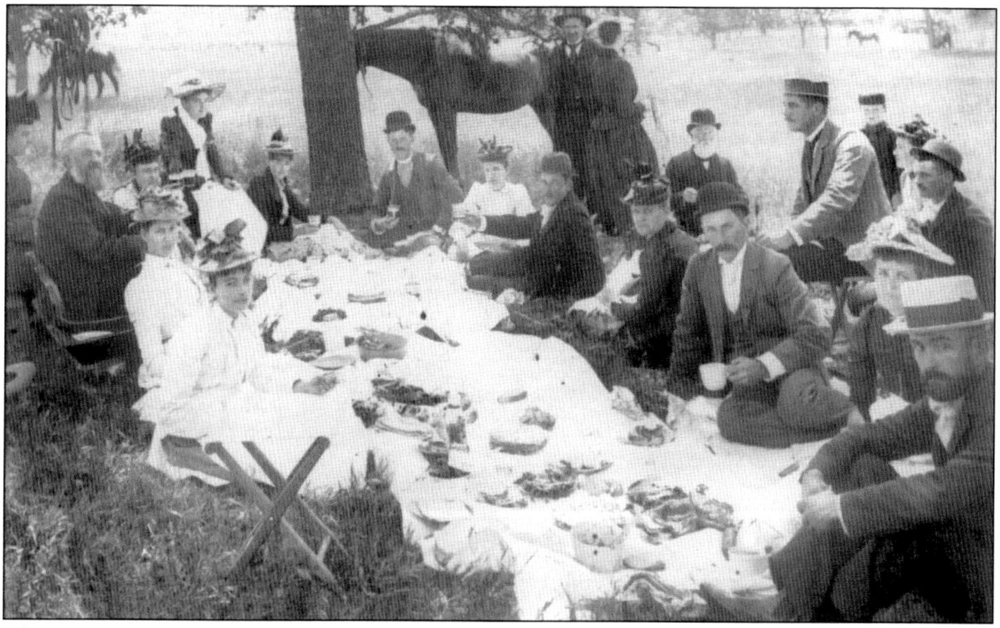

The grove of oak trees that is now Elk Grove Park was known throughout Northern California as Graham's Grove, a favorite picnic ground. The Granger's Picnic drew hundreds of people in their horse-drawn buggies to spend a shady day under the great old oaks. At the picnic seen here in 1894 are the Sims and Foulks families and their guests. The property was sold in 1903, and plans were made to cut the trees for lumber. A young woman, Jennie McConnell, enlisted the aid of citizens to save the trees and start a park. She sold shares for $5 apiece and bought the property. An open-air dance platform, baseball diamond, and horse trough were built, and the park became a center of community activity.

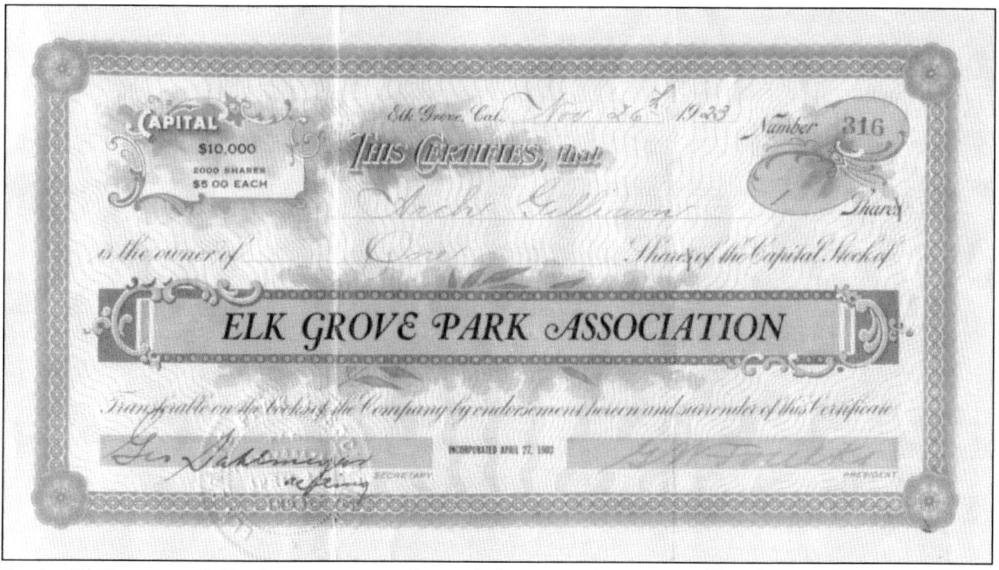

By the 1930s, it was difficult to maintain the park, but a new law enacted by the California legislature in 1935 helped keep it running. The Elk Grove Park was the first park district in the state to operate on tax money. Elk Grove citizens quickly embarked on the development of the park, and now there are many additional parks operated by the Elk Grove Community Services District.

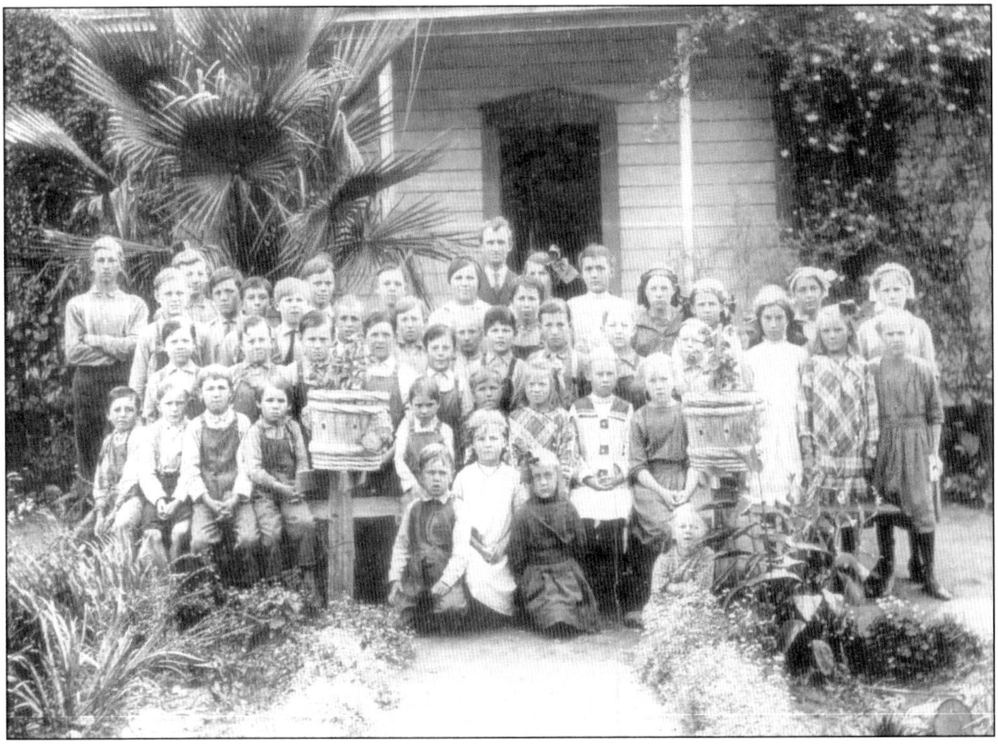

In 1914, students pose in front of Point Pleasant School, which later merged with the Franklin School.

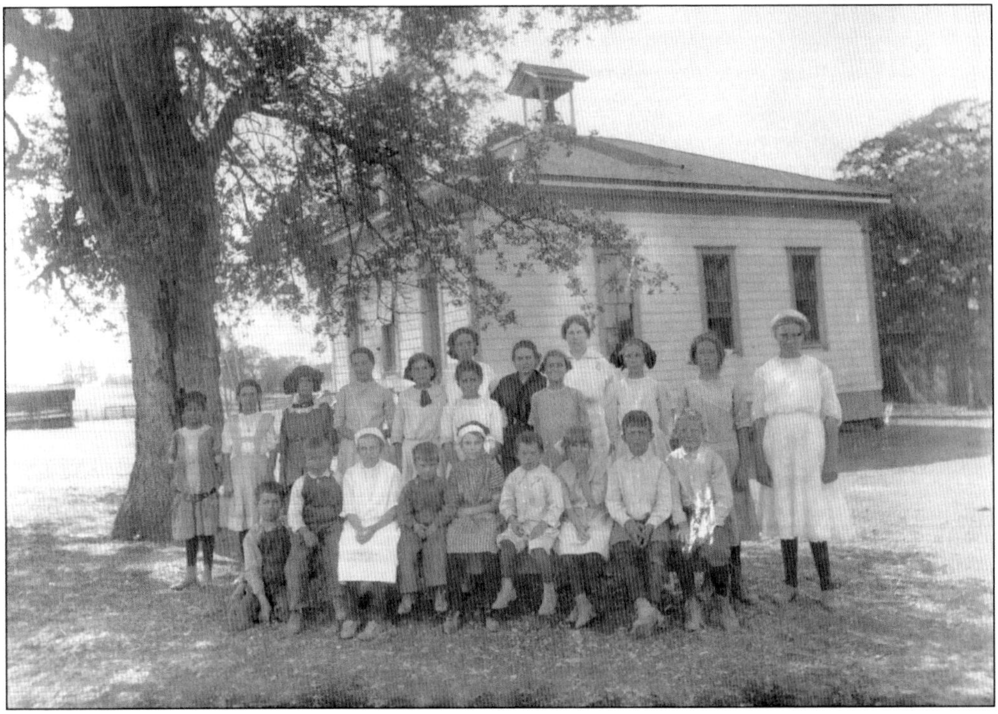

The Lee School (in Wilton) and its students are pictured here in 1914. The school building is now a residence, and the children of the area attend the C. W. Dillard School.

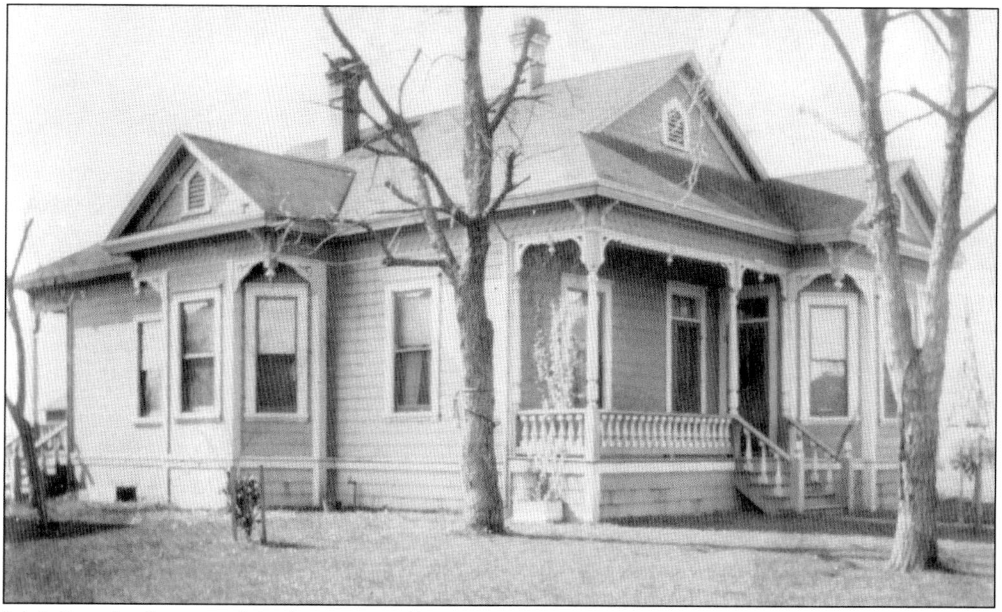

J. M. Derr built most of the houses in Elk Grove in the first half of the 20th century. This house was built in 1902 for Ernest Springsted. Later Dr. Hugh Beattie, Elk Grove's resident doctor, purchased the home. (Courtesy of Elk Grove Historical Society.)

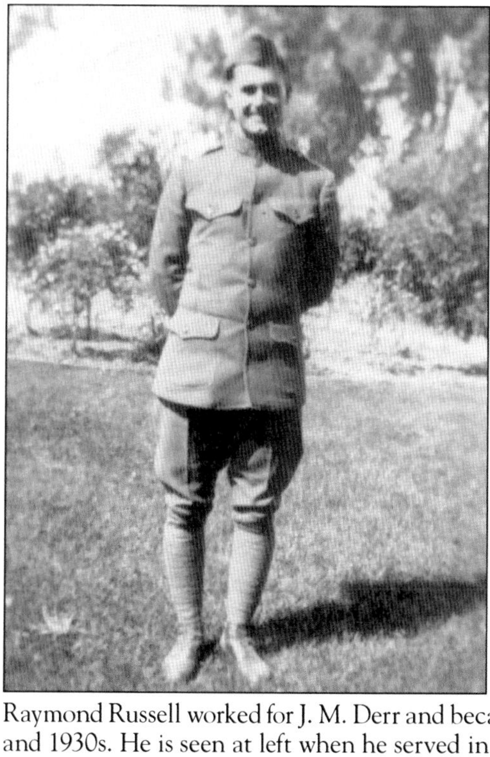

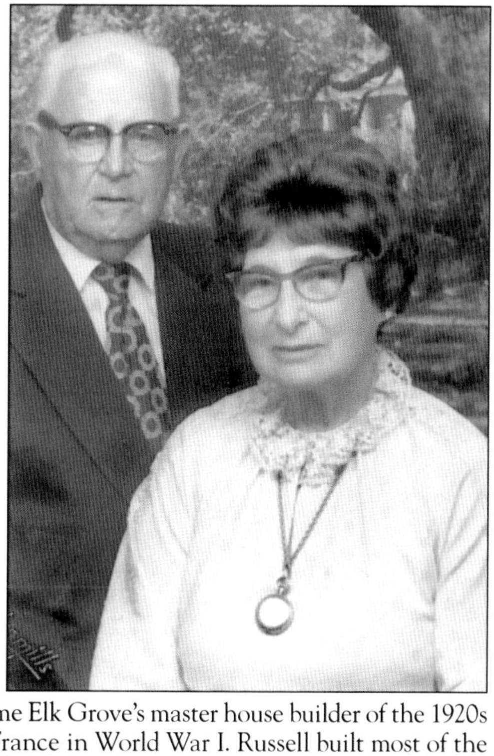

Raymond Russell worked for J. M. Derr and became Elk Grove's master house builder of the 1920s and 1930s. He is seen at left when he served in France in World War I. Russell built most of the Craftsman houses in town, including those south of Main Street in the area once called Nob Hill. Russell and his wife, Marge, are pictured at right. Jim and Virginia Ring fondly remember Russell as "Uncle Toots." (Courtesy of Jim and Virginia Ring.)

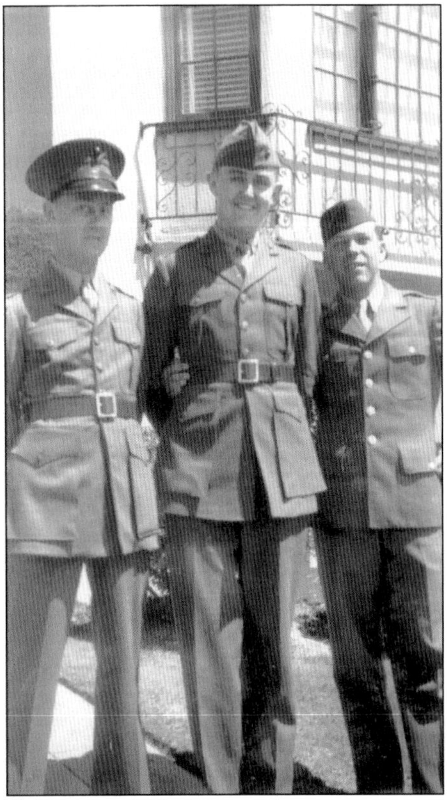

World War II had a great impact on Elk Grove, as it did in communities across the nation. Pictured here is George Signorotti (left) with two Marine buddies. After the war, George married Virginia, who was from Montana. The Signorotti family became well known for raising and marketing hops at their ranch along the Cosumnes River. (Courtesy of Virginia Signorotti.)

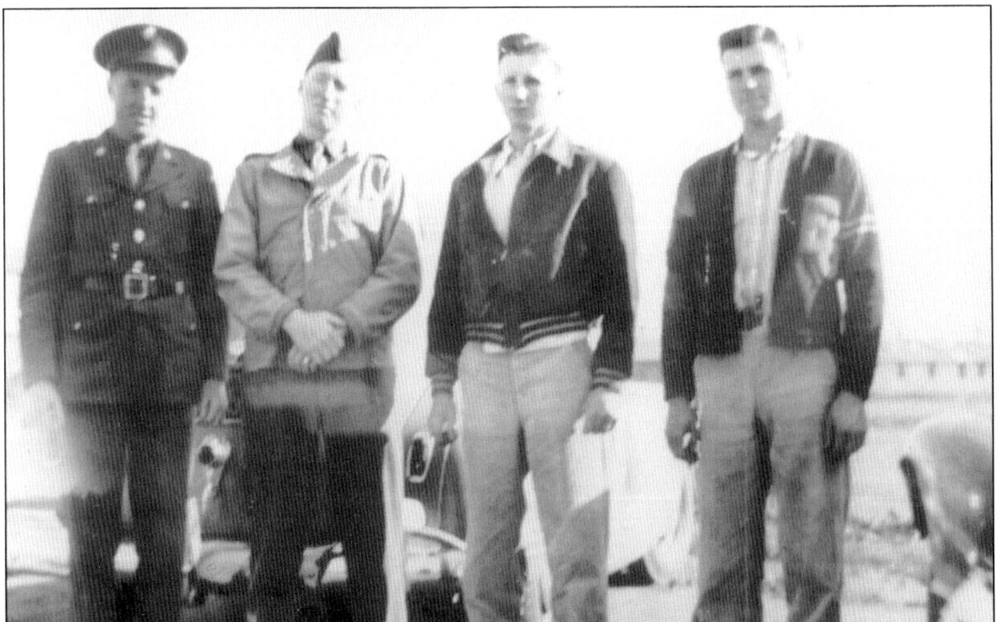

In this photograph, two Morse military men—Arch in the U. S. Army and Dave in the Air Force—are home on leave with their brothers Burt and George, who farmed with the rest of their family. (Courtesy of Dave and Jane Morse.)

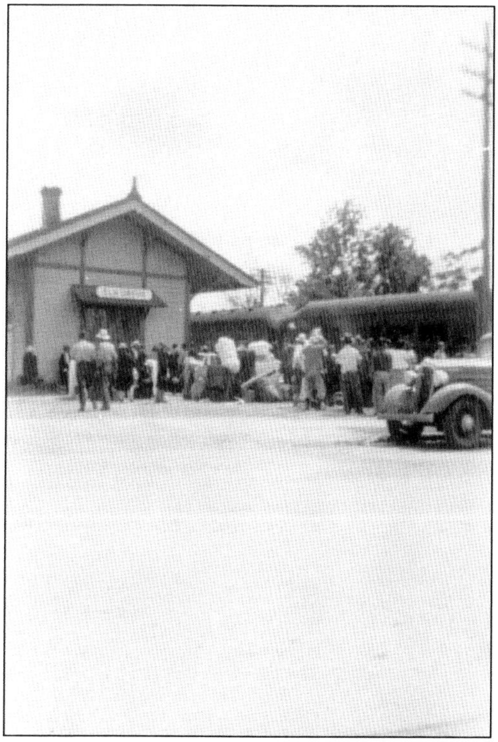

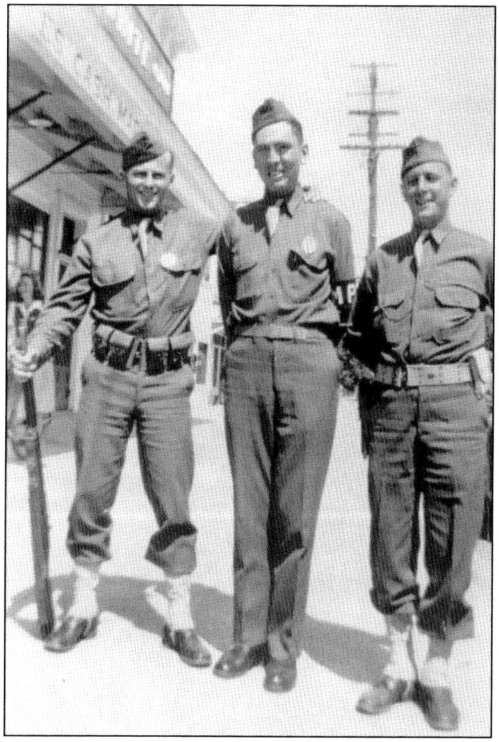

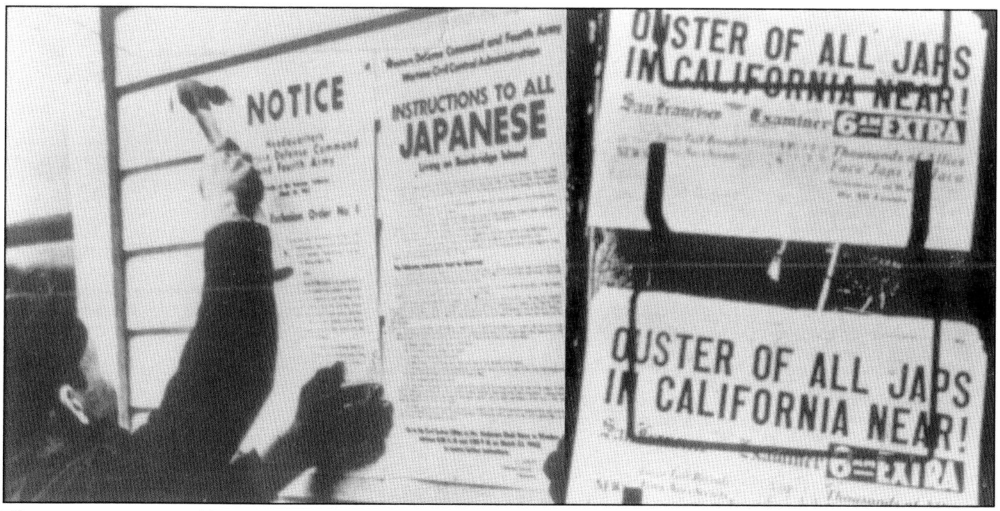

The experiences of Japanese Americans families in Elk Grove and Florin in the years of World War II mirrored those of all persons of Japanese descent in California and the West Coast. In the spring of 1942, all the families left the strawberries ripening in the fields and boarded trains that took them to internment camps. Executive Order 9066, signed by President Roosevelt, authorized their removal for the duration of the war. The photographs at the top of this page were taken by Frances Cumpston at the railroad station in Elk Grove in May 1942. U. S. Army soldiers oversaw the relocation in Elk Grove as well as in Florin. Notices were posted in many places informing people of the procedure. Many local families were sent to internment camps in Arkansas. This was a painful chapter in the lives of Elk Grove and Florin residents—for those of Japanese descent as well as their friends and fellow students.

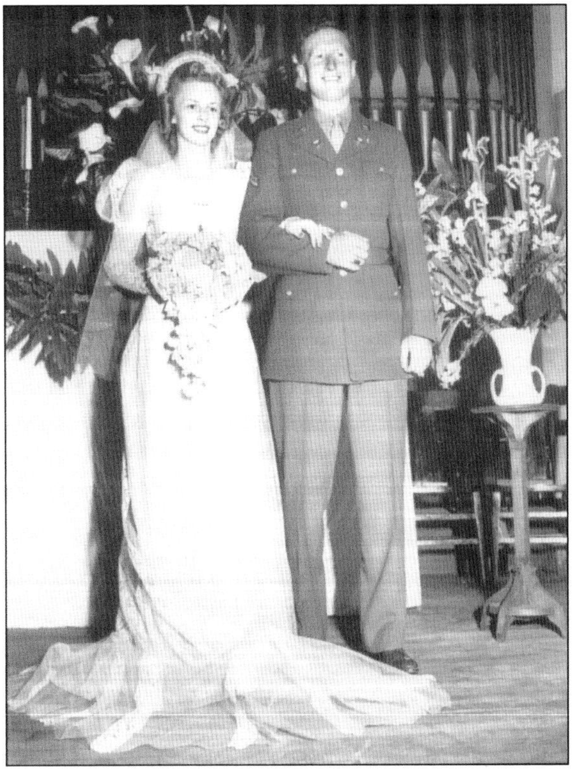

Wedding bells rang for many Elk Grove area young men and women during the war and when it was over in 1945. Pictured here are Dave and Jane Derr Morse in 1943. (Courtesy of Dave and Jane Morse.)

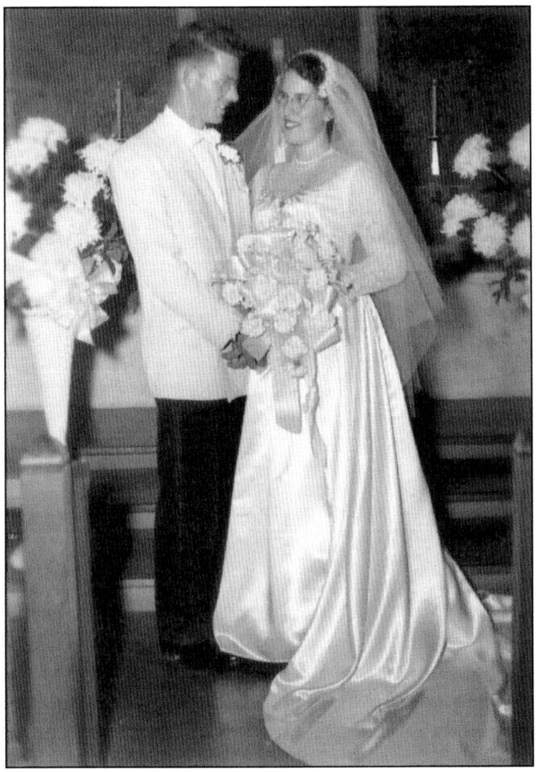

Jim and Virginia Ring were married in 1952. (Courtesy of Jim and Virginia Ring.)

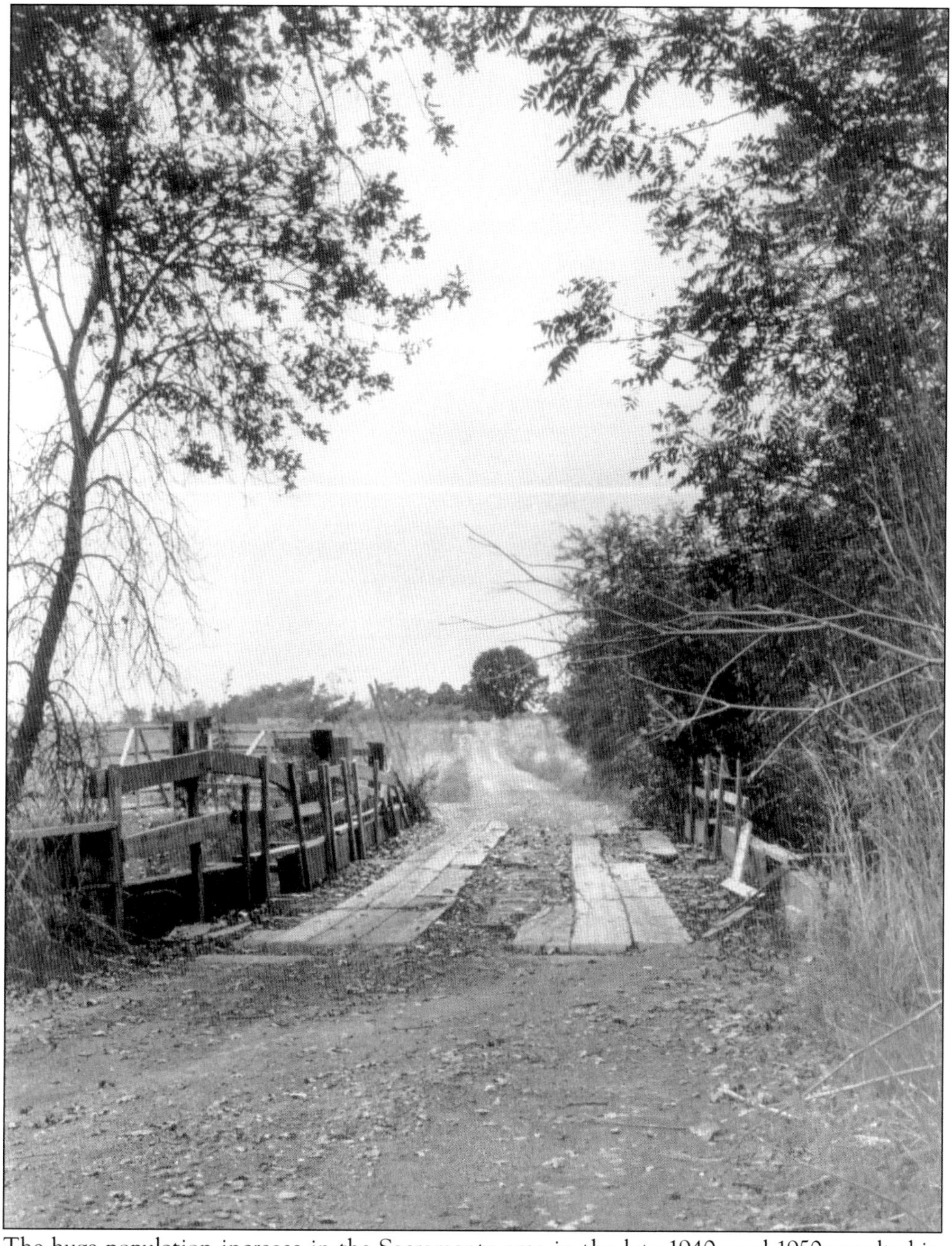

The huge population increase in the Sacramento area in the late 1940s and 1950s resulted in many houses being built along Stockton Road, now Highway 99. By the 1960s, it was becoming apparent that the growing population of the postwar years would bring about many changes to small-town and country life. Today it is taken for granted that residents have a main California highway that heads south from Sacramento through the city of Elk Grove. However, it was not always this way. The busy multilane freeways of Highway 99 and Interstate 5 would be a shock to the early settlers of Elk Grove. They only had trails, such as those still found in some rural areas like the one pictured here.

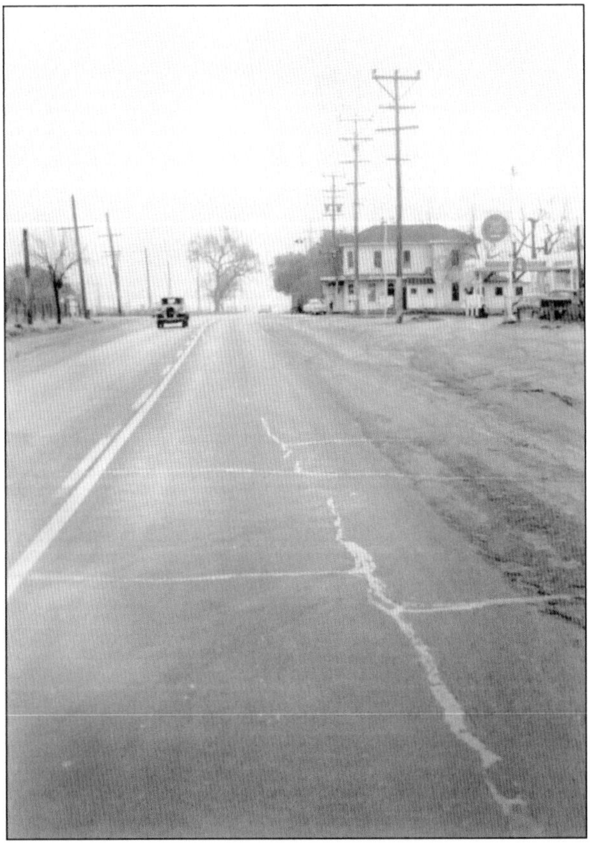

This photograph of Stockton Road at the entrance to Elk Grove was taken in 1953. The Elk Grove Hotel on the southwest corner of the intersection with today's Elk Grove Boulevard was torn down at that time. In 1957, the road became Highway 99 as part of the nationwide highway improvement program authorized by President Eisenhower. (Courtesy of Lucile Christesen.)

The Elk Grove School still stands along Stockton Road and Highway 99, just north of Wal-Mart. It has been a residence for many years, and not many people would recognize it as a former school. Who knows how long it will be there?

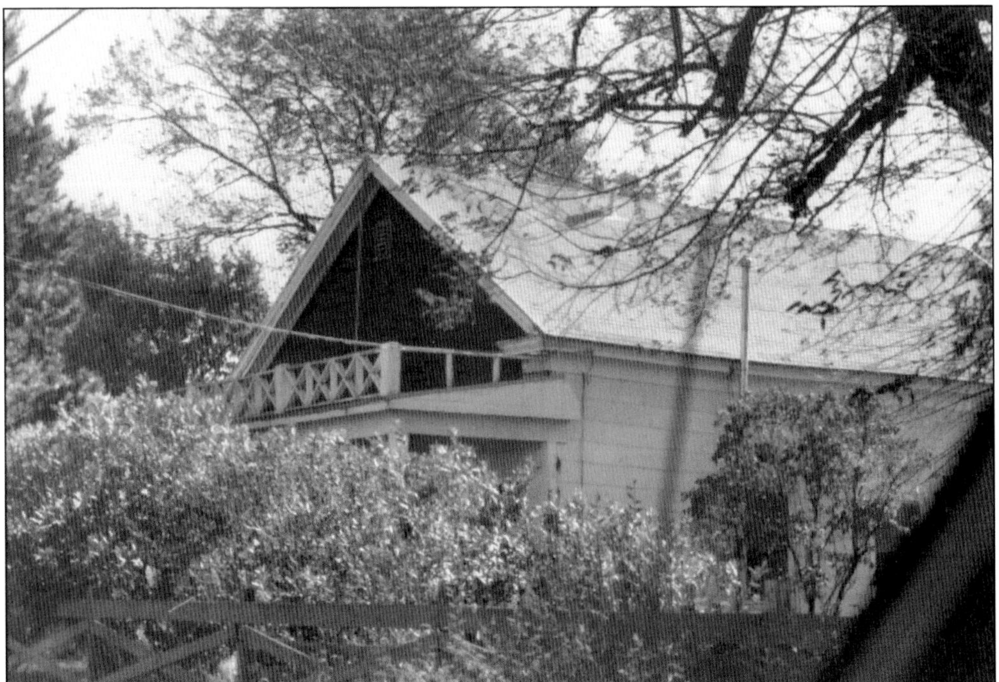

Ten

CHANGES 1951 TO 2006

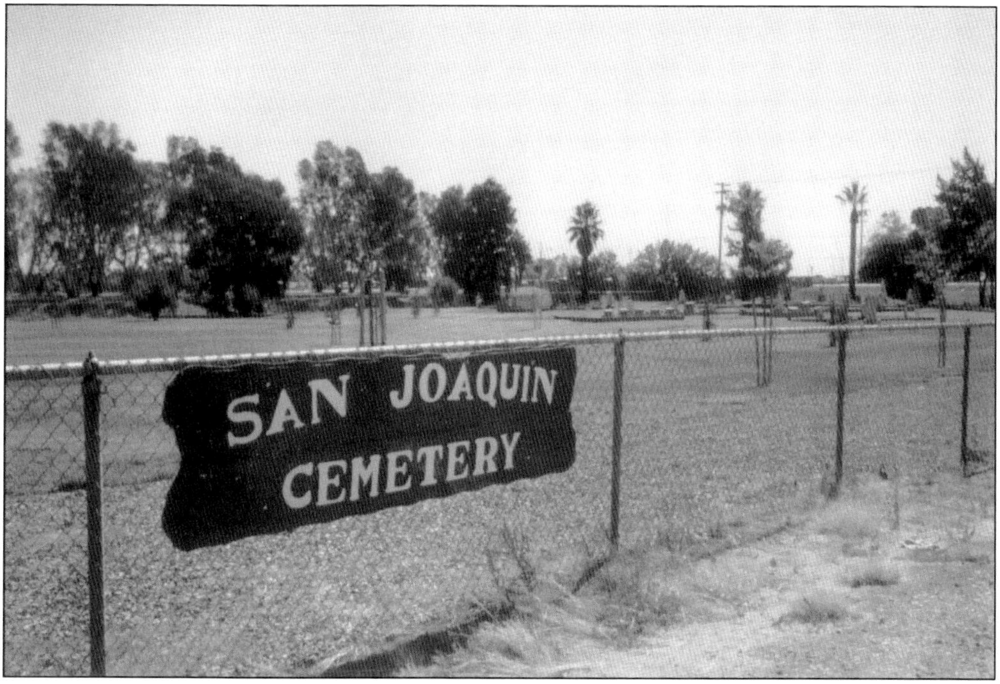

During the gold days, the trails that had once led to Monterey, the Mexican capital of California, became the route to Stockton. Upper Stockton Road is now Highway 99, and the frontage road is still called Stockton Road. One of the casualties of the new highway in 1957 was the razing of the original Elk Grove Hotel and Stage Stop, later rebuilt by the Elk Grove Historical Society. Two places still exist as reminders of the days long gone. One is the Elk Grove's Monterey Trail High School at Calvine Road and not far from Highway 99. The other is the cemetery, pictured here at Highway 99 and Sheldon Road. Its name, San Joaquin, is the only reminder that all of Elk Grove and Florin was once the township of San Joaquin.

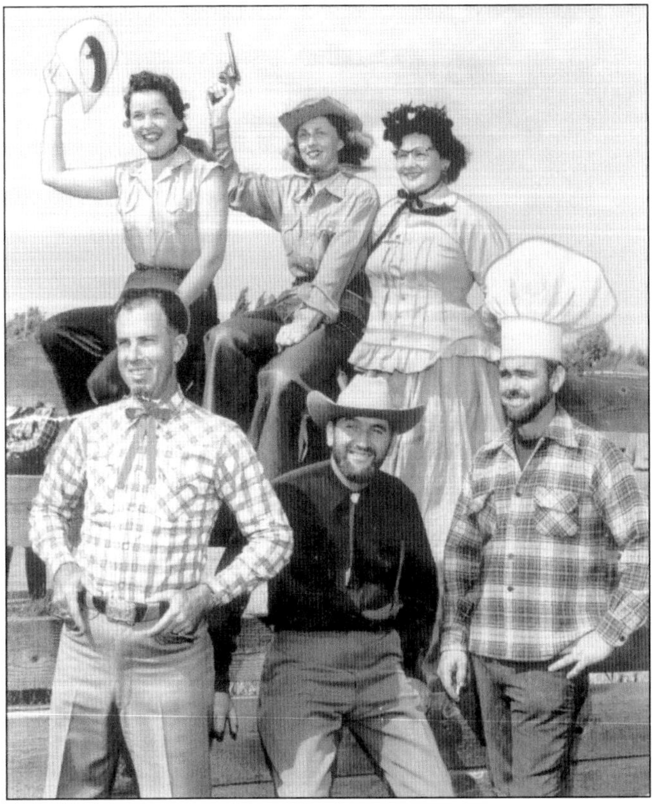

The Western Festival has been part of Elk Grove since 1957 when the parents at Elk Grove Elementary School, under the leadership of principal/ superintendent Raymond Case and Mothers' Club president Sue Morse (now Mikles), decided to have a fund-raiser. The founders, pictured here, created the Western Festival with the theme: Working together for our children, our school, our home, and our community. They had a parade, booths, food, and family entertainment—all of which have continued through the years on the first weekend in May. In 1966, Ronald Reagan rode his horse in the festival parade when he was running for governor of California. (Courtesy of Dave and Jane Morse.)

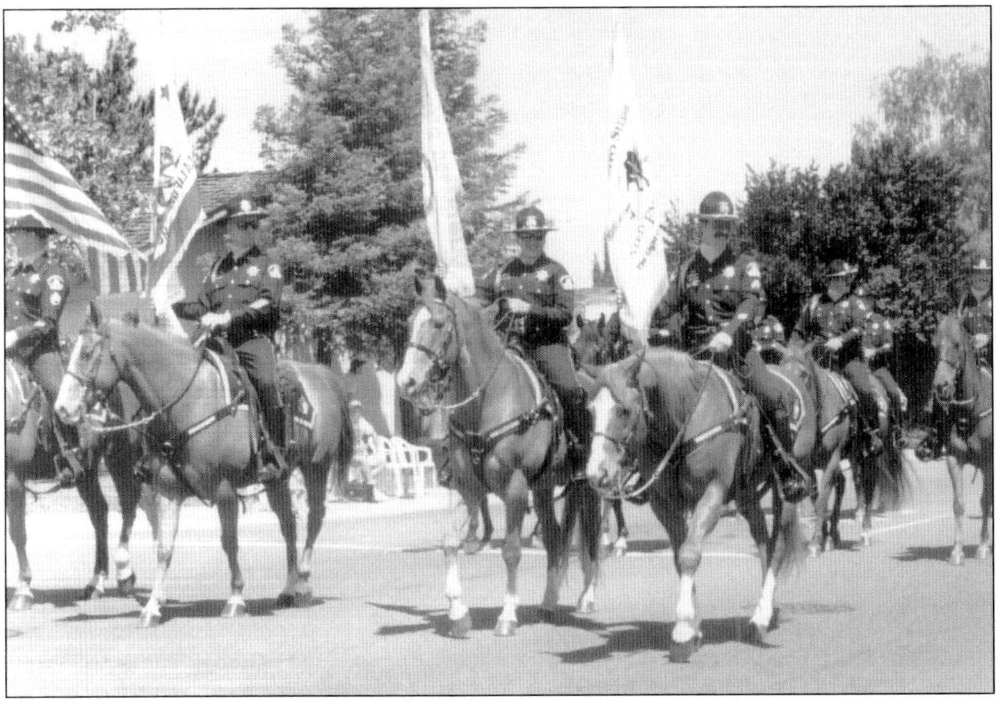

Pictured here is the Sacramento County Sheriff's Mounted Patrol, a regular group in the parades.

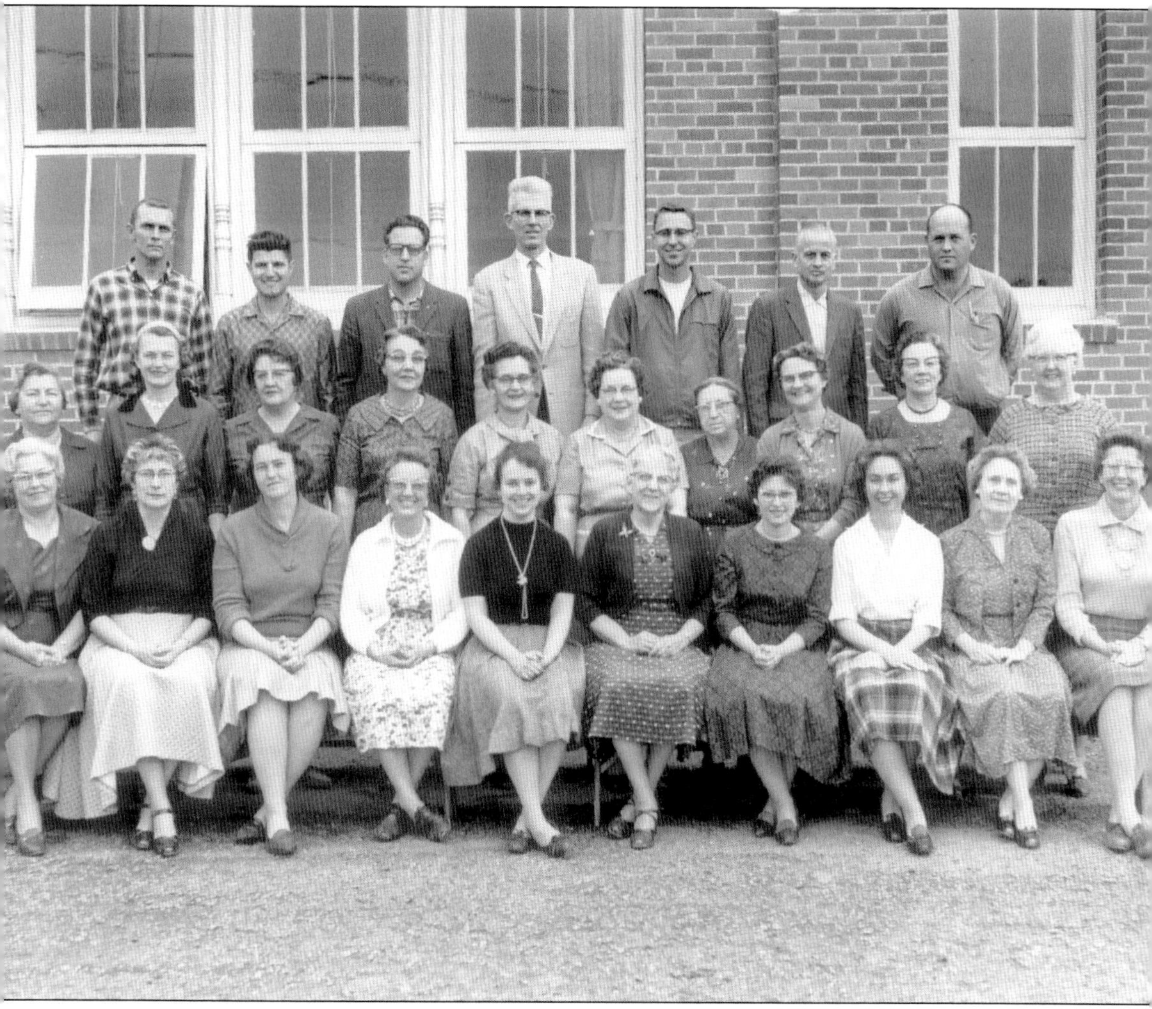

In 1959, the little elementary districts in the Elk Grove area merged with their high school district to create the Elk Grove Unified School District. The unification of school districts was happening all over California in the 1950s in an effort to provide greater services for students and at the same time reduce expenses. A vote of Elk Grove and Cosumnes-area citizens resulted in the unification of elementary districts with Elk Grove Union High School. The parents at Cosumnes River, Dillard, Franklin, Pleasant Grove-Reese, and Sierra Enterprise, each with one school (although most were mergers of other small districts), voted for unification. Florin did the same with its new Isabelle Jackson School, and Elk Grove followed suit with its new Anna Kirchgater School. The nine schools joined Elk Grove High School as a district of 3,000 students. Today the district has more than 60,000 students and 60 schools. Here teachers at Elk Grove Grammar School pose for a photograph in 1960. Raymond Case, the principal and former superintendent, is in the center of the back row. Everyone who enters the Elk Grove Community Services Building, the former Elk Grove Elementary School, is likely to notice the magnificent display of rhododendrons, camellias, and azaleas each spring. The flowers and Raymond Case Elementary School are lasting tributes in his honor.

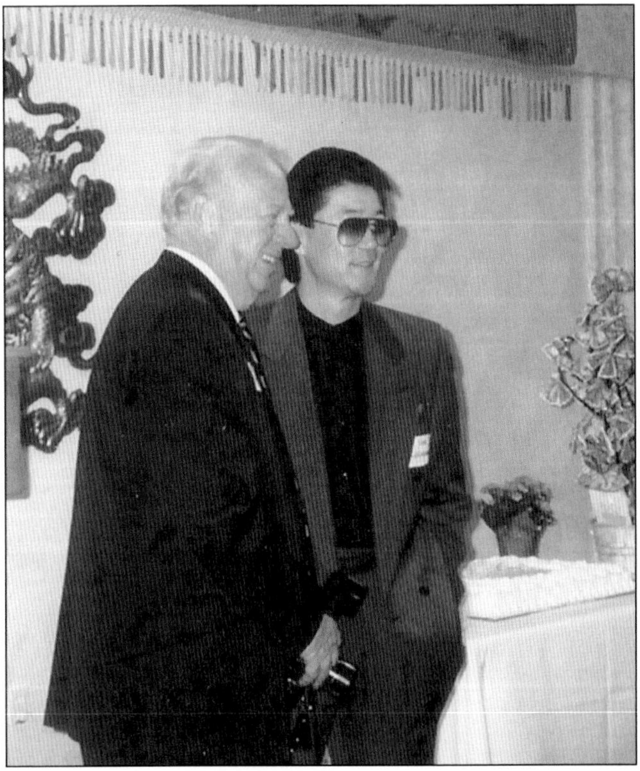

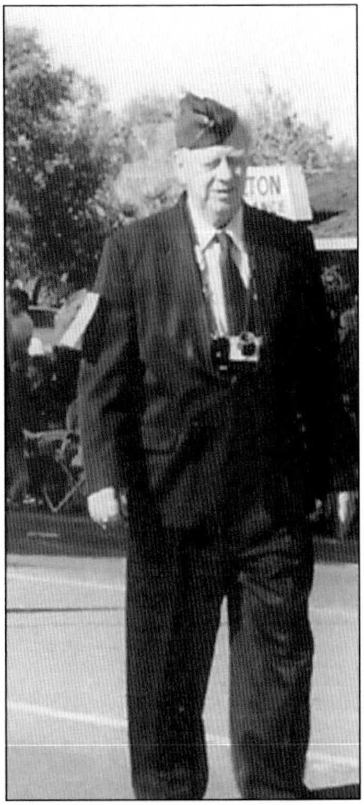

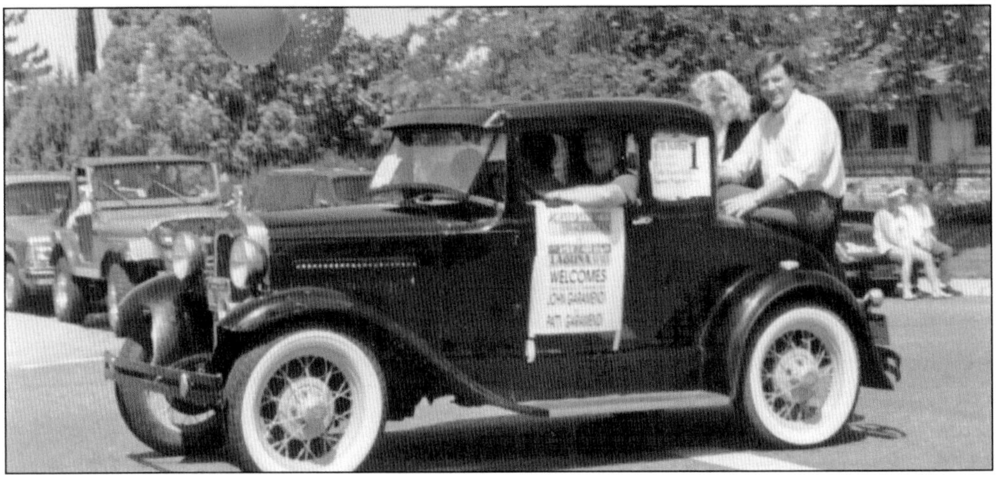

In 1959, Roy Herburger began a long association with the *Elk Grove Citizen* when he and his wife, Mary, bought the weekly newspaper and its sister paper, the *Galt Herald*. From an original distribution of 600, the *Citizen* has increased to 65,000 and is distributed twice a week instead of only weekly. The newspaper is now in the hands of two generations of Herburgers with son David as the publisher/general manager. The Herburgers are active community members who have dedicated the newspaper to serving the community. Roy is pictured above left with Tom Nakashima, a graduate of local schools who is actively involved with Sacramento radio and a frequent master of ceremonies at Elk Grove functions. On the right is Roy celebrating Veteran's Day. The *Citizen* welcomed John and Patti Garamendi back to California after serving in the Clinton administration in a Western Festival parade.

The Elk Grove Chamber of Commerce has been in existence since 1954. When the booklet pictured here was published in 1981, there were 225 businesses as chamber members. Today there are nearly 1,000, with more added each month. The chamber of commerce has been involved with the Citizen of the Year program since its beginning in 1955. Each year a local person is selected as the citizen of the year in recognition of community service.

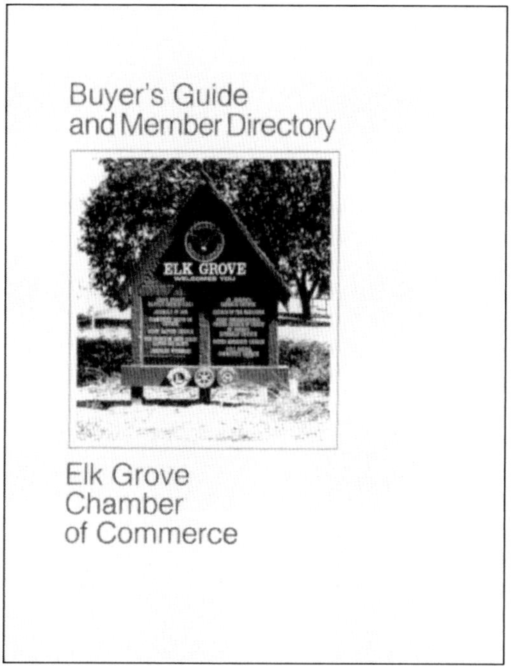

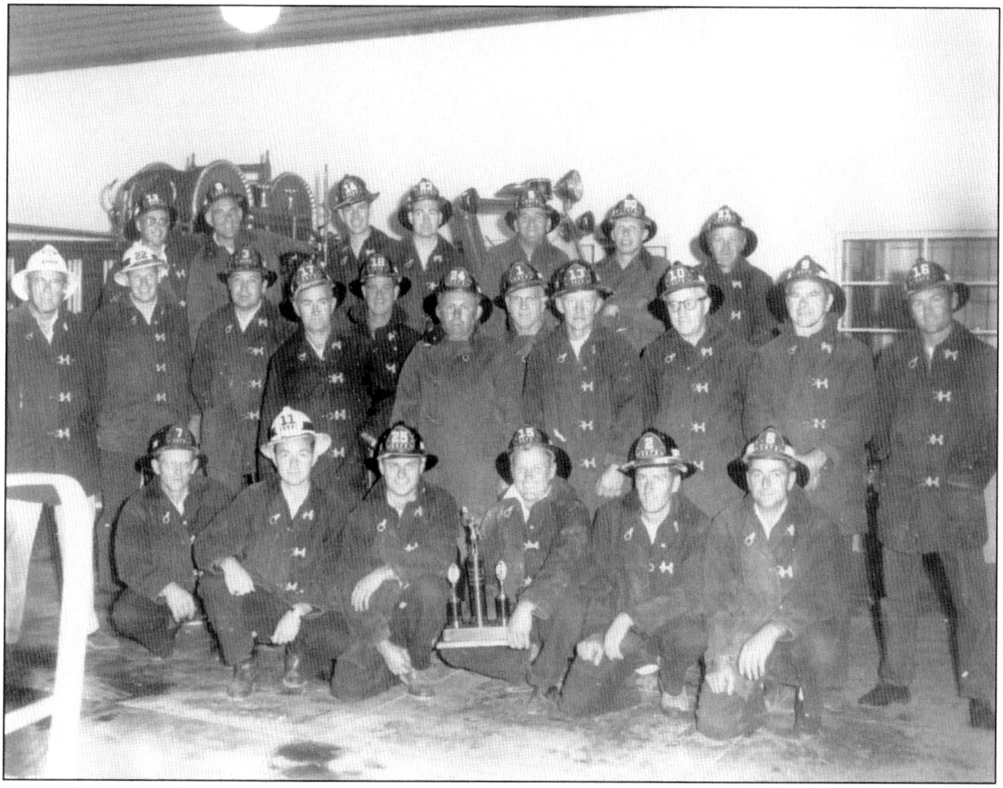

The Elk Grove Volunteer Fire Department, pictured here, was recognized in 1959. Longtime members of the fire department are Gerald Derr, former chief, and John Zehnder, whose sons have continued the family tradition of firefighting. (Courtesy of Gerald Derr.)

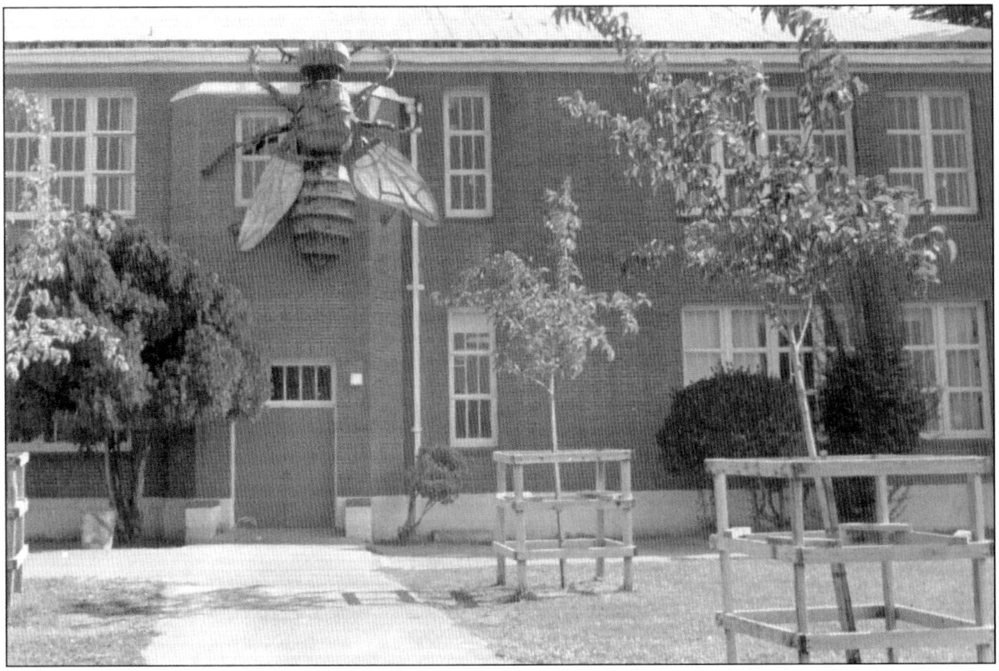

Art has always played a large role in Elk Grove although at times it has taken unusual forms. The brick building on the Joseph Kerr campus was originally the science building, and in 1973, a visitor appeared on the wall one morning. The giant fly was created by the world-famous artist known as Christo on a bridge in Sacramento. Through the efforts of several local residents, it was brought to Elk Grove and placed in this prominent place on Elk Grove Boulevard and Elk Grove-Florin Road.

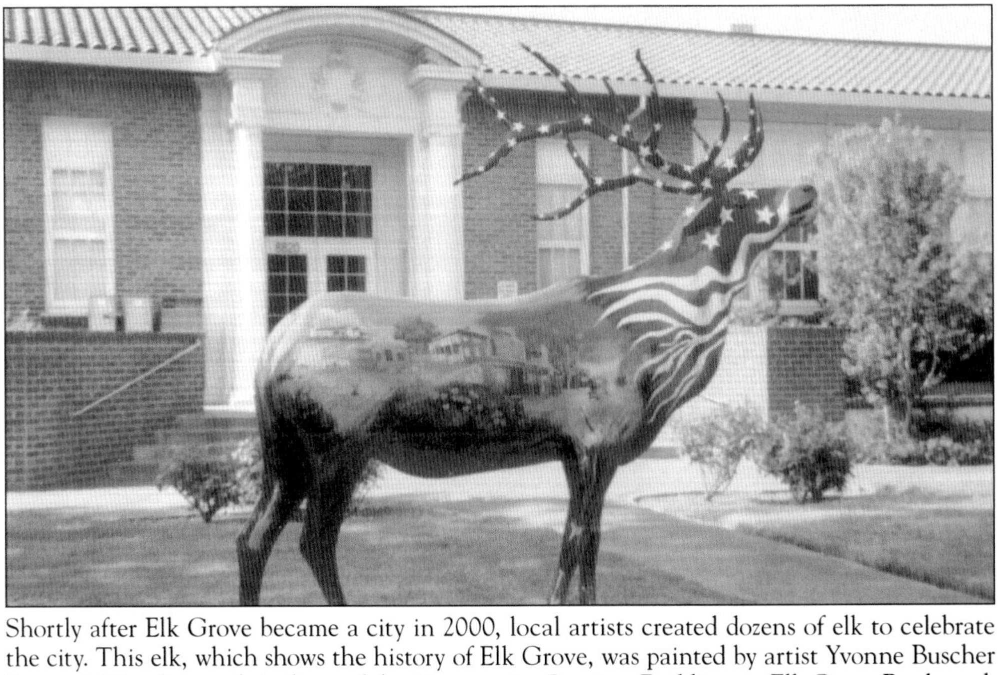

Shortly after Elk Grove became a city in 2000, local artists created dozens of elk to celebrate the city. This elk, which shows the history of Elk Grove, was painted by artist Yvonne Buscher Bonacci. The elk stands in front of the Community Services Building on Elk Grove Boulevard, the former Elk Grove Grammar School.

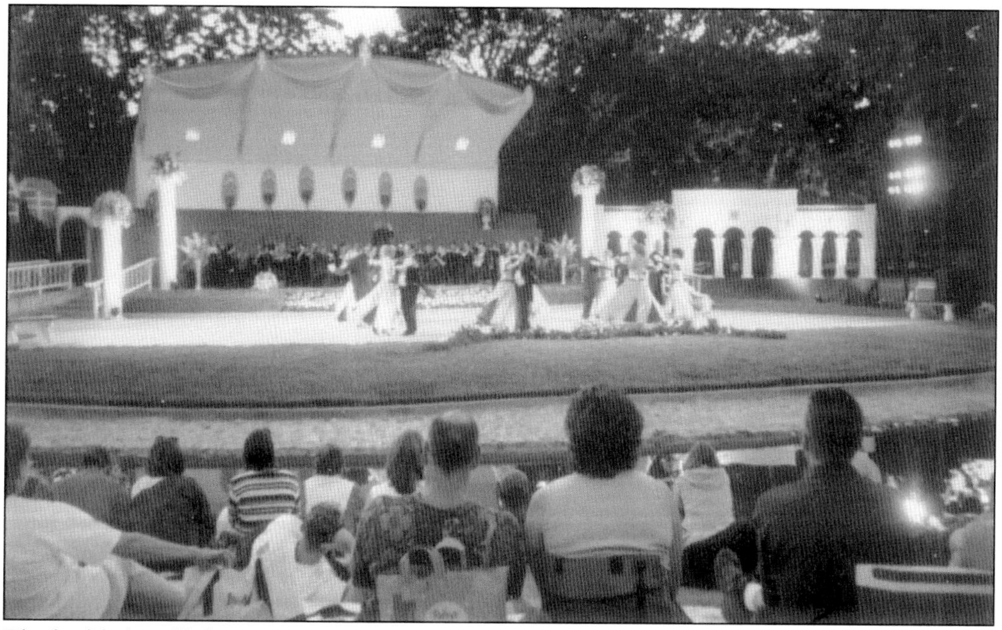

The highlight of July every year in Elk Grove is the Strauss Festival held in Elk Grove Park on what is now known as Strauss Island. Begun from an idea brought forth by Iris Zimbelman in 1987, the dancers and musicians perform four evenings during the last week of July to record crowds. (Courtesy of Jane and Dave Morse.)

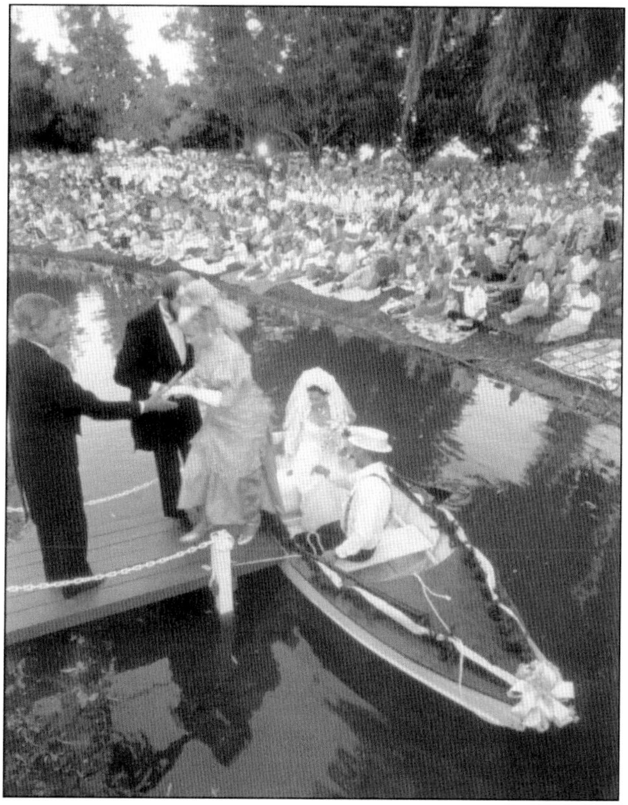

In 1989, Jane Morse, one of the dancers, along with her husband, Dave, steps out of the boat to approach the stage. The Strauss Festival is entirely managed by a host of volunteers, and the festival continues to be a free event for the thousands that attend. (Courtesy of Jane and Dave Morse.)

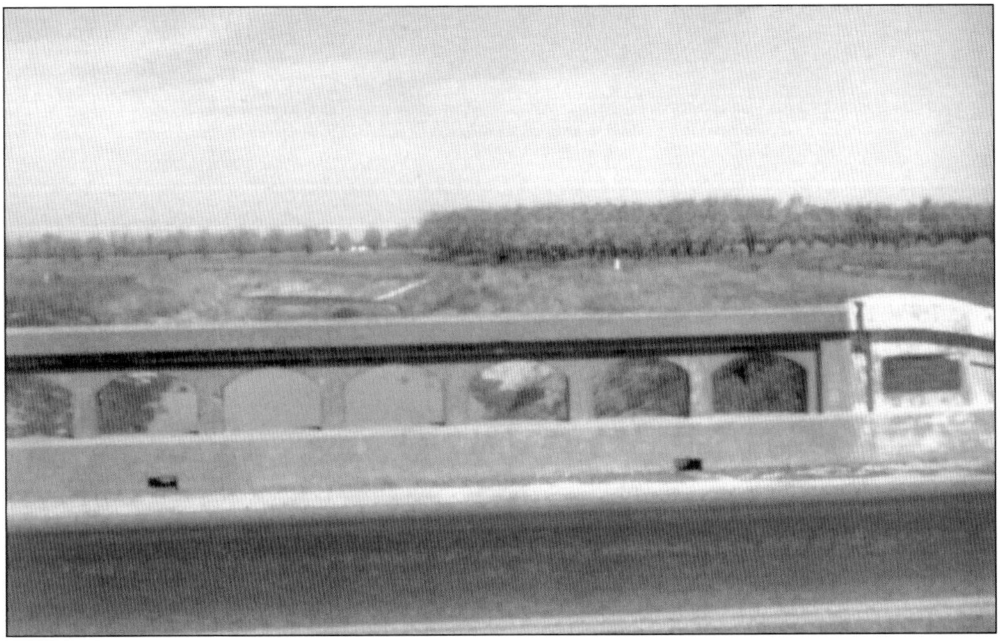

There have been many signs of change in the past decades of Elk Grove. The Williamson orchard covered a large acreage from what is now a shopping center on Elk Grove Boulevard to the site of James McKee Elementary School. Apples, pears, and plums were the main fruits, and many Elk Grove residents spent time picking fruit and packing it. The photograph here, taken in the early 1970s, shows the bridge on Elk Grove Creek and the Williamson orchards disappearing to the north.

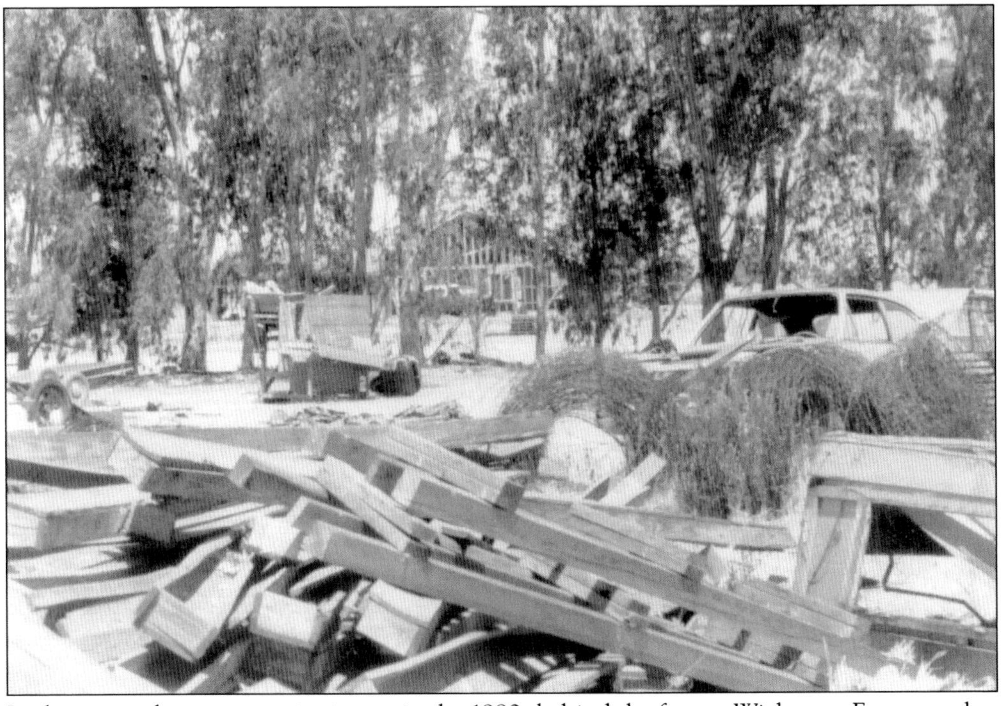

In this image, houses are springing up in the 1980s behind the former Wightman Farm on what is now Big Horn Boulevard in West Elk Grove's Laguna.

As changes continue to take place in the Elk Grove area, efforts are made to preserve the natural environment. In 1996, a new player entered the world of the Cosumnes River. The Cosumnes River Preserve has 13,000 acres of river land under its protection and management. There is a web site at www.consumnes.org, and at 13501 Franklin Boulevard there is a visitor center. (Courtesy of Nestor Lara in *History Happened Here.*)

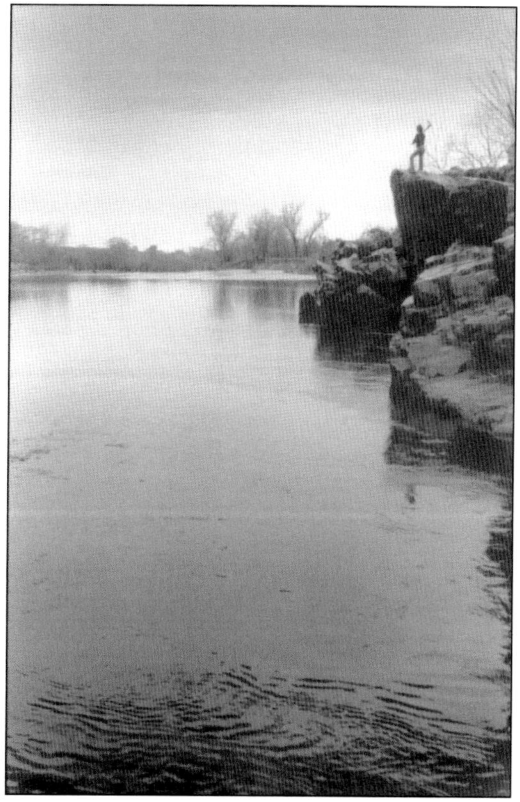

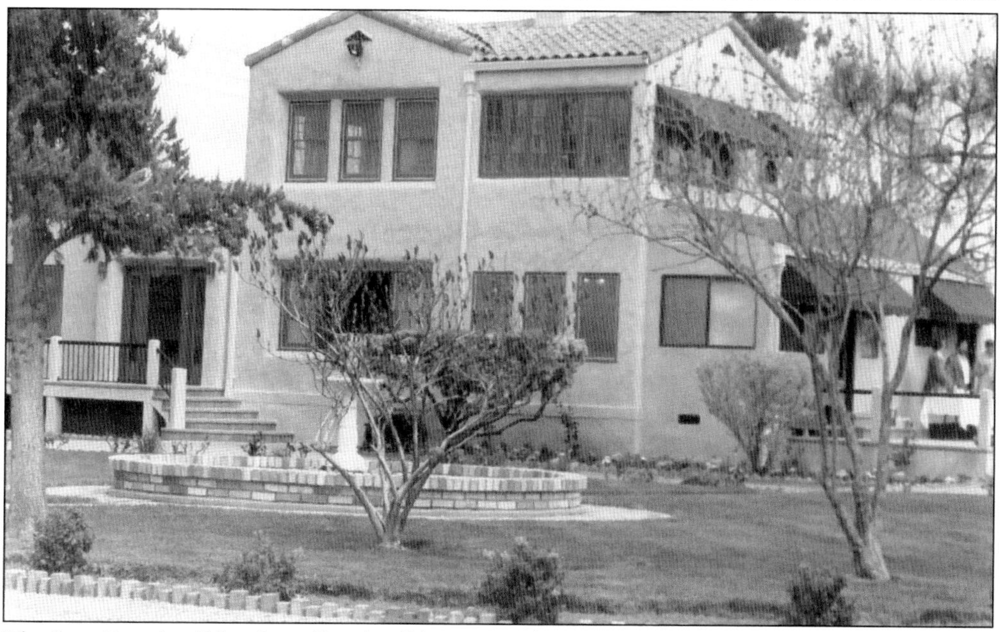

The Lent Ranch off Stockton Road will become a shopping center in the near future, but it may not be called the Lent Ranch Mall, much to the dismay of many local residents. The beautiful 1930s-era house pictured here was that of Lent family and is now the home of Robert and Lisa Lent, active community volunteer workers.

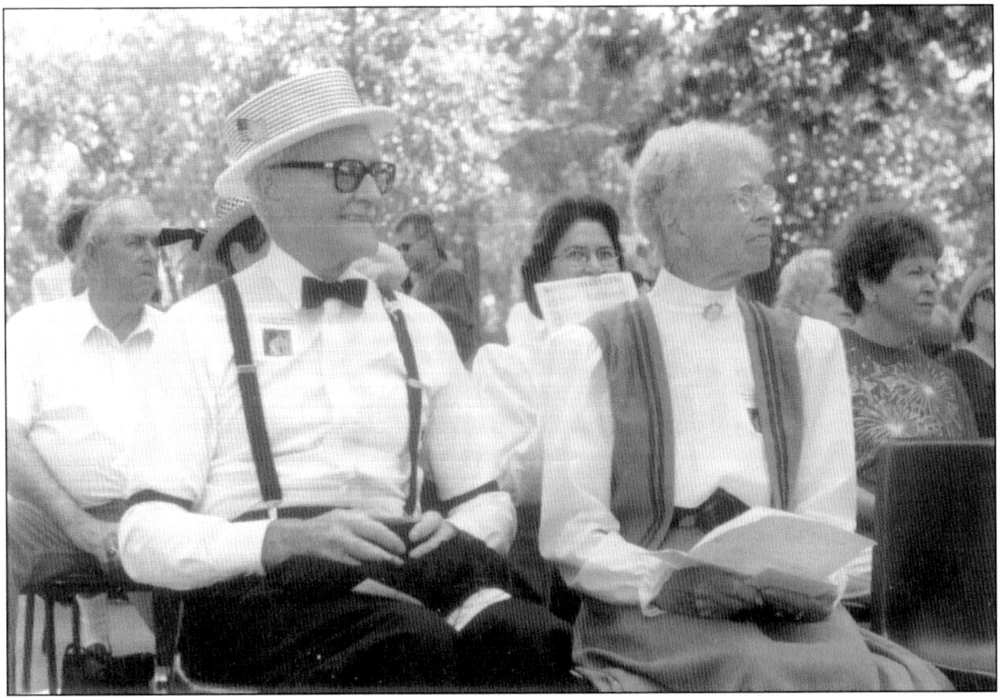

Through the years, Elk Grove has benefited from an impressive amount of community involvement. Students are encouraged to participate in community activities, and the Elk Grove Community Foundation, which provides scholarships for students, is widely supported. Social, church, and school groups continually involve all family members. Arnie Zimbelman and Frances Fite, the organizer of the Rhoads School programs, are pictured here at the anniversary celebration of the moving of the school to Elk Grove Park. Below are Virginia Ring and Dorothy Hrepich guiding visitors to the school.

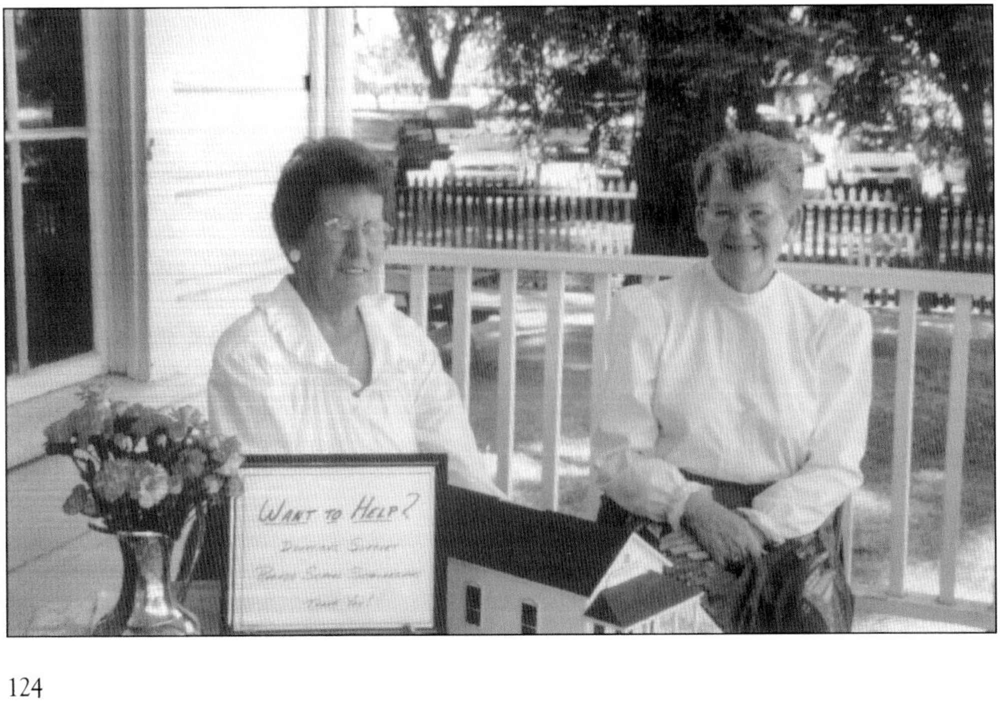

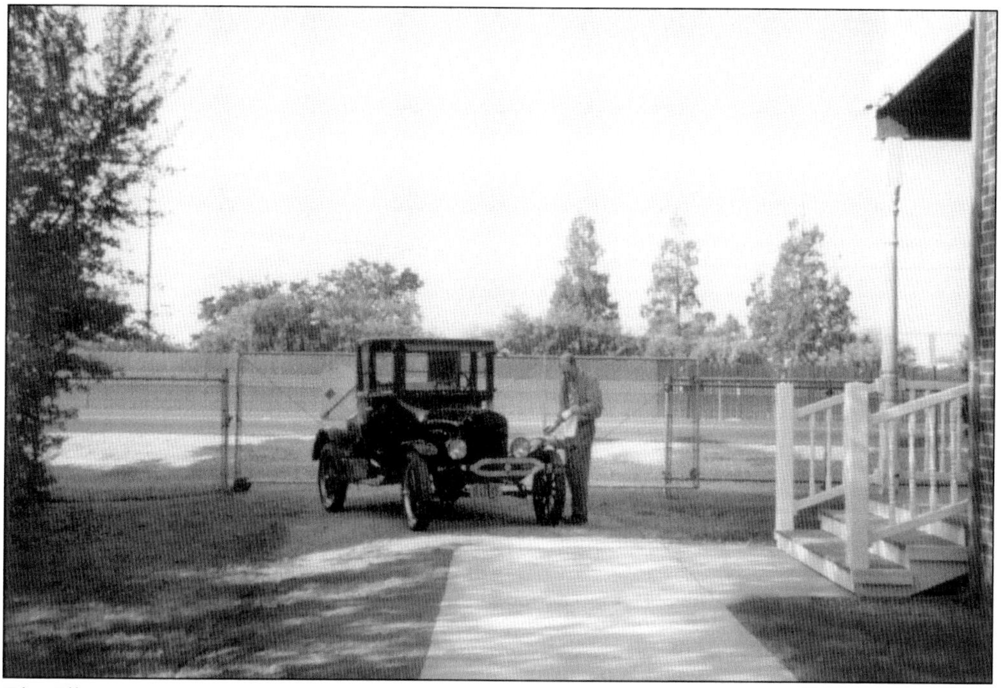

The Elk Grove Historical Society involves both old-timers and newcomers in its many projects. Pictured here is Milton Webb, past president of the historical society, who is the local expert on vintage automobiles, especially his Ford Model T.

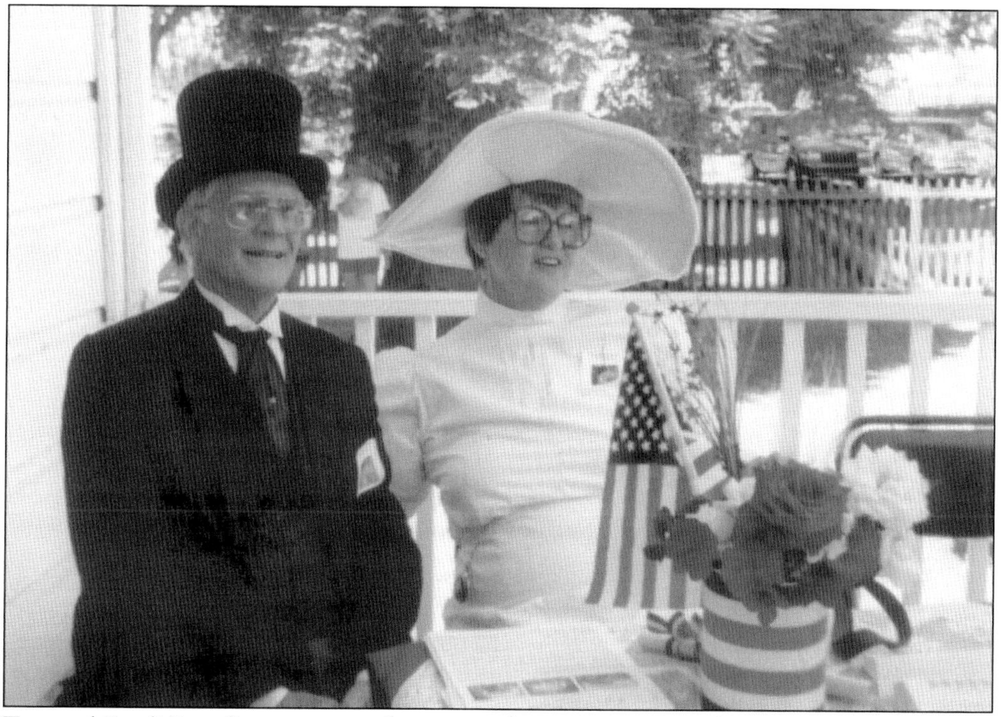

Tom and Sandi Russell encourage volunteerism for community members through the society as well as through other organizations.

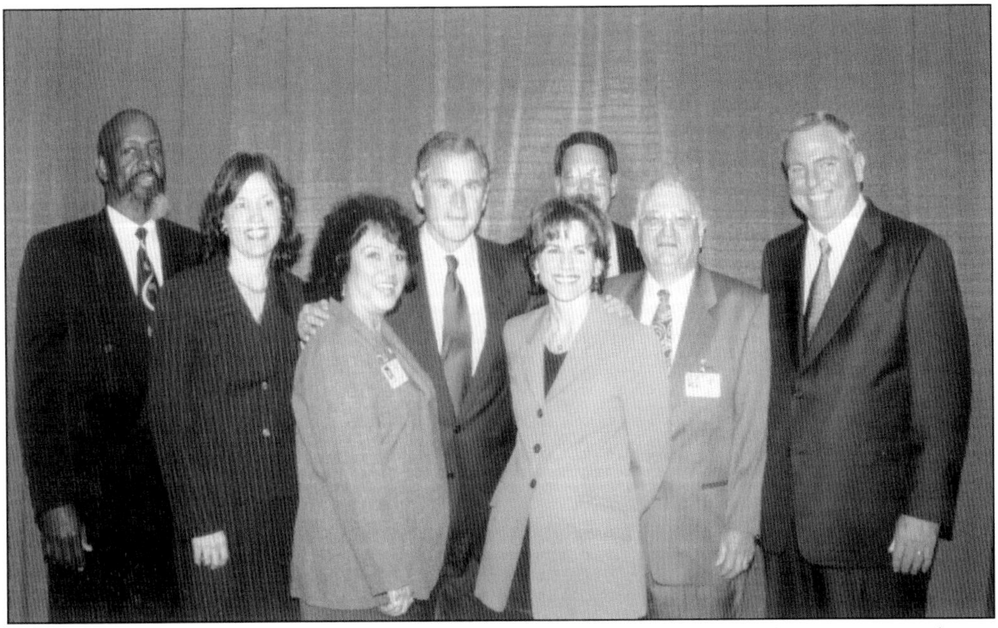

Pictured here with the Elk Grove Board of Education and superintendent Dave Gordon is George W. Bush when he visited the district during his campaign for president in 2000. The school district is the largest employer in south Sacramento County. The 320 square-mile district includes the city of Elk Grove, portions of the cities of Sacramento and Rancho Cordova, and part of Sacramento County. In 2006, the district has 61,162 students and is one of the largest school districts in California. (Courtesy of Elk Grove Unified School District.)

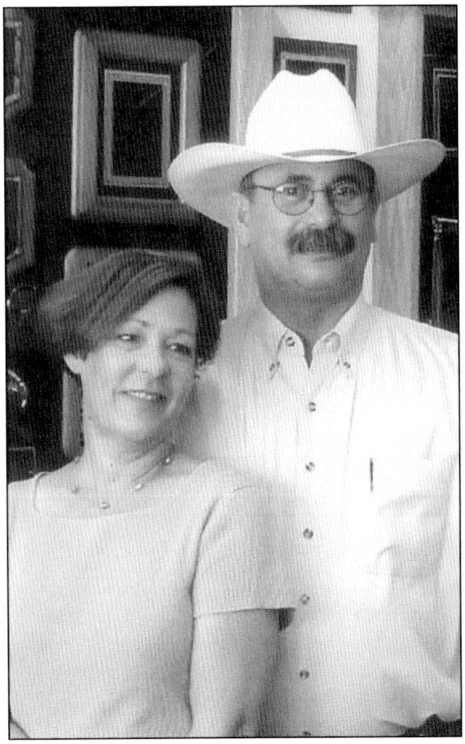

Many graduates of local schools have stayed in Elk Grove to raise their families, send their children to the schools they attended, and become the business people and entrepreneurs of the future. Typical of this trend are Paula and Frank Maita, who are pictured here. Their previous involvement in agriculture has changed to a Main Street business along with huge amounts of community volunteerism. Frank is on the City of Elk Grove Planning Commission and was president of the Old Town Merchants. Paula is active in many Old Town projects as well as her grassroots awards business.

In 2005, the City of Elk Grove embarked on an extensive revitalization project for Old Town Elk Grove and Main Street/Elk Grove Boulevard. The sign says the town was established in 1868. That is the year the railroad came through the area, and in 1876, businesses began to move to the railroad tracks.

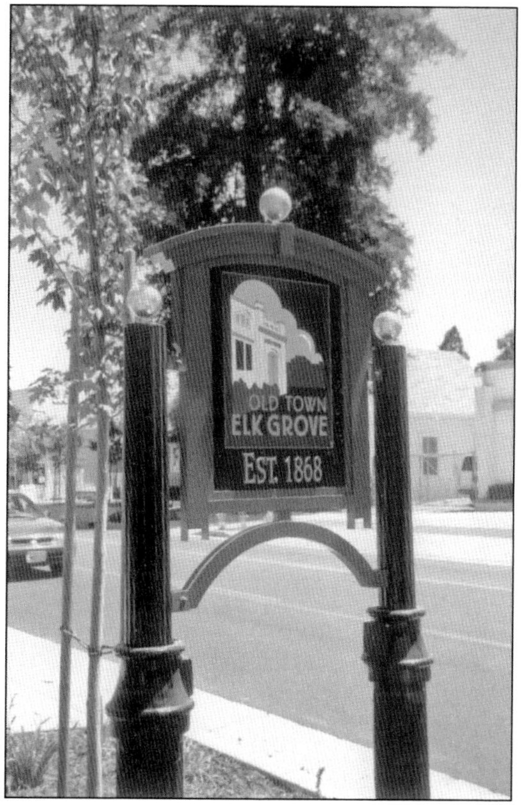

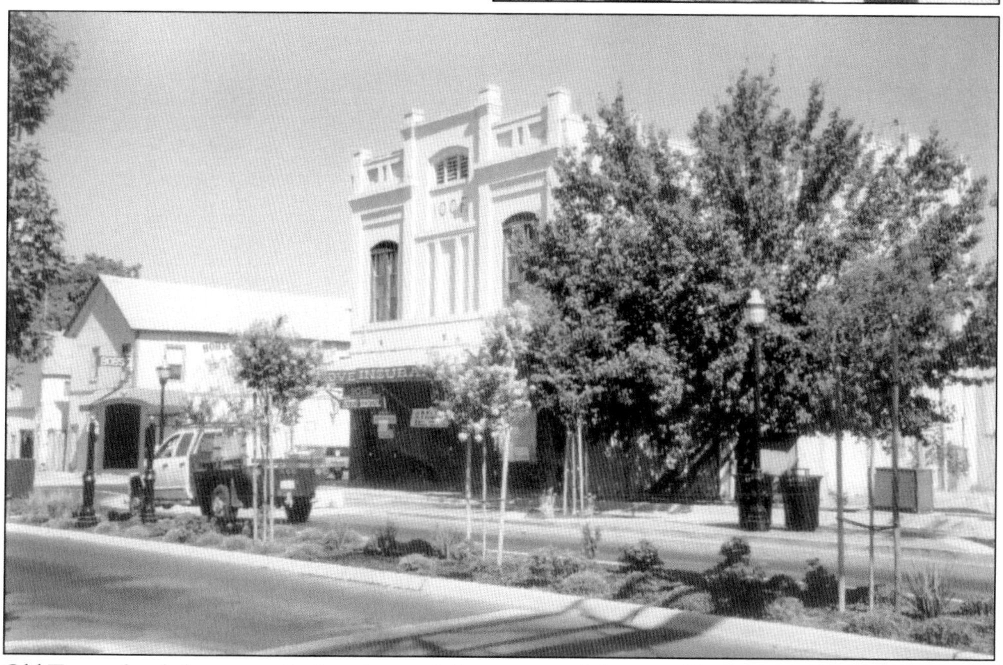

Old Town clearly has a new look today, and the variety of shops and businesses reflect the changes in a positive way. This is the original Odd Fellows Building, which has been at that site for more than 100 years.

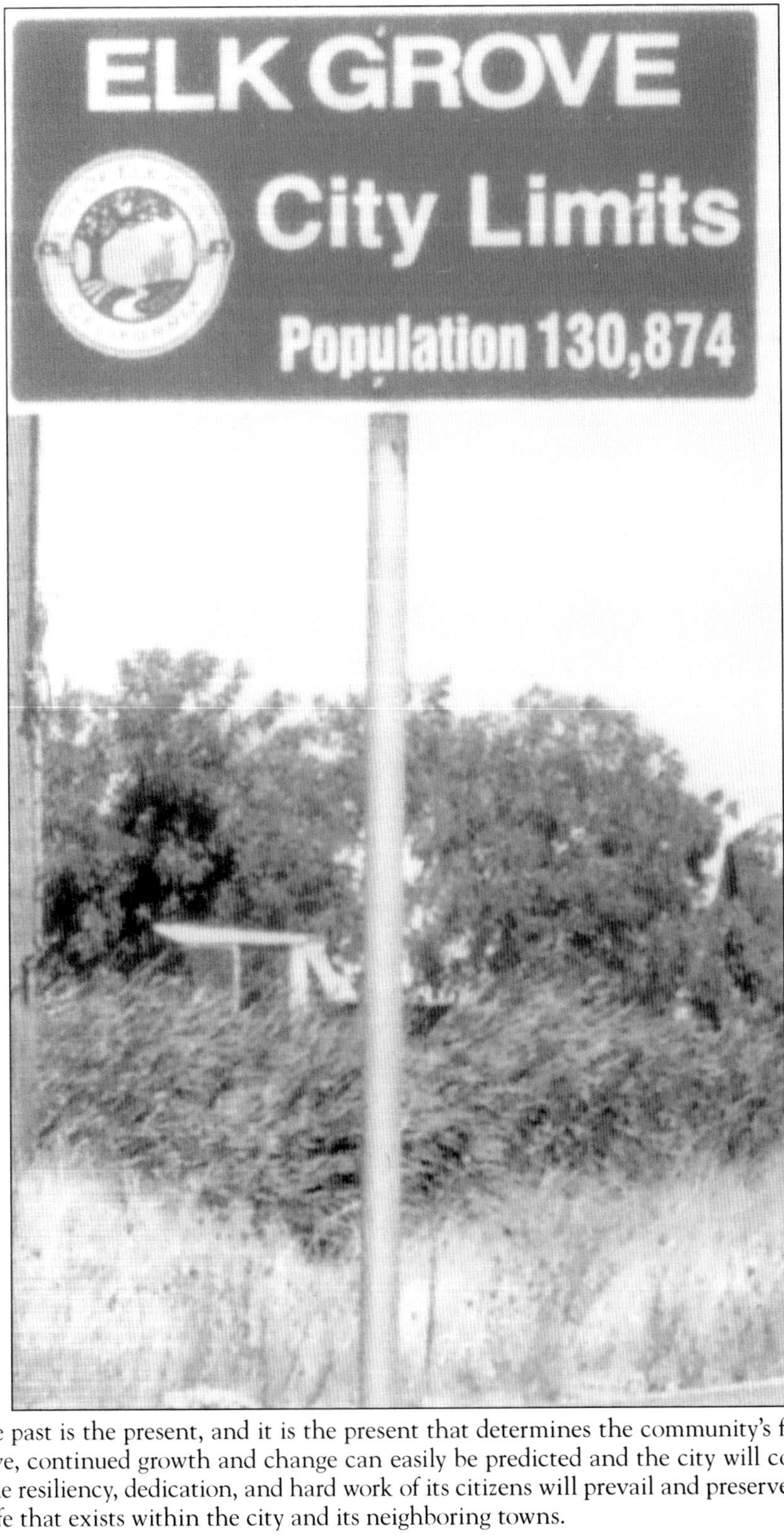

From the past is the present, and it is the present that determines the community's future. For Elk Grove, continued growth and change can easily be predicted and the city will continue to grow. The resiliency, dedication, and hard work of its citizens will prevail and preserve the great way of life that exists within the city and its neighboring towns.